Claim
Administration
Principles and Practices

SECOND EDITION

Jo Ann S. Appleton, FLMI, ALHC

INTERNATIONAL CLAIM ASSOCIATION

ISBN 1-877595-00-4

Library of Congress Catalog Card Number: 89-080609

Printed in the United States of America

Preface

The second edition of *Claim Administration: Principles and Practices*, like the first edition, is designed to provide individuals with a foundation in the basic principles of claim administration for life, health, and other types of insurance products. In the ten years since the first edition of *Claim Administration* was published, claim administration has changed dramatically. Advances in automation have changed the way claims are processed. Increases in the number of fraudulent claims have underscored the importance of careful claim administration. A proliferation of new types of insurance products and increases in the average face amounts of insurance policies have added complexity to the claim administration process.

In the second edition of *Claim Administration: Principles and Practices*, we have expanded the information presented in the original text to include information about these topics. In addition, we have greatly expanded the information presented in the original text about medical expense and disability claims. We have used a new approach, structuring the book along product lines in order to address similarities and differences in the claim process for each type of insurance product. The reader should note, however, that the descriptions of the claim examination and payment processes in this textbook are illustrative only and are not designed to represent the methods followed at any particular company nor to serve as models for claim examiners to follow.

Throughout the text, each insurance term is highlighted in ***bold italics*** when it is first used and is accompanied by a definition or explanation. Insurance statistics are cited throughout the text to help explain evolving trends within the insurance industry. Unless otherwise noted, statistics that relate to the United States are taken from the *1988 Life Insurance Fact Book*, published by the American Council of Life Insurance (ACLI) and the *1988 Update: Source Book of Health Insurance Data*, published by the Health Insurance Association of America (HIAA); statistics relating to Canada are taken from the 1987 edition of *Canadian Life and Health Insurance Facts*, a publication of the Canadian Life and Health Insurance Association (CLHIA).

This book was developed to serve as an assigned reading for one course in the Claims Education Program of the International Claim Association. The Claims Education Program is designed to provide an introduction to life and health insurance and a thorough understanding of claim administration in life and health insurance companies. A diploma from the International Claim Association and the designation of Associate, Life and Health Insurance Claims (ALHC), recognize successful completion of the program.

ORGANIZATION

The second edition of *Claim Administration: Principles and Practices* is divided into five sections:

Section One—Introduction overviews the general claim decision process. In addition, this section presents the basic characteristics and policy provisions of life and health insurance coverages so that readers will be familiar with these products before being introduced to the technical intricacies of the claim process for a particular insurance product. This part of the book also examines topics that are relevant to all types of insurance coverages, such as when insurance coverages begin and end, and misrepresentation in the application.

Section Two—Life Claim Administration focuses on the evaluation and payment of life insurance claims. Claims for supplementary life insurance benefits are also discussed.

Section Three—Medical Claim Administration explains the examination and payment of medical expense and dental claims. Medical and dental benefits and government-sponsored medical programs are described.

Section Four—Disability Claim Administration presents the claim process for disability claims. Definitions of disability, rehabilitation of disabled individuals, and disability settlements are discussed in this section.

Section Five—Other Types of Claims covers a variety of other types of insurance claims, including credit insurance claims, reinsurance claims, and claims for annuity and endowment benefits.

ACKNOWLEDGMENTS

The second edition of *Claim Administration: Principles and Practices* is a project of the International Claim Association. All of the members of the

International Claim Association Education Committee should receive special recognition for their involvement in this textbook project. I would like to express my sincere appreciation to W.J. West, CLU, ALHC, who chaired the ICA Education Committee when work was begun on this edition of the text, and to Carroll D. Smith, ALHC, who chaired the Curriculum Subcommittee and then the ICA Education Committee during this text project. My special thanks go to Jan E. LeRoux, Curriculum Subcommittee Chairperson, who served as the coordinator for this project, reviewed the entire manuscript, gave me much encouragement and support during the text development process, and whose contribution to the book was nothing short of outstanding.

My thanks go to the members of the textbook review panel who spent many hours reviewing manuscript copy. Their suggestions, insights, corrections, and encouragement were essential to the book's development.

Textbook Review Panel

Bruce E. Hodsoll, CLU, FLMI, ALHC
Director of Claims
Berkshire Life Insurance Company

John A. Houser, III, FLMI, ALHC, RHU
Director—Individual Benefits
UNUM Life Insurance Company

Jan E. LeRoux
Director of Claims
The Prudential Insurance Company of America

Debra A. Schempp
Federal Compliance Analyst
Phoenix Mutual Life Insurance Company

John V. Urbaitis, FLMI, ALHC
Senior Staff Claim Consultant (Retired)
John Hancock Life Insurance Company

Additional Reviewers and Technical Advisors

In addition to the members of the textbook review panel, many other individuals in the industry lent their expertise to various aspects of the text. I would like to express my appreciation to the following individuals: James F. Adams, ALHC, Assistant Vice President, Individual Claims, State Mutual Life Assurance Company of America; John C. Broshar, FLMI, Second Vice President, Munich American Reassurance Company; Lorne Harding, FLMI, ALHC, Manager, Policy Administration Operations, Manufacturers Life

Insurance Company; G. Robbie Robinson, Manager, Dental Claims, John Hancock Life Insurance Company; Carolynn E. Semon, ALHC, Life Claims Consultant, State Mutual Life Assurance Company of America; and Patsy E. Turpin, Director, Group Claims, Life Insurance Company of Georgia.

The following industry organizations and insurance companies have been extremely helpful in the development of this text by providing information or allowing us to use or adapt material owned by them: the American Council of Life Insurance (ACLI), the Canadian Life and Health Insurance Association (CLHIA), the Health Insurance Association of America (HIAA), the Phoenix Mutual Life Insurance Company, the Prudential Insurance Company of America, and the State Mutual Life Assurance Company of America.

Finally, much of the material in this book was drawn from the text *Claim Administration: Principles and Practices* (1980), by Charles H. Cissley. Therefore, it is appropriate to acknowledge all of the people who contributed to the development of that text.

LOMA Staff

The second edition of *Claim Administration: Principles and Practices* was developed for the ICA by LOMA. The following LOMA staff members deserve special mention for the work they performed on this text: Lana S. Kendig, FLMI, ALHC, read the entire manuscript and made many helpful suggestions; Jane L. Brown, FLMI, ALHC, served as one of the primary editors during the text's development and also coordinated the development of the glossary; Richard Bailey, FLMI, served as the production editor; Dani L. Long, FLMI, ALHC provided invaluable support during the text's development and production; Kristin M. Turner was largely responsible for compiling the glossary and also provided excellent administrative support. Robert D. Land, FLMI, while no longer a LOMA staff member, deserves recognition for copyediting the manuscript. Alexa Selph, also not a LOMA staff member, developed the index. Finally, my most sincere appreciation goes to Katherine C. Milligan, FLMI, ALHC, Manager, Curriculum Department, who reviewed the entire manuscript, and without whose support and guidance this text would not have been possible.

Jo Ann S. Appleton, FLMI, ALHC
Atlanta, Georgia
May 1989

Contents

SECTION TWO: LIFE CLAIM ADMINISTRATION

SECTION THREE: MEDICAL CLAIM ADMINISTRATION

SECTION FOUR: DISABILITY CLAIM ADMINISTRATION

SECTION

1

Introduction

1

The Claim Decision Process

Insurance products provide individuals and organizations with protection against some of the economic consequences of loss. In effect, a person who purchases insurance is buying the promise of the insurance company to pay a specified amount in the event that certain conditions occur. A claimant considers the payment of a claim as the fulfillment of the promise undertaken when the policy was sold. Prompt and courteous payment of valid claims contributes directly to customer satisfaction and thus to the long-term success of the insurance company.

In 1987, insurance companies in the United States and Canada disbursed more than $135.8 billion in life and health insurance benefits. Some of these claims were for relatively small amounts, such as a few dollars for a prescription drug. Other claims were much larger, such as multimillion-dollar life insurance settlements that included benefits for accidental death.

Claim administration, therefore, is an important function in a life and health insurance company. This chapter describes the claim administration function, including the claim decision process and claim investigation.

CLAIM EXAMINATION

Claim examiners, also called claim approvers and claim specialists, in conjunction with their managers, are responsible for deciding the company's liability for each claim. Claim examiners review each claim to ensure that it is valid; they deny claims that are invalid or fraudulent. Insurers pay most claims immediately. Payment of a small percentage of claims is delayed by the need to obtain additional information. Finally, on a still smaller percentage of claims, insurers must deny liability under policy terms.

During the process of examining a claim, a claim examiner usually has three overall objectives:

- to be sensitive to the position of each claimant, who presumably has suffered a loss, possibly a grievous one,
- to pay each claim as quickly as possible while still ensuring adequate investigation, and
- to minimize the cost of the claim administration process.

A claim examiner is trained to be courteous in all conversations and correspondence with the claimant. Even when circumstances prevent routine payment of the claim, a cooperative attitude on the part of the claim examiner will help assure that the claim is settled without undue stress to the claimant.

An insurance company has a responsibility to its insureds to provide prompt and equitable payment of claims. In addition, the laws of most jurisdictions mandate prompt settlement of claims. For example, a majority of states in the United States have enacted delayed interest statutes that require insurers to add interest to the proceeds payable, if a claim is not paid within a certain number of days after the company receives sufficient proof of loss. However, the claim examination process should not be so speedy that proper controls over the legitimacy of claims are lost. Not every claim deserves to be paid. Some claims are submitted under erroneous interpretations of policy provisions, and a small percentage are filed with fraudulent intent. The claim examiner must balance the need for prompt claim decisions with a need for effective claim control.

In addition, not every claim warrants the same amount of examination. An efficient claim processing system will identify those claims that, for any of several reasons, should be looked at more closely. If a claim examiner were to scrutinize every claim with the same degree of thoroughness, processing costs would rise, and, ultimately, so would premium rates.

How well these three objectives are met on a continuing basis depends very much on the professional conduct and training of claim examiners and the management of the claim department. In order to assure a high level of service and professionalism among claim personnel, many insurance companies have developed a philosophy to provide some general principles for claim practices. A company's claim philosophy may be written or unwritten, but it generally includes all of the guidelines shown in Figure 1–1, the "Statement of Principles" developed by the International Claim Association (ICA).

ICA Statement of Principles

The International Claim Association, in recognition of the need to continue public trust and confidence in the insurance industry, reaffirms the following principles:

1. Any individual who has, or believes he has, a claim is entitled to courteous, fair, and just treatment; and shall receive with reasonable promptness an acknowledgement of any communication with respect to his claim.

2. Every claimant is entitled to prompt investigation of all facts, an objective evaluation, and the fair and equitable settlement of his claim as soon as liability has become reasonably clear.

3. Claimants are to be treated equally and without considerations other than those dictated by the provisions of their contracts.

4. Claimants shall not be compelled to institute unnecessary litigation in order to recover amounts due, nor shall the failure to settle a claim under one policy or one portion of a policy be used to influence settlement under another policy or portion of a policy.

5. Recognizing the obligation to pay promptly all just claims, there is an equal obligation to protect the insurance-buying public from increased costs due to fraudulent or nonmeritorious claims.

6. Procedures and practices shall be established to prevent misrepresentation of pertinent facts or policy provisions, to avoid unfair advantage by reason of superior knowledge, and to maintain accurate insurance claim records as privileged and confidential.

7. Reasonable standards shall be implemented to provide for adequate personnel, systems and procedures to effectively service claims. These standards shall be such as to eliminate unnecessary delays or requirements, overinsistence of technicalities, and excessive appraisals or examinations. Claim personnel shall be encouraged and assisted in further developing their knowledge, expertise, and professionalism in the field of claim administration.

Figure 1-1. "Statement of Principles" of the International Claim Association.

As mentioned previously, the majority of states have enacted statutes that impose penalties on insurers who fail to settle claims promptly and equitably. Some states have adopted verbatim the National Association of Insurance Commissioners (NAIC) Model Unfair Claims Settlement Practices Act, shown in Figure 1–2. Other states have used portions of the Model Act in their statutes but have added more specific and restrictive time standards for certain actions by insurers, such as furnishing claimants with proof-of-loss forms.

The Claim Decision Process

There are many different types of claims, each of which requires flexibility on the part of the examiner in the examination process. Consideration of a disability claim, for example, necessarily raises different questions than does examination of a life claim. Nonetheless, a claim examiner is likely to follow a basic claim decision process that will hold regardless of the size or type of the claim, or the size of the company. This process involves obtaining satisfactory answers to seven questions prior to approving a claim:

1. Was the policy in force when the loss was incurred?
2. Was the "insured" actually covered by the policy?
3. Is the policy contestable?
4. What was the nature of the loss?
5. Is the loss covered by the policy?
6. What benefits are payable?
7. Who receives the benefits?

Although these questions might seem simple, complicated problems can arise when the examiner attempts to answer any of them. The problems could relate to provisions of the policy, the loss which occurred, or to the interpretation of laws and court decisions. Given the variety of policies and the wider variety of possible circumstances, any number of different problems can arise during the claim decision process.

Verifying Policy Status

As the first step in the claim decision process, the examiner verifies that the policy under which the claim is filed was actually in force at the time the loss occurred. This verification is usually routine because most companies now maintain this information electronically. Using computers, claim personnel can quickly and easily access policy status information. In most cases, a review of the records shows that the premiums have been paid promptly and regularly, so there is no question as to the in-force status of the policy. When problems do arise, they generally involve two questions:

Unfair Claim Settlement Practices

Committing or performing with such frequency as to indicate a general business practice any of the following:

(a) misrepresenting pertinent facts or insurance policy provisions relating to coverages at issue;

(b) failing to acknowledge and act reasonably promptly upon communications with respect to claims arising under insurance policies;

(c) failing to adopt and implement reasonable standards for the prompt investigation of claims arising under insurance policies;

(d) refusing to pay claims without conducting a reasonable investigation based upon all available information;

(e) failing to affirm or deny coverage of claims within a reasonable time after proof of loss statements have been completed;

(f) not attempting in good faith to effectuate prompt, fair and equitable settlements of claims in which liability has become reasonably clear;

(g) compelling insureds to institute litigation to recover amounts due under an insurance policy by offering substantially less than the amounts ultimately recovered in actions brought by such insureds;

(h) attempting to settle a claim for less than the amount to which a reasonable man would have believed he was entitled by reference to written or printed advertising material accompanying or made part of an application;

(i) attempting to settle claims on the basis of an application which was altered without notice to, or knowledge or consent of the insured;

(j) making claims payments to insureds or beneficiaries not accompanied by statement setting forth the coverage under which the payments are being made;

(k) making known to insureds or claimants a policy of appealing from arbitration awards in favor of insureds or claimants for the purpose of compelling them to accept settlements or compromises less than the amount awarded in arbitration;

(l) delaying the investigation or payment of claims by requiring an insured, claimant, or the physician of either to submit a preliminary claim report and then requiring the subsequent submission of formal proof of loss forms, both of which submissions contain substantially the same information;

(m) failing to promptly settle, when liability has become reasonably clear, under one portion of the insurance policy coverage in order to influence settlements under other portions of the insurance policy coverage;

(n) failing to promptly provide a reasonable explanation of the basis in the insurance policy in relation to the facts or applicable law for denial of a claim or for the offer of a compromise settlement.

Figure 1-2.   NAIC Unfair Trade Practices Act, Section 4, subsection (9).

had coverage commenced under the policy before the loss occurred, or had coverage under the policy terminated before the loss occurred?

Verifying Coverage of the Insured

Once the in-force status of the policy has been established, the next step of the claim process is to verify that the person suffering the loss was actually covered under the policy. This step is necessary to protect the insurance company from fraudulent and mistaken claims.

A **fraudulent claim** occurs when a claimant intentionally uses false information in an attempt to collect policy proceeds. Until quite recently, fraud was not a significant factor in the examination of claims. However, fraudulent claims have increased to the point where the NAIC has promulgated a Model Insurance Fraud Statute and Model Legislation to Create a Fraud Unit in a State Department of Insurance. Legislation following either or both of these models has been enacted in at least 17 states and is under consideration in several others.

The Model Insurance Fraud Statute defines insurance fraud and also requires that claim forms include the following statement:

> Any person who knowingly, and with intent to injure, defraud or deceive any insurance company, files a statement of claim containing any false, incomplete, or misleading information is guilty of a felony.

The Model Legislation to Create a Fraud Unit calls for a special bureau or division in a state's Insurance Department that has extensive investigative authority including subpoena powers, arrest powers, search and seizure authority, etc. Currently, four states—New York, California, Idaho, and Florida—have established such fraud bureaus.

Nonetheless, the vast majority of problems encountered by examiners during this stage of the claim decision process are genuine mistakes on the part of the insured. When these types of errors occur, they likely involve policies that cover more than one person, such as family policies or group policies. Under both family policies and group policies, the policy may be in force, but a person seemingly insured actually may not be included in the policy coverage.

Examining for Misrepresentation

An insurer ordinarily relies on statements made in policy applications. If such statements are false, they may result in the company's issuing a policy it would not otherwise have issued. Upon learning the truth, the insurer may have the right to cancel the policy on the grounds that no valid contract ever existed. The legal process of cancelling an insurance contract because of material misrepresented in the application is called **rescission**. Companies in both the United States and Canada must meet strict legal requirements in order to rescind a policy. One of these requirements is a limit on the time during which an insurer may contest or challenge the validity of a policy because of misrepresentation in the application. This time limit, usually two or three years, is called a **contestable period**.

As a standard practice, many companies scrutinize any claims arising during the contestable period. Such claims, of course, may be perfectly legitimate; as such, they would be honored. However, there is always the possibility that, when applying for insurance, the insured was aware of adverse information and withheld or falsified that information on the application. Most often, falsified information involves the medical history or condition of the insured; however, it also could involve the insured's occupation, hobbies, or any other factor that influences insurability.

Verifying the Loss

Having determined that the insured was covered by an in-force policy and that there was no misrepresentation, the examiner turns next to the loss that has been claimed. Specifically the examiner seeks proof that the loss did occur, along with sufficient detail to describe the exact nature of the loss.

Verifying Policy Coverage of the Loss

If a claim examiner is satisfied that a loss has occurred, the next step is to verify that the loss was covered by the policy. In some situations, the claim examiner might complete this step before verifying the loss. For example, if the claimed loss is clearly excluded from the policy, the examiner could decline the claim solely on that basis, without determining whether the proof of loss is satisfactory.

Determining the Amount of Benefits

As a rule, insurance companies try to adhere closely to the provisions of the insurance contract, in order to protect the interests of all parties concerned and to provide benefits exactly as intended. Ideally, the amount of liability should be clearly determinable, and in most claim situations, it is. However, at other times a number of factors must be considered in computing the amount of benefits. For example, accumulated dividends, interest payments, and premiums paid in advance may have to be added to a life insurance benefit. On the other hand, disability income payments may be reduced if the insured receives disability income from other sources such as Social Security or Workers' Compensation.

Determining the Recipients of Benefits

Once the amount of liability has been determined, the only step remaining in the claim decision process is to establish what person or persons will receive the benefits and in what share.

Life insurance policy proceeds are payable, in the manner designated, to the beneficiary or beneficiaries named in the policy. In many cases, the company can distribute the policy proceeds in exactly the way specified by the policyowner, but such distribution may not always be possible. For example, a beneficiary may be a minor or may be disqualified from receiving the policy proceeds because of statutory law. Medical expense and disability benefits ordinarily are payable under policy terms to the insured person but may also be assigned to a provider of services, such as a doctor or hospital.

Investigating Claims

Although not part of the formal decision process, investigation is a critical step in processing certain claims. In the majority of cases, the claim examiner evaluates a claim from the claimant's statement and from the submitted proof of loss. Using that information, the examiner determines whether the claim is legitimate and whether it meets the requirements of the policy. If the examiner has reason to doubt any aspect of the claim, further information may be required before a decision is made. The process of obtaining necessary claim information is known as a **claim investigation**. The purpose of a claim investigation is not to directly decide the merit of the claim, but rather to supply the information necessary to reach that decision. The process of investigation, then, is one of fact-finding, not one of decision.

The majority of claims do not require investigation. Of those that do, most require only short, simple searches that may involve no more than checking one medical record or interviewing one person. Investigations of this sort are typically performed by claim examiners themselves, working through written correspondence or by telephone.

Some claims require extensive investigation in order to establish all the relevant information. For example, a case in which an insured's death might have been accidental or suicidal would require extra investigation. Sometimes a claim examiner is able to conduct a complete investigation from the company office. Often, however, a field investigation is required in the locality where the insured lived or where the loss occurred. Some insurance companies have their own staffs of claim investigators for such field work; other companies utilize the services of professional investigation agencies.

The extent of the investigation to be conducted in connection with a claim depends on the exact type of claim involved, the kind of information needed to make a proper decision about the claim, and the difficulty encountered in obtaining that information. More specifically, the extent of an investigation is influenced by the

- amount of the insurer's liability,
- cause of the loss,
- circumstance of the loss,
- amount and type of information already available,
- age of the insured,
- place where the loss occurred,
- length of time the policy has been in force, and
- policy provisions.

The extent of the investigation, the information sought, and the techniques used to gather that information necessarily depend on the claim situation. Sources of information include hospitals and attending physicians, employers and unions, banks and neighboring businesses, landlords and tenants, and neighbors, relatives, and friends of the insured. Government agencies at all levels may also have important information about either the insured or the event of loss. Regardless of the sources being contacted, effective investigation requires courtesy, tact, and resourcefulness in order to obtain a true picture of the claim situation.

In recent years concern has grown over an individual's right to privacy within society. One aspect of this concern has been the need for insurers to secure valid authorizations to obtain claim investigation data from various sources. Also, a number of statutes and court rulings affect the techniques that may be employed in an investigation. For example, conducting an investigation under a false pretext is now prohibited in many jurisdictions. Many of the privacy regulations only formalize practices that insurers had already adopted on their own initiative. But those regulations have the weight of law, and violations may leave the insurer liable for the payment of damages.

Each step of a claim investigation should be carefully documented and retained in the claim file for that case. The documentation of an investigation should include

- the policy number and claim number, if any,
- the source contacted: hospital, physician, employer, or other source,
- the date of contact,
- the authorization to obtain necessary information, if such authorization is necessary,
- a copy of the request for information, if the request was made through correspondence,

- a report of the interview with the source, if one was conducted, and
- any other material information that has been obtained, such as police reports, vital statistics records, or newspaper clippings.

The documentation of an investigation should only contain information that is relevant to the claim. There should be no reference to ethnic origin unless that information is somehow relevant to the case. For example, in a contestable investigation it could be relevant that a Hispanic insured did not speak or understand English and that the application was taken by a non-Spanish-speaking agent. However, the fact that an insured and a spouse were of different races would not be relevant in most cases. Similarly, information about an individual's alleged morals or lifestyle is usually irrelevant to the decision of the case.

Hearsay evidence, or evidence based on what someone has been told but has not actually witnessed, that is uncovered during an investigation may properly be documented as a lead to more substantive evidence. Investigation reports, however, should not contain the personal opinions of the investigator or examiner. In the event of litigation over the claim decision, the contents of the claim file would likely be open to claimant's counsel, and the inclusion of personal opinions in the file is both unprofessional and potentially prejudicial to the position of the company.

References

"Fraudulent Claims." *1985 ICA Group Insurance Workshop Notes*, 17–18.
"Fraud Upon Insurance Companies." *1985 ICA Individual Health Insurance Workshop Notes*, 34–35.
Homer, Charles T. "Fair Claim Settlement Practices," *1987 ICA Life Insurance Workshop Notes*, 13–15.

2

Overview of
Life Insurance Coverages

Although claim examiners follow the basic decision process explained in Chapter 1 when examining all types of insurance claims, the focus and degree of the analysis varies according to the type of insurance claim. For example, an examiner processing a claim for benefits under a whole life insurance policy that has terminated must consider whether the policy might be in force under a nonforfeiture option. Since there are no nonforfeiture options under a term life insurance policy, they are not involved in the claim decision process for this product. An understanding of the various types of coverage available thus is important to the claim examiner. In this chapter, we review the basic types of individual and group life insurance coverage. Chapter 3 describes the general characteristics of group and individual health insurance coverage.

FORMS OF LIFE INSURANCE

Life insurance policies can be issued on an individual or group basis. *Individual life insurance* is issued to an individual in relatively unrestricted

This chapter has been adapted with permission from Chapter 3 of *Principles of Life and Health Insurance*, 2nd Edition (Atlanta, Georgia: LOMA, 1988), by Dani L. Long and Gene A. Morton.

maximum face amounts. Individual life insurance contracts typically cover only one person. However, special types of individual policies, such as family policies, may cover several lives.

Group life insurance covers a group of people under one contract, called the **master contract**. Thus, one master contract covers many individual lives. The majority of group life insurance policies are issued to businesses to cover the lives of employees; the group insurance contract is purchased by the employer for the benefit of the employees.

Individual Life Insurance

The two basic categories of individual life insurance commonly sold in the United States and Canada are term insurance and whole life insurance, each of which is available in many forms. *Term life insurance* is issued to provide coverage for a specified period or term. *Whole life insurance* is issued to provide coverage for the insured's entire lifetime, assuming premiums are paid as specified in the contract. Within each product category are several different forms of the basic product; these product classifications are often called plans of insurance.

Term Life Insurance

By definition, all term insurance products provide coverage for a specified, limited period of time. The term during which the policy is in force may be as short as the time required to complete a plane trip or as long as 30, 40, or more years. The term may be described as a specified number of years—1 year, 5 years, 10 years, 20 years—or it may be defined by specifying the age of the insured at the end of the term. For example, a term insurance plan that covers a person until the person reaches age 65 is referred to as "term to age 65," and the policy's coverage expires on the policy anniversary that falls either closest to or immediately after the insured person's 65th birthday. The *policy anniversary* is the anniversary of the date on which the policy was issued. For example, if a company issues a policy on January 5 of a given year, then every succeeding January 5 is the policy anniversary.

Term life insurance protection, or coverage, is usually sold as a policy, but it can also be provided by a *rider* added to or attached to a policy. A policy **rider**, which is also called an **endorsement**, is an addition to the insurance contract that is as legally effective as any other part of the policy. Riders are commonly used to provide some type of supplementary benefit or to increase the amount of the death benefit provided in a policy, although riders may also be used to limit or modify a policy's coverage. Some of the supplementary benefits that are commonly provided through riders will be described later in this chapter.

The life insurance benefit provided by a term life insurance policy can remain the same, decrease, or increase over the length of the contract. A *level term life insurance policy* provides a death benefit that remains the same over the period specified. For example, a five-year level term policy providing $10,000 of coverage specifies that the insurer will pay $10,000 if the insured dies at any time during the five-year period that the policy is in force. Premiums for level term insurance policies usually remain the same throughout each term of coverage.

A *decreasing term life insurance policy* provides a death benefit that starts at a set face amount and then decreases in some specified manner over the term of coverage. For example, the benefit during the first year of coverage of a five-year decreasing term policy or rider may be $10,000 and then may decrease by $2,000 on each policy anniversary; the coverage would be $8,000 during the second year, $6,000 in the third year, $4,000 in the fourth, and $2,000 in the last year. At the end of the fifth year the coverage would expire. The premium for decreasing term insurance usually remains level during the period of coverage.

The death benefit of an *increasing term life insurance policy* starts at one amount and increases at stated intervals by some specified amount or percentage. For example, an insurance company may offer a policy that has a death benefit which starts at $10,000 and then increases by 5 percent on each policy anniversary date throughout the term of the policy. Alternatively, the death benefit may increase according to increases in the cost of living as measured by a standard index, such as the Consumer Price Index (CPI). The premium for increasing term insurance generally rises with the amount of coverage. A policyowner usually is granted the option of freezing at any time the amount of coverage provided by an increasing term life insurance policy. This coverage may be sold as a single policy or, more commonly, as a rider to an existing policy.

By definition, term life insurance provides only temporary insurance protection. At the end of the specified period, the policy is no longer in force. Sometimes, however, a policyowner may wish to continue the coverage beyond the term specified in the policy. A *renewable term insurance policy* includes a renewal provision that allows the policyowner to extend the insurance coverage at the end of the specified term without submitting *evidence of insurability*, or proof that the insured person continues to be an insurable risk. If the policyowner has not exceeded (1) any upper age limitation for renewal of the policy or (2) the maximum number of renewals permitted, then the insurance company must renew the coverage at the policyowner's request. In such a renewal, the insurer cannot charge a higher premium rate based on the insured's physical condition even if the insured is suffering from a severe health problem. However, the insurer can, and usually does, charge an increased premium based on the current age of the insured. Since premium rates for new insurance coverage generally increase with the insured's age, the higher premium rate for renewal coverage is to be expected. The new premium rate will then remain the same throughout the new term of the policy.

Another type of term insurance policy that gives the policyowner the right to extend insurance coverage beyond the term specified is a **convertible term insurance policy**. The **conversion privilege** included in this type of policy allows the policyowner to change (convert) the term insurance policy to a permanent insurance policy without providing evidence of insurability. Even if the health of the person insured by a convertible term policy has deteriorated to the point that he or she would otherwise be uninsurable, the policyowner can obtain lifetime insurance coverage on the insured since evidence of insurability is not required at the time of policy conversion. The premium that the policyowner is charged for the permanent insurance policy cannot be based on any increase in the insured's degree of risk, except with regard to the insured's age.

Insurers usually do not permit conversion after the insured has attained a specific age, such as 55 or 65. In addition, conversion may be limited to the first five or eight years after policy issue. Finally, insurers may limit the death benefit of the converted policy to only a percentage of the original policy's face amount if the policy is converted after a certain period. For example, a 10-year term policy may permit conversion of 100 percent of the face amount only within the first five years of the term, and a smaller percentage, such as 50 percent of the face amount, if the policy is converted in the last five years of the term insurance coverage.

The privileges of renewal and conversion are of obvious potential value to the policyowner, but they are also of value to the insurance company. Most policyowners renew or convert their term policies not because they are in poor health, but because they want to continue their insurance protection. Therefore, insurance companies are able to keep the insurance in force without the expenses of initiating new sales and underwriting new business. Relatively few term insurance policies result in death claims because a term policy usually will (1) expire before the insured dies, (2) be converted to whole life insurance, or (3) terminate because renewal premiums have not been paid.

Whole Life Insurance

Unlike term life insurance that provides protection for a limited period of time and pays no benefits after that period ends, whole life insurance provides lifetime insurance coverage at a premium rate that does not increase with the age of the insured. In addition, whole life insurance policies differ from term life insurance policies in that, as a result of the premium pricing system, whole life insurance policies accumulate a savings element called the **cash value**. Each whole life policy guarantees that the cash value will accumulate in a specified manner. If a policyowner cancels whole life insurance coverage and surrenders the policy to the company, the policyowner can receive the net cash value of the whole life insurance policy, also known as the cash surrender value. The **net cash value** is the guaranteed cash value amount less any policy loans and any applicable surrender fees.

Sometimes, the owner of a policy that has a cash value may be unable or unwilling to continue making premium payments on the policy but will still desire some form of insurance protection. For the benefit of such policyowners, and in accordance with the Standard Nonforfeiture Law in the United States, life insurance companies include nonforfeiture options in their life insurance policies. **Nonforfeiture options** allow a policyowner who is surrendering a policy with a cash value to determine what is to be done with the policy's net cash value. The policyowner may choose to (1) receive the net cash value of the policy as cash, (2) use the net cash value to purchase paid-up insurance of the same plan as the original policy, (3) use the net cash value to purchase term insurance coverage for the amount of coverage available under the original policy, or (4) use the net cash value to pay an overdue premium on the original policy.

In addition, any whole life insurance policy that has accumulated a cash value may be used as security for a loan. The policyowner may request a loan, known as a **policy loan**, from the insurance company, or the policyowner may use the cash value of the policy as collateral for a loan from another financial institution. However, if the insured dies before a policy loan is repaid, then the unpaid amount of the loan plus any interest outstanding is subtracted from the policy benefit before the death claim is paid.

Modified Whole Life Insurance.   Since a policyowner's needs for life insurance may be greatest at the time when he or she is least able to afford whole life insurance, insurers commonly offer two methods of modifying whole life insurance policies. The first of these modifications of traditional whole life policies involves *modifying the premium* for a specified initial period, such as five years, by charging less than the policyowner would normally pay for a similar whole life policy. After the specified period, the premium increases to a stated amount that is somewhat higher than the usual (nonmodified) premium would have been. This increased premium is then payable for the rest of the life of the policy. The death benefit of the policy, however, remains the same during the entire period. For example, a $75,000 continuous-premium whole life policy issued on the life of a 23 year-old man might require a $500 annual premium payment. The premium for a modified whole life policy for the same amount might be $310 per year for the first ten years, with the premium increasing to $700 per year thereafter for the rest of the policy.

The second manner of modifying traditional whole life policies involves *modifying the amount payable as a death benefit*. Under this method, the death benefit is decreased by a specific percentage or amount at certain stated ages. In anticipation of reduced coverage at the older ages, an insurer will be able, from the time of policy issue, to provide a stated amount of coverage under a modified whole life policy for a lower premium than would be possible if the insurer were liable for the initial death benefit amount throughout the entire expected lifetime of the insured. For example, the death benefit of a modified coverage whole life insurance policy may begin at $100,000, decrease to $75,000 at age 60, decrease further to $50,000 at age 70, and then remain level for the rest of the insured's lifetime. As this example illustrates, during the period when the insured is at an advanced age, the death benefit of the policy will be at its lowest level. Usually, however, this period will also be the time when the policyowner's need for life insurance is lowest.

Universal Life Insurance.   Universal life insurance policies are a fairly new form of whole life insurance coverage. Within certain limits, the owner of a universal life policy can choose the policy's face amount and premium amount and can change these amounts after the policy is in force. Figure 2–1 illustrates the manner in which a universal life policy operates. Insurers deduct an expense charge from the premium paid for a universal life policy in order to cover the costs of administering it. The remainder of the universal life premium is credited to the policy's cash value. Each month, the insurance company deducts the mortality costs from the cash value and credits the remainder of the cash value with an interest payment at a specified rate. Both the amount of the mortality charges and the interest rate are subject to change over the course of the policy.

The owner of a universal life policy is permitted to specify the premium amount he or she will pay, as long as this amount falls within the limits specified by the company. The policyowner can also change the premium amount at any time, subject to similar restrictions. The *minimum* annual premium amount specified by the insurer applies only to the *initial* premium payment. However, although insurance companies do not specify minimum renewal premium amounts, if the renewal premium amount the policyowner pays is too low *and* the amount of money in the policy's cash value is insufficient to pay the policy's mortality and expense charges, then the policy will terminate.

Insurance companies also establish maximum premium amounts that can be paid for a universal life policy. These maximums are based on the amount of the policy's death benefit in relationship to the amount of the policy's cash value. The more a policyowner pays in premiums above the amount needed to pay the policy's costs, the greater the policy's cash value will be.

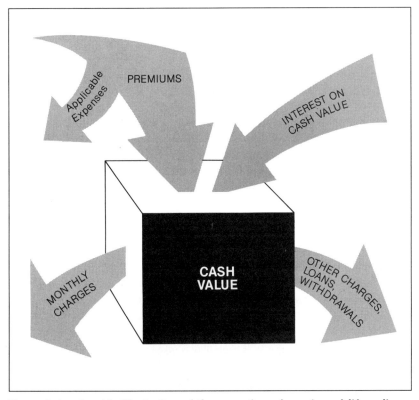

Figure 2-1.   Graphic illustration of the operation of a universal life policy.

In order to prevent the policy from being viewed strictly as an invest-ment contract, rather than as a life insurance contract, the policy's cash value is not permitted to exceed a specified percentage of the policy's death benefit. The specific percentage permitted depends on the insured's age. In the United States, the required difference between a policy's face amount and the policy's cash value is referred to as the ***TEFRA corridor***, because the Tax Equity and Fiscal Responsibility Act (TEFRA) of 1982 was the first legislation that stipulated this relationship in its definition of life insurance contracts. Insurance companies will not allow a policyowner to pay a premium amount that results in a cash value that exceeds the legislatively defined percentage of the death benefit.

In addition, most universal life policies in the United States include a provision specifying that if the cash value exceeds this percentage, then the death benefit of the policy will automatically increase to an amount that will meet requirements concerning the proper relationship between the cash value and the death benefit. In Canada, requirements concerning the cash values and death benefits of universal life policies are much stricter than these requirements are in the United States; consequently, universal life policies are not as popular in Canada as they are in the United States.

Variable Life Insurance.   A **variable life insurance policy** is similar to a traditional whole life policy in that premiums for most forms of variable life policies sold in North America remain level throughout the lifetime of the insured. However, most insurers also offer a single-premium or modified-premium variable life policy.

The major difference between a variable life policy and a traditional whole life policy is that the death benefit and the cash value of a variable life policy depend on the investment performance of a special fund, called a *separate account* in the United States, and a *segregated account* in Canada. Assets representing policy reserves of traditional whole life policies are considered part of the company's general account and are placed in a varied group of secure investments which provide a steady rate of return. Assets representing the policy reserves for *variable* life insurance policies are placed in **separate accounts**, which have few investment restrictions. Most variable life policies permit the policyowner to select from among several separate accounts and to change this selection at least annually. Each separate account follows a different investment strategy. For example, some accounts concentrate investments in high-growth stocks, while other accounts may concentrate on bonds. The values of the separate accounts increase or decrease depending on the returns from the separate investments. The death benefit and the cash value of variable life insurance policies depend upon how well the separate account investments do. Most variable life policies guarantee that the death benefit will not fall below a specified minimum. A minimum cash value is rarely guaranteed.

Purchasing variable life insurance, despite its minimum death benefit guarantees, is riskier for policyowners than purchasing a traditional whole life policy. For example, if the stock market fails to perform well, the variable life insurance policy may not provide as high a death benefit for a given premium as a traditional whole life policy will provide. Further, the cash value of a variable life product could fall to zero if investment results are extremely poor. However, there is a potential for substantial gain from a variable life insurance policy, and there is some evidence to support the idea that over time the face amount of a variable life policy will keep pace with inflation.

Variable Universal Life.   Variable universal life insurance policies, which are also called *universal life II* and *flexible-premium variable life* policies, combine the premium and death benefit flexibility of universal life with the investment flexibility and risk of variable life insurance. Like a universal life policy, a variable universal life policy allows the policyowner to choose the premium amount and the death benefit. Like a variable life policy, the cash value of a universal variable life policy is placed in a separate investment account. The policyowner chooses the investment account and may change the chosen option at least annually. The policy's cash value changes along with fluctuations in the investment earnings of the separate account. Most insurers allow the policyowner to choose whether his or her variable universal life policy's death benefit remains level or varies along with changes in the investment earnings of the separate account.

Supplementary Benefit Riders

The coverage provided by most individual life insurance policies may be expanded by adding supplementary benefit riders. Earlier in this chapter, we mentioned that term insurance coverage may be provided either by a term insurance policy or by a term insurance rider added to an existing policy. There are many additional benefits which, for an extra premium amount, can be provided by riders. In this chapter, we describe two important benefit riders that are widely used throughout the life insurance industry: guaranteed insurability riders and cost of living benefit riders. Other supplementary benefit riders are described in later chapters.

Guaranteed Insurability Rider.   The guaranteed insurability (GI) rider gives the policyowner the right to purchase additional insurance of the same type as the original policy on specified dates for specified amounts without supplying additional evidence of insurability. Normally, the rider states that the amount of coverage the policyowner may purchase on an option date is limited to the face amount provided under the original policy or an amount specified in the rider, whichever is smaller. For example, a guaranteed insurability rider on a $10,000 traditional whole life policy may state either that the owner has the right to purchase additional $10,000 whole life insurance policies when the insured is 30, 35, and 40 years old, or the rider may permit such purchases on the third, sixth, and ninth policy anniversaries. It may also permit the purchase of additional insurance policies when certain events occur, such as marriage or the birth of a child. When added to a universal life policy, the guaranteed insurability rider gives the policyowner the right to increase the universal life policy's face amount without providing evidence of insurability, rather than the right to purchase a new universal life policy.

The rider guarantees that the policyowner will be able to purchase additional life insurance coverage even though the insured may no longer be in good health. Also, many insurers provide a premium discount for policies purchased on any of the option dates specified in the guaranteed insurability rider.

While the right to purchase the extra coverage is automatic, the actual purchase is not; the policyowner who desires the extra coverage must take positive action to buy the new coverage. Most GI riders specify that if the policyowner does not exercise the option on one of the specified dates, that option is lost forever, though the policyowner can still exercise the next option when it comes due.

Some guaranteed insurability riders provide automatic temporary term insurance coverage for the period during which the option to purchase can be exercised. This term insurance coverage usually lasts 60 to 90 days and is designed to protect the beneficiary in cases in which the policyowner is delayed in taking the necessary action.

Cost of Living Adjustment Rider.   The cost of living adjustment (COLA) rider can be added to both term insurance policies and the various forms of whole life insurance policies. This rider specifies that the face amount of the policy will automatically increase every year that there is an increase in the Consumer Price Index (CPI). For example, if the CPI rises 5 percent during a year, then the death benefit of a $20,000 whole life insurance policy with a COLA rider would increase by 5 percent to $21,000. The premium rate for the coverage will also increase when the death benefit of the policy increases. No evidence of insurability is required for such coverage increases. If the CPI decreases during a year, the policy benefit generally remains level. Most COLA riders specify a maximum policy death benefit beyond which the benefit may not be increased regardless of increases in the CPI. Usually, the policyowner is permitted to refuse the additional coverage; however, many such riders specify that if the increase is refused, then the rider will terminate and no further increases will be made available.

Group Life Insurance

As mentioned at the beginning of this chapter, life insurance can also be provided on a group basis. Group life insurance provides life insurance coverage for a group of people under one master contract. The groups most commonly covered under a group contract are employer-employee groups. A group life insurance contract is a contract between the insurance company and the owner of the group master contract. The individuals insured under a group contract are not parties to the contract.

Traditionally, group insurance protection is provided by one-year renewable term insurance which provides the insured with no cash surrender values or nonforfeiture options. Although other types of group life insurance coverage are available, we describe only one-year renewable term coverage in this chapter because of its predominance in the group life insurance market.

One-Year Renewable Term Life Insurance

One-year renewable term life insurance is rarely offered as an individual life insurance product. The major disadvantage to such a product is the annual increase in premiums as the insured ages. Although the annual premium increases for an individual insured under a one-year renewable term life insurance product are slight from year to year at the younger ages, the increases are sizable after age 45. In the group market, however, one-year renewable term life insurance is used almost exclusively because the overall cost of the group premium seldom rises sharply since younger individuals are continually moving into the group plan.

Certificates of Insurance

Although individuals insured under a group policy are not parties to the group insurance contract, they still have a right to know the extent of their coverage under the group insurance contract. Group life insureds receive a certificate of insurance that outlines the insurance benefits that will be paid or the method for determining the amounts of insurance benefits that will be paid. The certificate of insurance also describes any policy provisions such as the conversion privilege or the waiver of premium for disability that are included in the group master contract.

Benefit Amounts.   To avoid *antiselection*, or the tendency of persons who have a greater likelihood of loss also to have a greater tendency to buy insurance, life insurance companies base group life insurance benefits on a schedule so that neither the individual insured nor the policyowner can select individual benefit amounts. In employee benefit programs, the amount of an employee's group life insurance is usually based on some objective factor such as the employee's position, seniority, or earnings. Figure 2–2 shows a representative group life insurance benefit schedule based on employee earnings.

Conversion Provision.   Group term life insurance certificates contain a conversion privilege which is similar to the one that may be included in individual term life insurance policies. If an insured group member loses his or her group coverage because of (1) termination of employment, (2) termination of membership in a classification of eligible employees, or (3) retirement, then the conversion privilege allows the insured to convert his or

Annual Earnings	Group Term Life Insurance Benefit
Less than $10,000	$ 10,000
$10,000 to 14,999	$ 20,000
$15,000 to 19,999	$ 25,000
$20,000 to 29,999	$ 40,000
$30,000 to 39,999	$ 75,000
$40,000 to 49,999	$100,000
$50,000 and over	$125,000

Figure 2-2.   Sample group life insurance benefit schedule basing benefits on amount of employee earnings.

her group coverage to individual whole life insurance coverage within a stated period, usually 30 to 45 days after the date of termination of coverage. The insured must pay a premium that is appropriate for the insured's age, but no extra premium may be assessed based on the health of the insured.

3

Overview of Health Insurance Coverages

Although health insurance policies were not issued in the United States and Canada until the middle of the 19th century, the growth in the number of such policies has been phenomenal. By the end of 1985, more than 181 million Americans—77 percent of the civilian noninstitutional population in the United States—were protected by one or more forms of private health insurance. Even though residents of Canada are covered by government health insurance programs, the majority of Canadians are covered by supplementary private health insurance as well.

Health insurance is a broad classification that includes two distinct types of insurance coverages: (1) *medical expense coverage*, which provides benefits for the treatment of sickness or injury; and (2) *disability income coverage*, which provides income benefits when the insured is unable to work or suffers a loss of income because of sickness or injury. While both types of coverages are classified as health insurance, the characteristics

This chapter has been adapted with permission from Chapter 12 of *Principles of Life and Health Insurance*, 2nd Edition (Atlanta, Georgia: LOMA, 1988), by Dani L. Long and Gene A. Morton.

of each coverage are quite different, and the claim processing methods for each type of coverage can vary considerably as well.

In this chapter, we present a brief overview of the characteristics of insurer-provided medical expense coverage and insurer-provided disability income coverage. We will also look at the characteristics that distinguish individual health insurance coverages from group health insurance coverages. In later chapters, we explore in greater detail many of the health insurance topics introduced in this chapter.

MEDICAL EXPENSE COVERAGES

Medical expense coverages were originally developed with separate benefits for hospital, surgical, and medical expenses. Each type of basic coverage provided very specific benefits. Then, insurers began offering a comprehensive major medical contract either as a stand-alone policy or in addition to the basic benefits. As insurers isolated other consumer needs, additional types of coverages were offered. Although the names of the specific insurance products may vary from insurer to insurer, medical expense coverages can usually be grouped into one of the following five major categories:

- basic *hospital-surgical-medical expense coverage*, which provides benefits related directly to hospitalization costs;
- *major medical coverage*, which provides broad and substantial protection for medical expenses;
- *social insurance supplemental coverage*, which provides benefits that complement existing government health insurance programs;
- *hospital confinement coverage*, which provides a predetermined flat benefit amount for each day an insured is hospitalized; and
- *specified expense coverage*, which provides benefits, such as dental benefits or prescription drug benefits, that reimburse the insured for expenses incurred by obtaining treatment for a condition specified in the policy.

With the exception of specified expense coverage, all medical expense coverages are available in the United States to both groups and individuals. In Canada, where all citizens are covered by government programs that pay benefits to cover the costs of most types of medical treatment, social insurance supplements and specified expense coverages are available to individuals and groups that want to add to the coverage provided by government programs.

DISABILITY INCOME COVERAGES

Disability income coverages provide specified income benefits when an insured person becomes unable to work or suffers a loss of income because of an illness or injury. (We describe disability benefits in greater detail in Chapter 14.) Disability income insurance can be issued on an individual or a group basis. Basic individual disability income policies typically provide a flat income benefit amount that is specified at the time the policy is purchased. Group disability policies, by contrast, generally specify income benefit amounts that are a percentage of the insured's earnings. In addition, benefits provided under group policies are usually reduced to reflect any amounts received by the insured from other sources, such as government disability income programs. Individual disability income benefits are not reduced in this manner.

GROUP HEALTH INSURANCE POLICIES

There are many similarities between group life insurance policies and group health insurance policies. Both are issued as master contracts to the master policyholder; under both types of policies, certificates of insurance are issued to the group members insured under the contract. As in group life insurance, the group health policyholder defines the classes of individuals eligible for coverage. Most employers who purchase group health insurance contracts define eligible group members as all full-time employees who are actively at work on the date that the coverage takes effect.

Most group insurers will tailor group health insurance policies to meet the needs of each master policyholder, thus allowing the policyholder flexibility in choosing the specific benefits that will be included in the policy. For group policies that provide disability income coverage, the policyholder can specify the elimination period, the benefit amount, and the maximum benefit period that will be included in the policy. For medical expense policies, the policyholder can specify the type of medical expense coverage (hospital-surgical, major medical, etc.), the benefit maximums, and the cost containment features to be included in the policy. Cost containment features such as preadmission testing and second surgical opinions are included in medical expense policies to influence insureds to hold down claim expenses by using the most cost-effective health care services available.

Group Health Insurance Policy Provisions

Several of the provisions found in group health insurance contracts, such as the grace period provision and the incontestability provision, are similar to ones found in group life insurance contracts. (As mentioned in Chapter 2, we discuss these provisions in detail in later chapters.) In this section, we describe certain contract provisions that differ in content from corresponding provisions found in group life insurance contracts. These provisions include (1) the physical examination provision, (2) the pre-existing conditions provision, and (3) the conversion provision.

The Physical Examination Provision

The physical examination provision grants the insurer the right to have an insured who has submitted a claim for benefits examined by a doctor of the insurer's choice, at the insurer's expense. Such an examination may provide the insurer with information about the validity of a medical expense claim or a disability claim made by the insured. In disability income policies, this provision also grants the insurer the right to require that a disabled insured undergo examinations at regular intervals so that the insurer can determine whether the insured is still disabled. A physical examination provision is usually included in both individual and group health insurance contracts.

Pre-existing Conditions Provision

A few group health insurance policies include a pre-existing conditions provision which states that benefits will not be paid for conditions caused by a pre-existing condition. In group policies, a **pre-existing condition** is usually defined as a condition for which an individual received medical care during the three months immediately prior to the effective date of the coverage. Group policies also specify that a condition will no longer be considered pre-existing if (1) the insured has not received treatment for that condition for three consecutive months, or (2) the person has been covered under the group plan for 12 consecutive months. Group policies generally specify that the pre-existing conditions provision will be waived for all group members at the time a contract becomes effective if the group was previously covered by a group health policy issued by another insurer. The content of the pre-existing conditions provision found in individual health insurance policies is different from the pre-existing conditions provision found in group policies and is described later in this chapter.

Conversion Provision

The conversion provision of a group health insurance certificate states that an insured group member who is leaving the group has a limited right to purchase an individual health insurance policy without presenting proof of insurability. The conversion right is limited in that an insurer can refuse to issue an individual policy if the individual coverage would result in the insured group member's being insured under two or more policies. Generally, the benefits provided by the converted individual policy will parallel the benefits available under individual health policies rather than the benefits available under the group contract. However, the elimination period included in individual disability income policies is waived if the insured is disabled at the time of conversion. Further, the pre-existing conditions provision traditionally included in individual health insurance policies is not included in individual conversion policies.

Cost Containment Features in Group Medical Expense Policies

The rapidly rising costs of health care in the late 1970s and 1980s resulted in increased claim payment amounts and, thus, in higher health insurance premium rates. In 1988, for example, many group health insurers increased their premium rates an average of 20 percent over 1987 premium rates. Group policyholders watching the costs of their medical expense plans escalate have become interested in incorporating a variety of cost containment features in their medical expense plans. Cost containment features that can be incorporated into medical expense policies include (1) deductibles, (2) coinsurance provisions, (3) coordination of benefits (COB) provisions, (4) second surgical opinion (SSO) programs, and (5) preadmission testing (PAT) programs. The ways in which all of these cost containment features affect claim handling are discussed in Chapter 12.

Deductibles

A *deductible* is the amount an insured must pay before an insurance company will make any benefit payments under a policy. By requiring an insured to share in the costs of medical expenses, a deductible encourages an insured to utilize medical services only when necessary. Both individual and group medical expense policies include deductibles.

Group policyholders can choose deductible amounts ranging from $100 to $1,000 per calendar year or can base deductible amounts on the amount of an insured's earnings. For example, the deductible for a person earning less than $20,000 might be $100, whereas the deductible for a person earning between $20,000 and $40,000 might be $300. In addition, policyholders can implement special deductibles for certain kinds of care. For example, a policyholder that wants to discourage unnecessary hospital admissions may require that an insured pay, in addition to the regular deductible, a separate deductible for each hospital admission.

Coinsurance Provisions

Coinsurance provisions are included in most group medical expense policies and are similar to deductibles in that they require an insured to share in the costs of medical expenses. A *coinsurance provision* specifies the percentage of covered expenses, usually 10 to 25 percent, that insureds under the group plan must pay and the percentage of covered expenses, usually 75 to 90 percent, that the group plan will pay. In addition, coinsurance provisions usually specify an overall maximum limit such as $1,000 that an insured will have to pay in any calendar year before the insurer will pay 100 percent of the insured's medical expense claims. For example, assume that Isaac Douglas is insured under a medical expense policy with a $200 deductible, an 80 percent coinsurance percentage, and a $1,000 maximum annual limit. If, after satisfying the deductible for his policy, Isaac incurs another $500 of covered medical expenses, then he will be responsible for paying $100, and the insurer will be responsible for paying $400 of the medical expenses.

Some group policyholders have recently increased their insureds' coinsurance percentage, thinking that an insured would be more likely to utilize cost-effective medical care if required to contribute more to its costs. Other group policyholders have taken another approach and decreased the insured's coinsurance percentage when the insured utilizes certain kinds of care such as an outpatient surgical center instead of in-hospital surgery.

Coordination of Benefits Provisions

Coordination of benefits (COB) provisions were developed to avoid instances of overinsurance. **Overinsurance** occurs when a person insured under two or more insurance policies can collect total benefits in excess of actual losses incurred. For example, a person covered as a dependent under one group policy and as a primary insured under another group policy could file for benefits for the same medical expenses under both policies and could collect more in benefits than was incurred in medical expenses.

COB provisions are included in all group medical expense contracts. The COB provision defines the plan that is the primary provider of benefits in situations in which the insured group member has duplicate group medical expense coverage. The **primary provider of benefits** is the medical expense plan that is responsible for paying the full benefit amounts promised under the plan. Once the plan designated as the primary provider has paid the full benefit amounts promised, then the insured can submit to the secondary plan (1) the claim and (2) a description of the benefit amounts paid by the primary plan. The secondary plan will then determine the amount payable for the claim under the terms of its coverage. COB provisions are discussed in greater detail in Chapter 12.

Second Surgical Opinion (SSO) Programs

Many health insurance policies provide full coverage for nonemergency surgery only if the insured has obtained a confirming second opinion before undergoing the surgery. The reason for SSO programs is that significant amounts of elective surgery are unnecessary. For example, one study conducted over an eight-year period found that about one-third of those voluntarily seeking a second surgical opinion, and 18 percent of those required to seek such an opinion, did not receive confirmation for the operation from the second opinion.[1]

Insurers usually reimburse the insured for the costs of the second opinion (or even a third opinion) and require no deductible or coinsurance payments. Other insurers allow a set dollar amount for the costs of the second or third opinions. However, even if there are conflicting opinions about the necessity of the surgery, the decision to elect or reject surgery remains with the insured. The SSO program merely determines the percentage of the costs that the group plan will pay.

Preadmission Testing (PAT)

X-rays, lab tests, and other tests necessary for an insured's surgery or hospital admission are much less expensive if the tests are done on an outpatient basis prior to the insured's hospital admission. Health insurance policies frequently provide higher benefit levels or waive deductibles or coinsurance requirements for tests done on a preadmission basis. An insured may still elect to have the tests done on an inpatient basis but must share in the costs through deductibles or coinsurance payments.

INDIVIDUAL HEALTH INSURANCE POLICIES

Although insurers do not offer individual health insurance applicants the number of coverage variations that are available to group policyholders, an individual applicant is permitted to make some choices concerning the benefit levels and renewal provisions that will be included in the individual policy. For medical expense policies, the insurer usually allows the applicant to choose the deductible amount. For disability income policies, the insurer generally offers several possible combinations of elimination periods and maximum benefit periods.

Types of Policies

Both individual medical expense policies and individual disability income policies can be classified on the basis of the type of renewal provision included in the policy. According to the terms specified in the renewal provision, health insurance policies are classified as either (1) cancellable, (2) optionally renewable, (3) conditionally renewable, (4) guaranteed renewable, or (5) noncancellable.

---

[1] "Second Surgical Opinion." *1983 ICA Group Insurance Workshop Notes*, 3–4.

Cancellable

In a cancellable policy, the renewal provision grants an insurer the right to terminate an individual policy at any time, for any reason, simply by notifying the insured that the policy is cancelled and by refunding any advance premium that the policyowner had paid. Some states in the United States have declared that cancellable health insurance policies are illegal. In all Canadian provinces other than Quebec all individual medical expense insurance policies are cancellable.

Optionally Renewable

An insurer has the right to refuse to renew an optionally renewable health policy on a date specified in the policy. This date is usually either the policy anniversary date or any premium due date. An insurer is also permitted to add coverage limitations and/or increase the premium rate for any class of optionally renewable individual health insurance policies.

Conditionally Renewable

A conditionally renewable health insurance policy grants an insurer a limited right to refuse to renew a health policy at the end of a premium payment period. A refusal to renew must be based on one or more specific reasons stated in the policy contract but cannot be related to the insured's health. The age or employment status of the insured are often listed as reasons for refusal.

Guaranteed Renewable

An insurer is required to renew a guaranteed renewable health insurance policy, as long as premium payments are made, until the insured reaches the age limit stated in the contract, usually age 60 or 65. Premium rates may be increased for a whole class of guaranteed renewable policies but not for an individual insured.

Noncancellable

Noncancellable policies are guaranteed to be renewable until the insured reaches the age limit specified in the contract, usually 60 or 65. An insurer does not have the right to increase the premium rates for a noncancellable policy under any circumstances. The noncancellable classification is usually available only in disability income policies.

Individual Health Insurance Policy Provisions

Many of the policy provisions found in individual health insurance policies are similar or identical to provisions found in group health insurance policies. For example, both group and individual medical expense policies include physical examinations provisions. In this section, we describe a few of the individual health insurance policy provisions that differ substantially or entirely from the policy provisions found in group health insurance policies.

Pre-existing Conditions Provision

Most individual health insurance policies contain a pre-existing conditions provision which states that until the insured has been covered under the policy for a certain period, usually two years, the insurer will not pay benefits for any health conditions that were present and known to the insured before the policy was issued. The pre-existing conditions provision is designed to prevent antiselection by those individuals who might seek to purchase an individual health insurance policy to provide benefits for a known health problem. In an individual health insurance policy, a *pre-existing condition* usually is defined as an injury that occurred or a sickness that first appeared or manifested itself before the policy was issued *and* that was not disclosed on the application. Some policies specify that the insured person must have experienced symptoms of the condition during either a two- or five-year period before the policy was issued in order for the insurer to exclude that condition from coverage. A sample pre-existing conditions provision is shown in Figure 3–1.

Any condition that an insured disclosed on an application is not considered to be a pre-existing condition. An insurance company will pay benefits for the treatment of such a disclosed condition unless the policy specifically excludes the condition from coverage.

In addition, the Uniform Individual Policy Provisions Law Model Bill specifies that after an individual policy has been in effect for three years, no claim may be denied nor benefits reduced because of a pre-existing condition. In some states, that period is two years. Many policies use a period that is shorter, such as one year.

Pre-existing conditions.   Benefits for a charge that results from a covered person's pre-existing condition, as defined in this policy, will be provided only if that charge is a covered charge and is incurred by that person after coverage for that person has been in force for two years. However, if a condition is excluded from coverage by name or specific description, no benefits will be provided for any charges that result from that condition even after those two years.

Figure 3–1. A sample pre-existing conditions provision.

The Overinsurance Provision

Individual health insurance policies commonly include overinsurance provisions, also known as insurance with other insurers' provisions. Overinsurance provisions allow an insurer to make a proportional reduction in the amount of its benefit payment to an insured, when the insured has other health insurance coverage of which the insurance company had not received notice prior to acceptance of the application. This provision takes effect only if the insurer *was not notified* of the other coverage at the time of application. If a company applies this provision to a claim and reduces benefits, the company will return a pro-rata portion of the premiums that have already been collected.

Claim Provisions

Individual health insurance policies are required to include provisions that define both the insurer's and the claimant's obligations with respect to claim procedures.

The notice of claim provision requires the claimant to provide timely notification of a loss to the insurer. In the United States, the insurer must be given notice of a claim within 20 days after the occurrence of a loss covered by the policy, or as soon thereafter as is possible. Where it is not reasonable for an insured to give such notice to the insurer within 20 days, later notice will generally be accepted.

The claim forms provision specifies that the insurer must provide the claimant with the proper claim forms within 15 days of the date notice of loss is received. If claim forms are not provided, the claimant need only provide a written description of the nature and extent of the loss.

Another provision specifies that a claim will be paid immediately upon receipt of proof of loss unless periodic payments are involved. In Canada, the insurer must pay benefits within 60 days of receipt of proof of loss for a medical expense claim and within 30 days of receipt of proof of loss for a disability income claim.

References

Vadakin and Lipton. *The Health Insurance Answer Book* (Greenvale, New York: Panel Publishers, Inc., 1986), 71–93.

4

Determining When Coverage Begins

In insurance sales transactions, particularly individual life and health insurance sales transactions, insurers reserve the right to evaluate the risk involved in each application before issuing an insurance policy. The process that insurers use to assess and classify the potential degree of risk that a proposed insured represents is called **underwriting**. Because of the potential for antiselection, insurers reserve the right to modify the terms of coverage or even to reject an application if the underwriting process indicates that the applicant has a higher than acceptable probability of loss.

During the underwriting of individual insurance, an applicant may suffer a loss that would be covered under the terms of the policy as applied for. In such situations, the claim examiner must determine if the policy was in effect during the period after the signing of the application but before policy issue. If the insurance company did not accept any legal *consideration*, or initial premium payment, at the time the application was signed and submitted, then no valid contract existed and the proposed insured was not covered by the policy. On the other hand, if the insurer accepted an initial premium payment with the application, a loss during the underwriting period may be covered through interim, or temporary, coverage. Whether such temporary coverage exists depends upon many factors including: (1) the type of premium receipt issued, (2) court rulings regarding premium receipts, (3) the existence of a temporary insurance agreement, (4) the method and adequacy of the initial premium payment, (5) agent actions and statements, and (6) changes in the policy or in the applicant's status after the date of application.

PREMIUM RECEIPTS

Insurance companies commonly issue a premium receipt to an applicant who submits the initial premium with an insurance application. The premium receipt usually provides some temporary insurance coverage during the underwriting period. Although the wording of premium receipts varies from company to company, the two basic types of premium receipts commonly used by insurance companies are binding receipts and conditional receipts.

Binding Receipts

An insurance company that issues a **binding receipt** is willing to start coverage on the date of the policy application subject to later termination if the insurer finds that the proposed insured is uninsurable. A binding receipt provides temporary insurance that remains in effect at least until the insurer reaches an underwriting decision. In some cases, the binding receipt remains in effect until the applicant is notified of the underwriting decision. A claim that arises for a loss occurring prior to the underwriting decision would be evaluated in the same manner and according to the same criteria as a claim arising for a loss occurring after policy issue.

Binding premium receipts are common in the property and liability lines of insurance because there is comparatively little opportunity for antiselection by applicants for those products. For example, a soliciting agent selling a fire insurance policy is usually able to ascertain to some degree the insurability of the structure involved. By contrast, life and health insurance applicants may be aware of health impairments that are not readily apparent to the agent. Therefore, most life and health insurers are reluctant to issue binding receipts. They are more likely to issue a form of premium receipt that provides interim coverage on a conditional basis, rather than a binding basis.

Conditional Receipts

A **conditional receipt** specifies standards or conditions the proposed insured must satisfy before the insurer will accept the applicant as an insurable risk. If the conditions are met, coverage becomes effective as of the date named in the receipt. If the conditions are not met, the insurer has no liability. In legal terminology, specified standards or conditions that must be met before the proposed insured's insurance coverage comes into being are called *conditions precedent*, because the fulfillment of these standards precedes the responsibility of the insurer to provide insurance coverage. Two types of conditional premium receipts are approval receipts and insurability receipts.

Approval Receipts

The approval receipt specifies that the proposed insured will be covered from the issue date of the approval receipt but only if the application is approved by the company. Wording varies, but one example is

> The insurance for which this application is made shall take effect on the date of this receipt or the date of the medical examination (if required), whichever is later, if the applicant is approved for insurance as set forth in the application.

Under the wording of this type of receipt, if a life insurance applicant dies before the insurer approves the risk, the insurer can deny liability for the claim. Suppose, for example, on June 1, Marsha White applies for a life insurance policy on her own life, pays the initial premium, and receives a conditional receipt of the approval type. On June 4, Marsha undergoes the required physical examination. On June 5, before any underwriting decision has been made, Marsha dies accidentally. Under the wording of an approval receipt, the company, upon learning of Marsha's death, could reject the application even if the results of her medical examination show that Marsha was in good health on June 4.

Because of the restricted coverage provided by approval receipts and liberal interpretations of these types of receipts by U.S. courts, conditional receipts of the approval type are rarely used today.

Insurability Receipts

An insurability receipt provides coverage only if the company ultimately approves the application or determines the proposed insured to be insurable. If the proposed insured is determined to be insurable, then the insurer will provide coverage retroactively from the later of the premium receipt date or the date of the medical or paramedical examination, if an examination is required. The receipt might be worded as follows:

> The insurance for which this application is made shall take effect on the date of this receipt or the date of the medical examination

(if required), whichever is later, if in the opinion of the company
the insured is insurable under its rules and practices for the plan
and the amount applied for.

Although the wording of the insurability receipt is close to that of the
approval receipt, the difference is significant. For example, if in the previous
example Marsha White had been issued an insurability receipt instead of
an approval receipt, the company would be required to proceed with *post
mortem* (after death) underwriting of the application. If the *post mortem*
evaluation indicated that Marsha was insurable on June 4, when the medical
examination was completed, then the conditions precedent would have
been satisfied; coverage would extend back to June 4 and would have been
in effect when Marsha died.

Problems can arise, however, when the company has to determine an
applicant's insurability after death. Suppose that Marsha died on June 3,
after completing the application but before undergoing the medical examination. In such a case, it is impossible for the company to determine
Marsha's insurability; hence, according to the wording of the receipt, the
company has no liability to pay a death claim. Nonetheless, claim examiners
usually review the circumstances surrounding such a death, particularly
if the proposed insured appeared to be a healthy person and died accidentally, to ascertain possible liability should the beneficiary take the claim
to court.

In situations in which an applicant who was issued an insurability receipt
dies after completing an application but before undergoing a required
medical examination, a claim examiner should consider the following
questions:

1. At the time of the application, was the applicant advised by the
   agent that a medical examination of the proposed insured was
   necessary?
2. If the medical examination was ordered by the home office
   underwriter, had the request been conveyed to the proposed insured before the date of death?
3. How long a period elapsed between the completion of the application and the date of death?
4. If there was a delay in undergoing the medical examination,
   what was the reason? Was the delay caused by procrastination
   by the proposed insured, failure of the agent to provide
   guidance, or nonavailability of the examining physician?

If the answers to any of these questions suggest that the company contributed in any way to the failure of the proposed insured to undergo the
required medical examination, then the insurer is more open to challenge

for denying claim liability than if the delay were wholly the fault of the proposed insured. As a matter of practice, some companies return initial premiums on all applications for which underwriting is not completed within a specified period of time, such as 60 days, with a letter stating clearly the reasons for the return of premium.

Situations arise in which the proposed insured undergoes the required medical examination but dies before all of the requested tests have been administered. For example, the underwriter may require additional blood pressure readings or urinalysis, but the proposed insured dies before the tests can be made. Once again, it is impossible to determine insurability, and the claim examiner needs to consider the circumstances. Were the additional tests really necessary to the evaluation of the proposed insured's risk, or were they simply to lend additional validity to the underwriting decisions? Was there a delay on the part of the company in informing the proposed insured of the need for additional tests? Or did the proposed insured delay the tests after being clearly informed of their necessity? A diligent search for answers to these questions can help the claim examiner determine the company's liability for a claim.

Finally, the proposed insured might have successfully completed the medical examination but died before a requested inspection report was received by the company. In such a situation, the application should be underwritten *post mortem*. If the inspection report shows that the application should have been approved as applied for, the claim should be paid.

But what if the inspection report reveals information to indicate that the proposed insured would not have been issued insurance as applied for? When a *post mortem* rejection is based on the inspection report, it may be necessary, if the case results in litigation, to prove the actual truth of all derogatory material in the inspection report. Therefore, the claim examiner should ensure that allegations in the inspection report, as well as statements from all other sources of necessary information, such as hospital records or attending physicians' statements, are factually stated, clearly relevant, and reported exactly as given.

Legal Decisions on Premium Receipts

Over the past 25 years, insurers have witnessed a continuing trend by U.S. courts to interpret the language in conditional receipts in ways not intended by insurance companies. In Canada, courts are more likely to adhere strictly to the language used in conditional premium receipts.

Initially, the approval type of conditional receipt found disfavor with U.S. courts because the courts did not want life insurance companies to arbitrarily deny an applicant coverage simply because of the applicant's death. The courts used various arguments including ambiguity of the language of the receipt, reasonable expectations of the applicant, unfair acts of the insurance company, and the fact that the applicant is paying something for nothing, to support their decisions in cases on this topic.

The insurability type of receipt would seem to avoid courts' concerns about arbitrary rejection of applicants since, under the requirements of the insurability receipt, the insurer applies standard underwriting criteria to evaluate the proposed insured, even if such underwriting is performed on a *post mortem* basis. Yet, legal decisions in at least 20 states have now rendered all conditional receipts, whether approval receipts or insurability receipts, nearly useless in limiting an insurer's liability during the underwriting period.

One of the most significant departures from a literal interpretation of the wording of conditional receipts can be found in the 1978 Pennsylvania Supreme Court decision in the case of *Collister* vs. *Nationwide Life Insurance Company.* In this case, the proposed insured died nearly seven weeks after completing the application, but without having taken the medical examination. The insurer denied the claim on the basis of failure to complete the conditions precedent, specifically, the required medical examination. The Pennsylvania Supreme Court said, in a divided opinion, that insurers must prove, "by clear and convincing evidence, that the consumer could not reasonably have expected to receive immediate coverage in return for the payment of the required premium." The court reached this decision despite the fact that the premium receipt contained these words on its front:

CONDITIONAL FIRST LIFE PREMIUM RECEIPT: NO INSURANCE WILL BECOME EFFECTIVE PRIOR TO POLICY DELIVERY UNLESS THE ACTS REQUIRED BY THIS RECEIPT ARE COMPLETED. NO AGENT OF THE COMPANY IS AUTHORIZED TO CHANGE ANY ACT REQUIRED.

On the reverse side were the words:

IMPORTANT

The company reserves the right to require a medical examination. Until you can provide proof that you are insurable, the Company provides no insurance.

If you are requested to have an examination, don't delay. Make arrangements promptly. There is no insurance until a satisfactory examination has been made and all the conditions of this receipt are completed.

It appears to be clear from the decision in *Collister* that courts who liberally interpret the wording of conditional receipts will interpret a conditional receipt as if it were a binding receipt regardless of the wording used in the receipt. Therefore, attempts by insurers to clarify conditional receipt language seem to hold little promise for creating a more favorable legal environment.

TEMPORARY INSURANCE AGREEMENTS

The uncertain legal status of conditional receipts has led a number of insurers to introduce temporary insurance agreements as an alternative to the conditional premium receipt. *Temporary insurance agreements*, also known as temporary insurance receipts and interim insurance agreements, typically provide a guaranteed amount of temporary life insurance coverage for a specific period of time, usually the time during which the policy is being underwritten.

A temporary insurance agreement provides an applicant with coverage in an amount equal to the lesser of (1) the amount of all death benefits applied for in the application, or (2) the life insurance company's maximum acceptance amount for the temporary insurance agreement, usually $100,000 to $500,000. Further, such agreements specify that if the proposed insured commits suicide during the term of coverage or if the application contains a material misrepresentation or a fraudulent statement, then the coverage is void.

All temporary insurance agreement forms include questions about the proposed insured's health. Figure 4–1 shows an example of the health questions included in a representative temporary insurance agreement. In order for an agreement form to be acceptable to an insurer, all health questions must be answered "No," and no question may be left blank. As a practical matter, most agreement forms have only two basic health questions, as follows:

1. Has the proposed insured seen any physician or other practitioner within the past year to have surgery performed or recommended?
2. Has the proposed insured had or been treated for heart disease, stroke, or cancer within the past two years?

If the proposed insured cannot satisfactorily answer all questions on the agreement form, he or she will not be covered under the temporary insurance agreement, and the insurer's agent is not authorized to accept any initial premium payment.

Temporary insurance coverage begins on the date an applicant satisfactorily completes the temporary insurance agreement form and makes pay-

ABC LIFE INSURANCE COMPANY
TEMPORARY INSURANCE AGREEMENT   No.050636

IMPORTANT: This Agreement provides a limited amount of insurance for a limited period of time if all of its conditions are met. No agent has authority to waive or change the terms of this Agreement.

Received from _____ in connection with an application for insurance having the same number as this Agreement:

$_____—Life Insurance or Annuity $_____—Disability Insurance

HEALTH QUESTIONS

1. Within the past 90 days, has any applicant been a patient in a hospital or other medical facility, had surgery, or been advised to be hospitalized or have surgery?   Yes No ☐ ☐

2. Within the past 2 years, has any applicant been treated for heart trouble, stroke, or cancer, or been advised by a medical professional to have such treatment?   Yes No ☐ ☐

3. If disability insurance is applied for, within the past 2 years has any applicant been unable to perform the duties of his occupation for 10 or more consecutive days due to sickness or injury?   Yes No Not Applicable ☐ ☐ ☐

If any Health Question is answered "yes," give question(s) and name of applicant(s) "yes" refers to: _____ _____. No insurance is provided under this Agreement on that applicant(s).

If any Health Question is not answered, this Agreement is void.

CONDITIONS

Insurance on an applicant, up to the Amount Limitation, will begin on the Effective Date if:

1. There is no material misrepresentation in the application or answers to the Health Questions; and

2. All of the Health Questions are answered "No" or "Not Applicable" with respect to that applicant; and

3. The payment received is at least 10% of the standard annual premium for the policy applied for at Life's published rates. Except that, if 10% of the standard annual premium is less than $15, the payment received must be at least $15. If payment is by a check which is postdated or not honored on presentation, this Agreement is void.

If an applicant dies by suicide, while sane or insane, the death benefit will be only the amount of premium paid.

EFFECTIVE DATE

"Effective Date" means the latest of:

1. the date of the application;

2. the date of the last medical exam initially required under ABC Life's underwriting rules. Any required medical exam must be completed within 30 days after the date of this Agreement; if not, this Agreement will be void with respect to that applicant.

AMOUNT LIMITATION

The total amount of insurance which may take effect on any applicant under this and all other Temporary Insurance Agreements is $100,000 of life insurance (including accidental death) and $1,000 per month of disability income.

TERMINATION OF TEMPORARY INSURANCE

Insurance under this Agreement will terminate with respect to all of the applicants on the earliest of:

1. The date that insurance begins under the policy applied for or under a policy issued other than as applied for;

2. 10 days after a policy other than as applied for is offered to the Proposed Insured or Owner;

3. 5 days after ABC Life mails a letter of declination to the Proposed Insured or Owner;

4. 60 days after the date of the application.

ALL PREMIUM CHECKS MUST BE MADE PAYABLE TO ABC LIFE. DO NOT MAKE THE CHECK PAYABLE TO THE AGENT OR LEAVE THE PAYEE BLANK.

I have read this Agreement and understand and agree to its terms. I understand this receipt provides no insurance unless all of its conditions are met and all required medical exams are completed. I declare that the answers to the Health Questions are true and complete to the best of my knowledge and belief.

_____   _____
Date   Proposed Insured

By_____   _____
Soliciting Agent   Owner (if other than Proposed Insured)

IF YOU HAVE NOT RECEIVED YOUR POLICY WITHIN 60 DAYS OF THE DATE OF THIS AGREEMENT, CONTACT ABC LIFE AT P.O. BOX _____, ATTN: UNDERWRITING DEPARTMENT.

Agent's Note: Send original to Home Office with application and give copy to Proposed Insured (Owner, if other than Proposed Insured).

COMPANY COPY

SNAP OUT THIS STUB WITH TISSUE SHEET ATTACHED BEFORE COMPLETING TEMPORARY INSURANCE AGREEMENT

Figure 4-1. Sample temporary insurance agreement form.

ment of the required portion of the first year's premium on the policy applied for. Coverage usually terminates at the earliest of

- 90 days from the date of the agreement; or
- the date insurance becomes effective under the policy applied for; or
- the date a policy, other than as applied for, is offered to the applicant; or
- the date the company mails notice of termination of coverage to the designated person.

Temporary insurance agreements have several favorable claim aspects. First, the exposure period for the company is short, and second, the amount of coverage usually granted under the temporary insurance agreement is limited. In addition, companies using the temporary insurance agreement forms have not experienced a significant amount of misrepresentation or fraud, possibly because of the inclusion of health questions in the agreements. And, most importantly for claim personnel, the courts appear to regard temporary insurance agreements as less ambiguous than conditional premium receipts.

METHODS OF PREMIUM PAYMENT

Most individual insurance policy applications state clearly that ". . . no insurance applied for shall become effective unless the policy shall have been issued by the company and the first premium paid in full . . . ." In most instances, premium payments are paid in full by personal check and pose few claim problems for the insurer. However, claim problems do occur when a bank does not honor a check used to make premium payments, when an applicant chooses an alternate premium payment method, when an applicant pays the wrong amount, or when an applicant delays paying the initial premium.

Payments by Personal Check

Payments made by personal check usually pose no claim problems. The major exception involves payments made by checks that a bank does not honor because of insufficient funds in the applicant's account. In many cases, a policy may have already been delivered in good faith by the company before the applicant's check is returned. Technically, in such cases, the consideration requirements for a valid insurance contract have not been met and there is no insurance in effect. However, companies typically allow the applicant a specified period of time to make a proper payment before

voiding the contract. Claim problems often occur, as the following example illustrates, when the insured experiences a loss during this interim
period.

> On September 1, Michael Bateson applied for life insurance, paid
> the required initial premium by check, and satisfactorily completed
> the required medical examination that same day. Michael died on
> September 5. On September 12, the check was returned by the bank
> marked "insufficient funds."

In this situation, it can be argued that the insurer is not liable for the
policy claim because Michael did not submit the required consideration.
In actuality, much depends upon an insurance company's regular claim practices. If an insurer regularly waives its rights and allows applicants a specified
period of time to make late payment before formally voiding a contract,
then the courts might view as arbitrary a decision to refuse late payment
solely on the basis of death.

A company's liability for a claim such as the one illustrated in the example above may also depend to a great extent on whether the policy has
been delivered. Many courts hold that if a policy has been delivered before
a check is returned, such unconditional delivery estops, or legally prohibits,
the insurer from denying that the policy was in force. In such jurisdictions,
the company might have to accept liability for the claim and pay the death
benefit after subtracting the initial premium. However, if a loss occurs before
the policy is delivered, the company would have stronger grounds for denying liability.

Some companies seek to prevent claim problems of this sort by using
conditional premium receipts which state that receipts are issued on the
condition that any check or other order for payment of money is good
and collectible. Other companies use temporary insurance agreements
which usually state that there is no coverage under the agreement form
should the check or draft submitted as payment not be honored by the bank.

Payroll Deduction

Payroll deduction plans, also known as salary deduction plans, may cause
claim problems in situations in which a loss occurs after an application
is signed but before the first premium has been collected by the insurer.
Under a payroll deduction plan, an individual applicant signs an application for insurance and authorizes his or her employer to deduct a specified
amount from the applicant's wages on a regular basis to pay the insurance
premiums. However, in many cases, the amount deducted per pay check
is less than a full premium payment. If a loss occurs prior to the employer's

making the first full payment to the insurance company, is the insurance company liable for the claim? Consider the following example:

> On May 1, Hortense Smith authorized a deduction of $10 from each weekly paycheck toward a monthly premium of $40 for individual disability coverage. After the first two deductions were made in May, Hortense suffered a covered loss.

In this example, at the time of the covered loss, the employer has not deducted enough from her pay to make the initial premium payment to the insurer. The insurer, therefore, has not received any premium payment. However, Hortense may consider her authorization of the premium deduction to constitute payment to the insurer. In general, if there is no special wording regarding a premium deduction, companies will consider such applications to have been written on a "binding" basis and will honor claims such as that of Hortense. However, if the application states that there is no coverage until a full monthly premium has been paid, then that provision should govern the situation.

Bank Loans

Sometimes an agent sells a policy on a nonprepayment basis; simultaneously, the applicant signs a form requesting a bank loan. The amount of the loan is usually equal to one or more annual premiums. If the loan is approved, the amount is paid to the insurer.

Suppose the proposed insured dies after satisfying insurability requirements but before the loan is approved. There are different views on the liability of the insurer for such a claim. Under one view, the negotiations amount to a commitment of money to the insurer, warranting coverage after insurability had been established. By another view, such a commitment is not absolute because the applicant can withdraw the loan request, or the lending institution may not approve the loan. By this view, there would be no claim liability. However, if a company were willing to use the bank loan arrangement to attract business, it might encounter a sentiment in court that the insurance was indeed prepaid.

Dividend Accumulations

In some cases, the applicant chooses to use dividend accumulations on an in-force policy to pay the initial premium for a new policy. If the amount of dividend accumulations is sufficient to cover the initial premium of the new policy, and if the applicant authorizes in writing the use of the dividends for payment of the initial premium, then payment of the initial premium is accomplished. If a conditional receipt is given, and if the company determines that the applicant is insurable, coverage will be effective back to the date specified in the receipt. In a situation in which a conditional receipt is not given, if both the application and the payment agreement are executed simultaneously, many companies would assume that coverage dated back to the date of the application.

Policy Loans

An applicant may give a written statement requesting that the loan value, or the surrender value, of an in-force policy be used to pay the first premium on a new policy. If insurability is established, the claim liability is the same as though the premium had been paid by dividend accumulations. Should an applicant fail to submit a written statement authorizing the use of a policy loan for prepayment of the premium, the application for the new policy would be looked upon as a nonprepaid application.

Brokerage Business

Some insurance brokers will accept a life insurance application without prepayment but will immediately bill the applicant for the amount of the premium. If the proposed insured proves to be insurable but dies before the policy is delivered and the initial premium collected, the application is considered to be a cash on delivery (COD) policy, with no liability on the part of the insurer for a death claim.

Pre-authorized Checks (PAC)

Under a pre-authorized check (PAC) plan, a policyowner authorizes an insurer to draw checks from the policyowner's bank account in order to pay premiums. Premium prepayments under PAC plans are similar to cash prepayments in that if a risk is accepted by the underwriters, a loss occurring prior to the actual issuance of the policy is likely to be covered.

Partial Prepayments

Some companies accept partial premium prepayments and issue conditional receipts, which may establish interim coverage for the proposed insured. The interim coverage is usually for a period that the amount of premium paid would buy. Other insurers accept partial prepayments but issue only general money receipts which state specifically that no liability is undertaken. In recent years, a growing number of court decisions have held that it is unconscionable for an insurer to accept a money deposit without giving some specific consideration in return. Courts have also held that partial prepayments constitute ambiguity, and the courts have permitted the introduction of verbal testimony to establish an insurance contract. Because of this trend toward establishing liability where none had been intended, many companies no longer accept partial prepayments. But, at times, an agent may inadvertently quote and collect a partial prepayment, with the applicant believing that a full prepayment has been made. For purposes of determining the start of coverage, the insurer will have to treat such an application as being prepaid.

Minimum Deposit Arrangements

The applicant for a policy that has a first-year cash value may pay only the difference between the annual premium and the policy's net cash value at the end of the first year. The first-year value is thus used as a loan to pay the balance of the initial premium. Such a transaction is known as a *minimum deposit arrangement*. When accompanied by payment of the amount of the difference, the minimum deposit is satisfactory prepayment of the premium, and it will establish interim coverage under a conditional receipt.

Delayed Prepayments

Claim problems can arise when an application is taken without prepayment, but a premium prepayment is made before the policy is issued. For example, assume that Ruby Mandelli applied for a life insurance policy on March 1. On March 10, Ruby gave the agent the amount of the initial premium. On March 15, Ruby died before the policy was issued. Under these circumstances, the question of liability is strongly influenced by the type of receipt given. If Ruby received a conditional receipt, and if she is subsequently found to have been an insurable risk, then the insurer should probably accept liability. In general, as mentioned previously, courts are opposed to insurers' holding money while not providing any specific consideration, such as temporary coverage. Some companies seek to avoid this problem altogether by including wording on their conditional receipts to the effect that temporary coverage is possible only if payment is made on or before completion of the application. Other companies firmly prohibit the payment of any premium after the application has been submitted but before the application is approved.

AGENT'S ACTIONS AND STATEMENTS

Premium receipt forms customarily contain wording that prohibits the soliciting agent from waiving any of the conditions in the receipt. One example reads: "No change may be made in the terms and conditions of this receipt, and no statement purporting to make such a change shall be binding on the insurer." Nonetheless, much of the litigation involving premium receipts focuses on alleged statements made by soliciting agents. For example, a claimant may state that the agent, in providing a conditional receipt, said, "Now you're covered."

A clear statement on the receipt form regarding the lack of an agent's authority to waive conditions is usually sufficient for the courts to rule that any statements to the contrary are inadmissible because, in contract law, oral statements may not be used to change the terms of a written contract whose language is clear. Courts have usually held this to be true even when the agent makes a mistake in explaining the conditions involved.

However, the oral statements of the agent may be admissible, in some situations, as evidence in litigation seeking to establish liability of the insurer. If, for example, a court determines that the wording of the receipt is vague or ambiguous, then an agent's statements may be admitted as evidence in an attempt to determine the applicant's understanding of the meaning of the conditional receipt. Further, some courts have held that conditional receipts should be interpreted in view of the "reasonable expectations" of the applicant; such courts are therefore willing to admit agents' statements as evidence.

In evaluating a claim that involves questionable statements or actions on the part of an agent, the claim examiner should inquire into the following aspects of the sales and underwriting process:

- *Is the wording on the premium receipt and policy application forms clear?* Ambiguity will be construed against the insurer and can open the way for legal admission into evidence of an agent's statements.
- *Is the agent's lack of authority to waive any conditions clearly and prominently stated on the form?* Such a clarification lessens the chance of admitting the agent's statements of waiver into evidence.
- *Do agents' training materials and written company procedures emphasize the need for proper explanations of conditional receipts and interim coverage?* A documented record of company policy and practice may aid in establishing the good faith of the company.
- *In processing the application, were there any unnecessary delays during which the company held the premium money?* Particularly important here are delays (1) by the agent in submitting the application and the premium to the home office, and (2) by the home office in notifying the applicant of the rejection and in returning the premium. Explanations for unnecessary delays would help in establishing the company's good faith.
- *Has the company followed a practice of tolerating erroneous statements by agents?* If company sales brochures are worded more loosely than are the premium receipts, or if the agents are not adequately supervised, the company may be estopped, or prevented, from relying on the written terms of the receipt.

MODIFICATIONS IN POLICY APPLICATIONS

Sometimes a prepaid application for which a conditional receipt has been given cannot be approved exactly as applied for, but the insurance company is willing to issue the applicant a policy that specifies a higher-than-standard premium rate or a policy that contains exclusions, riders, or reduced benefits. The insurer, in such situations, is rejecting the applicant's original offer for a policy and is making a counteroffer to the applicant. Until the insurer's counteroffer is accepted—i.e., until the proposed modifications to the coverage or to the premium amount are accepted by the applicant and any additional premium paid—there is no contract between the applicant and the insurer. Therefore, the insurer is generally not liable for losses that occur before the insurer's counteroffer is accepted by the applicant.

Sometimes, however, policy applications are rejected because of minor technical problems, e.g., the wrong state's version of a policy application was signed. In such cases, and depending upon the established philosophy and practices of the company, the insurer may choose to accept liability for a loss prior to acceptance of the insurer's counteroffer.

CHANGE OF CONDITION OR INSURABILITY PROVISIONS

In the United States and in all of the Canadian provinces except Quebec, applications for insurance customarily include provisions which state that the policy shall not become effective until (1) the application is approved, (2) the policy is delivered, and (3) the first premium is collected. If the premium is not submitted with the application or if the premium is inadequate, a fourth qualification—that the policy be delivered during the continued good health of the insured—is typically included in applications. In the province of Quebec, an insurance policy comes into force upon acceptance of the application by the insurer, not upon delivery of the policy.

The requirement of continued good health is specified in either a change of condition provision, or an insurability provision in the application. According to a **change of condition provision**, all conditions described in the application must still be true at the time of policy delivery in order for the policy to become effective. In the case of the **insurability provision**, in order for the policy to become effective, the insured must still be insurable at the time of policy delivery according to the underwriting rules and practices of the company.

When an application is submitted without acceptable prepayment, the agent who delivers the approved policy usually asks the applicant questions regarding the health, habits, and occupation of the proposed insured. If the answers at the time of delivery are different from those given on the application, the agent will not deliver the policy but will submit the policy to the company's underwriting department for a review of the risk to determine if the changes in the proposed insured's status warrant any changes in the policy coverage or the policy's premium rate.

Agent's Actions

Claim examiners should explore the circumstances of policy delivery carefully in situations in which it is suspected that the insured had experienced a change in condition, but the policy was delivered anyway. It may be that the agent did not make the necessary inquiries at the time of delivery. If this is the case, the insurer may have a difficult time using the "change of condition" or "change of insurability" defense in court. If the applicant was not requestioned because the agent did not notice any change, the company may be able to reject a claim after the company presents sound evidence of an actual change. However, the agent may have delivered the policy to someone other than the proposed insured, without making any inquiry regarding the proposed insured's health. Another possibility is that the agent may have been told that the proposed insured was ill, but the agent delivered the policy anyway. In some cases, policies have actually been delivered to an insured who was hospitalized. When policy delivery is made by an agent who has knowledge of an applicant's illness, the insurer will find it difficult to deny coverage unless there is evidence of collusion between the insured and the agent.

GROUP INSURANCE

When determining whether coverage has started under a group life or health insurance policy, group claim examiners look at different factors than those considered by individual claim examiners. Although under both types of policies the receipt of the initial premium is usually a condition precedent to the start of coverage, conditional or binding receipts are generally not used in connection with group policies. Instead, the effective date of coverage is usually specified in the application and is included as a part of the policy; moreover, the effective date of coverage is often set to meet the needs of the group policyholder. The effective date may be set as part of a collective bargaining agreement between the policyholder and a labor union, or it may be set to coincide with the date on which existing coverage with another carrier is terminated. Group insurers commonly accept liability for claims incurred after the effective date agreed upon, even though underwriting may not be completed by then. Thus, claim examiners usually have few problems in determining when group insurance coverage begins for a covered group.

Initial Eligibility

Nevertheless, claim problems do occur during the process of determining whether an individual group member is covered. Although most group policies provide that all group members are eligible for coverage immediately under a new policy, the claim examiner, seeking to determine whether coverage has commenced for a group claimant, must still consider the specific policy provisions regarding initial eligibility.

Actively-At-Work Provisions

Group life and health insurance policies commonly include provisions, referred to as **actively-at-work provisions**, that require employees to be actively at work on the date their insurance would normally become effective in order to receive insurance coverage. For a new policy, this date would be the date the policy takes effect. For a new employee joining an existing group, this date would be the first full day of employment. If an employee is not actively at work on the day the plan takes effect, then the employee becomes eligible for insurance coverage on the day he or she returns to work. When a claim examiner is trying to determine if an employee has satisfied the actively-at-work requirement, the examiner must first look closely at the definition of the actively-at-work provision included in the contract.

According to one definition, an insured is actively at work if he or she is "actively performing the duties of his or her occupation." However, another definition describes *actively at work* as "actively performing all of his or her duties at the usual place of business on a full-time basis—full-time being at least 30 hours per week." It should be obvious that the outcome of a claim may differ substantially depending upon the type of definition used in the contract.

For example, consider an executive who is confined to a hospital prior to the effective date of her company's group life insurance policy, and who remains confined until the date of her death. If, while in the hospital, the executive conducted business by phone, dictated letters, and reviewed company reports, was the executive actively at work? Under the first definition, the death claim might very well be payable. Under the second definition, since the executive did not fulfill the requirement of working at the usual place of business, the claim could be properly denied.

When handling claims involving actively-at-work questions, the claim examiner should obtain all of the facts pertinent to the insured's employment, including

- a copy of the insured's job description,
- a letter describing the extent of the insured's travel and work outside of the office,

- a record of the insured's work attendance and absence, and
- any documents such as letters, memos, vouchers, etc., that the insured may have written or signed on or after the coverage's effective date.

Waiting Periods

Some group insurers require new individuals joining a group to complete a **waiting period**, also known as a *probationary period*, which is a period of time, usually one to six months, that must pass after a new employee is hired before that employee is eligible for insurance coverage. Waiting periods are designed to prevent an individual with a current physical problem from joining a group and then immediately filing a claim resulting from the pre-existing illness. Claim examiners handling claims filed under policies with waiting periods must ensure that the claimant has satisfied any specified waiting period. In most cases, the employer's records are used to verify that the claimant has satisfied the waiting period.

Evidence of Insurability

A person who is eligible for group coverage but does not elect coverage when the policy first becomes effective may still obtain coverage by satisfactorily answering a series of medical questions. The reason for requiring medical questions is that the potential for antiselection is greater among those who wait to join the plan. If the person's coverage is approved and a claim question arises during the coverage's contestable period, the claim examiner must gather sufficient information to determine if a misrepresentation occurred when the evidence of insurability was submitted.

References

Collister vs. *Nationwide Life Insurance Company,* Pennsylvania Supreme Court, Eastern District. No. 244, 1976.

Kimball, Gary. "Conditional Receipts," *1983 ICA Life Insurance Workshop Notes,* 41–43.

"Liability on Claims Occurring Prior to the Effective Date of Coverage, " *1975 ICA Individual Health Insurance Workshop Notes,* 11–15.

Sullivan, George D. "Interim Insurance," *1987 ICA Life Insurance Workshop Notes,* 196–203.

Wolf, Jim. "Group Life Perspectives," *1986 ICA Life Insurance Workshop Notes,* 58–63.

5

Misrepresentation in the Application

An application for individual insurance includes statements made by the proposed insured about the proposed insured's medical history, occupation, financial status, and other insurance in force. Insurance companies rely on these statements during the underwriting process to determine whether to issue the policy as applied for. If the proposed insured misrepresents a fact that is **material**, or relevant, to the underwriting decision, and the insurer issues a policy to the applicant that the insurer would not have issued had the truth been stated in the application, then the insurer has a legal right to rescind the contract.

According to contract law, if one party to a contract makes a misrepresentation and thereby induces the other party to enter into a contract that he or she would not have entered into had the truth been known, then the party who has been misled has the right to rescind the contract because the two parties never had a true meeting of the minds. When an insurer rescinds an insurance policy because of material misrepresentation in the insurance application, the insurer is said to be asserting the defense of misrepresentation. Whether a particular loss—death, injury, or illness—would have been covered under the terms of the policy is thus irrelevant, for there was no policy in force.

POLICY CONTESTS

A court action to determine whether a valid insurance policy exists is called a policy contest. In a policy contest, the insurer seeks to initiate a legal suit to rescind a policy. Upon rescission of the policy, the insurer returns to the policyowner the premiums that had been collected.

A court action to contest the validity of a particular claim is called a contest of a policy claim. In a contest of a policy claim, the insurer argues that a particular claim is not payable for any of several possible reasons, such as a policy exclusion. The insurer does not return premiums to the policyowner because the valid policy contract remains in existence.

To avoid confusion, throughout this chapter the term *contestability* in its various forms will refer to the process of contesting the validity of the policy because of misrepresentation in the application. A contestable claim is one that arises during the period while the policy is still contestable and for which liability may legally be denied if there is proof of misrepresentation in the application.

REQUIREMENTS FOR CONTESTABILITY

To successfully contest an insurance policy in most U.S. jurisdictions, an insurer must prove three elements of misrepresentation:

- falsity of the application either through a misstatement or a concealment of facts;
- materiality of the misstatement, or materiality of the concealment, to the acceptance of the risk; and
- reliance by the insurer upon the misstatement or concealment of facts.

In addition, some jurisdictions require knowledge on the part of the applicant of the materiality of the misrepresentation.

Canadian law differs somewhat from U.S. law in the area of policy contestability. Canadian law requires only that there be a false statement in the application and that the misstatement be material to the insurer's underwriting decision in order for an insurance contract to be voidable. The knowledge of the applicant as to the materiality of the misrepresentation is irrelevant.

Falsification of the Application

For an insurer to assert a defense of misrepresentation, the company must first prove that the application is in fact false, either because of a misstatement or a concealment of facts by the applicant.

To prove falsification, the company should generally have in its possession documented, written evidence sufficient to prove that false information was included in the application or that information omitted from the application was relevant to risk assessment. Usually this evidence consists of

- copies of physicians' office records, including consultation dates, complaints, findings, diagnoses, medications, and treatments prescribed;
- hospital records showing dates of admission, reason for confinement, and treatment;
- employer records showing time absent from work, gross income of the insured, and nature of occupational duties;
- copies of other insurance policies in force, and the nature and extent of coverages; and
- information about hobbies of the insured, including licenses issued to the insured to engage in a hobby, evidence of membership in clubs devoted to that hobby, or written statements from instructors and co-hobbyists.

In every case, the evidence of misrepresentation should be documented. Hearsay evidence may be useful in furnishing leads to persons who are able to give direct testimony; it may also be useful in corroborating other evidence. However, hearsay evidence alone cannot be the basis for contesting a policy, nor for denying a claim.

Materiality of the Misstatement

After finding that a statement in an application is false, the claim examiner must establish that the misrepresentation is material, or relevant. There are two quite different legal tests of materiality used in various jurisdictions: the materiality to acceptance of risk test and the materiality to cause of loss test.

Materiality to Acceptance of Risk Test

According to the test of materiality used in most jurisdictions in the United States and in Canada, if an insurer would have taken a different underwriting action on an application if the truth of the matter misrepresented had been known, the misrepresentation is considered to be material. A false statement may be regarded as material if the knowledge of it would naturally and reasonably have influenced the judgment of the underwriter toward any of the following three actions:

1. declining to issue any policy,
2. issuing the policy with a waiver or amendment excluding

    coverage for a specified physical condition or for pursuit of
    specified occupations or hobbies, or
3. issuing the policy at a premium rate higher than the standard
    rate or with reduced benefits.

A claim examiner who discovers a possible misrepresentation should
present the company's underwriter with the facts about the case. If, in the
underwriter's opinion, the policy could still have been issued as applied
for, then the false or omitted information is not considered to be material
and the policy cannot be contested successfully. However, if the decision
of the underwriter is that the policy would not have been issued as applied for, then the requirement of materiality may have been met. When
the underwriting decision indicates that the application should have been
declined, the insurer can easily establish materiality of the misrepresentation. However, if the underwriting decision is that the policy could have
been issued but that the premium rate should have been higher than it
was, then the issue of materiality is less certain or possibly nonexistent.
Some companies in this situation will disregard the small difference in rating
unless there is clear evidence of fraudulent intent by the applicant; still
others will pursue their right to contest the policy.

Materiality to Cause of Loss Test

In order to contest a policy on the basis of misrepresentation in Kansas,
Missouri, Rhode Island, and Puerto Rico, an insurer must prove that the
facts misrepresented on the application were related to the loss insured
against. For example, the matter misrepresented in a life insurance application must have had a direct tendency to shorten the insured's life expec-
tancy. Statutory requirements such as these are commonly termed **causal
relation requirements**. Although insurance statutes in Arkansas do not
contain a causal relation requirement, a recent court decision there supports a limited application of this concept.
    The causal relation requirement can be illustrated in the following
example:

> On an application for life insurance, Frank Wilden, the insured, stated
> that his health was excellent and that he suffered from no known
> medical impairments. Actually, Frank was being treated for arterio-
> sclerotic heart disease and hypertension. One year after the policy
> was issued, Frank died of colon cancer. In a *post mortem* under-
> writing decision, the company's underwriter states that, had the in-
> sured's medical history been known, the policy would not have been
> issued.

In Canada and in most states, the fact that an insured misrepresents a material fact relevant to the insurer's acceptance of the risk might well suffice to uphold rescission of the policy. But in Kansas, Missouri, Rhode Island, Puerto Rico, and possibly Arkansas, a company would have to establish that the fact misrepresented contributed to the loss experienced. In the above example, Frank's death from cancer is not related in any way to the facts misrepresented on his application for insurance. Therefore, in the aforementioned jurisdictions, the insurer would probably be required to pay the life insurance proceeds to the beneficiary of Frank's policy.

In jurisdictions requiring a causal relation for rescission of a policy, the claim examiner must be alert to a possible connection between the matter misrepresented and the nature of the loss. Cases in which such a connection appears possible may require medical or legal advice to determine whether an investigation is warranted.

Reliance by the Insurer upon Misrepresentations

An insurance company has a contractual right to rely on statements made in policy applications. However, in order for an insurer to rescind a policy because of material misrepresentations in the application, the company must prove that it relied to its detriment upon a false statement of fact in the application or upon the completeness of an application in which material facts were actually omitted. If the claimant can show that the insurer relied on some source of information other than the application, or had access to information that was of such a nature as to compel the insurer to inquire further, then the requirement for reliance may be missing.

For example, assume that an individual filed a group medical expense claim with an insurer three months before applying for a life insurance policy with the same company. If information in the medical expense claim contradicted information presented in the life insurance application, then the insurer may be presumed to be on notice as to the falsity of the answers in the life insurance application. In such a case, the insurer may be assumed to have knowledge of the facts and may have waived its right to a defense of misrepresentation.

A different type of problem arises when a company fails, through either an investigation or a medical examination, to detect a misrepresentation. For example, assume that on an application for life insurance, the insured, Karen Paisano, falsely denied any history of heart disease. A required medical examination failed to detect any indication of heart disease. Shortly after the policy was issued, though, Karen died of heart disease.

In this case, can the company plead reliance on the misrepresentation in the application, or did the company rely on the findings of the examining physician? In cases such as this one, a few courts have found that the requirement of reliance was satisfied. The fact that an insurer makes an independent investigation into the insurability of a proposed insured before issuing its policy, in the view of these courts, does not waive the insurer's right to rely on the truthfulness of statements in the application "unless the investigation discloses facts [that are] sufficient to expose the falsity of the representations of the applicant or which are of such a nature as to place upon the insurer the duty of further inquiry."

However, some courts have held that, by undertaking an investigation or requiring a medical examination, the insurer may have shifted reliance from statements of the applicant to findings of its own representatives. In one such case, the court held that the issue of reliance centered on whether the insurer relied solely on the answers in the application, solely on the medical examination, or partly on each. Therefore, it appears that when an insurance company has had the benefit of either an investigation or a medical examination of the insured, the question of reliance may be difficult to ascertain in a court action. Claim examiners should refer such cases to legal counsel prior to undertaking any rescission action.

Knowledge of the Materiality of the Misrepresentation

In addition to proving falsification, materiality, and reliance, insurers must, in some jurisdictions, prove that the applicant had knowledge of the materiality of the misrepresentation in order to establish a defense of misrepresentation. A majority of the jurisdictions within the United States require misrepresentation *either* to be made with the intent to deceive *or* to be material to the risk. The Massachusetts statute is representative of this type of statute and reads as follows:

> No oral or written misrepresentation or warranty made in the negotiation of a policy of insurance by the insured or in his behalf shall be deemed material or defeat or avoid the policy or prevent it attaching unless such misrepresentation or warranty is made with actual intent to deceive, *or* unless the matter misrepresented or made a warranty increased the risk of loss.

A few jurisdictions hold that the insurer must prove that the applicant knew that the matter misrepresented was false and that the applicant intended to deceive the insurer with the falsity. Innocent misrepresentations, made without the applicant's knowledge of the truth, may not be used to contest a policy. Insurance statutes in Ohio, for example, read as follows:

> No answer to any interrogatory made by an applicant in his application for a policy shall bar the right to recover upon any policy issued thereon, or be used in evidence at any trial to recover upon such policy, unless it is clearly proved that such answer is willfully false,

that it was fraudulently made, that it is material, and that it induced the company to issue the policy, that but for such answer the policy would not have been issued, and that the agent or company had no knowledge of the falsity or fraud of such answer.

Finally, the statutes of some states are somewhere in the middle between these two extremes. California, for example, does not require proof of intent to deceive, but the insurance company must show that the insured had knowledge that one or more answers were incorrect. In Michigan, a jury decides whether innocent misrepresentations by the applicant are sufficient to support rescission.

BARRIERS TO CONTESTABILITY

Even if an insurer satisfies all statutory requirements for contesting a policy, certain barriers may prevent an insurer from rescinding an insurance contract for misrepresentation in the application. Some of these barriers result from statutes; others arise primarily from court decisions.

Incontestability Provisions

The major barrier to asserting the defense of misrepresentation is the statutory prohibition against contesting policies beyond a stated period of time, normally two years. General legal contracts can be rescinded at any time upon discovery of a misrepresentation; however, laws in the United States and Canada require insurance contracts to contain a clause which provides that after a policy has been in effect for a specified period of time (1) from the date of issue, and (2) during the lifetime of the insured, the validity of the policy will be incontestable. In life and health insurance policies, such a clause is commonly referred to as an *incontestability provision*. A typical life insurance policy incontestability provision reads as follows:

> This policy shall be incontestable after it has been in force, during the lifetime of the insured, for a period of two years from the earlier of the policy date or the date of issue, except for nonpayment of premiums.

The wording "during the lifetime of the insured" is important insurance contract language. Without such wording, a beneficiary of a life insurance policy could delay filing a claim for policy benefits until after expiration of the policy's contestable period, and the insurer would be unable to assert a defense of misrepresentation.

A typical health insurance policy incontestability provision reads as follows:

> After two years from the date of issue of this policy no misstatements made by the applicant in the application for such policy shall be used to void the policy or to deny a claim for loss incurred or disability commencing after the expiration of such two-year period.

Identifying the Contestable Period

Most statutes provide that the policy becomes incontestable after it has been in effect for two or three years from the "date of issue." Many policy provisions use the same language. However, in many cases the date of policy issue and the date when the insurance became effective are different. Claim examiners sometimes must determine which date is the one from which the beginning of the contestable period should be figured. The majority of court decisions follow the principle of favoring the insured by beginning, and thereby ending, the contestable period at the earliest possible time. Generally, courts have found that

- if the effective date of insurance is later than the policy issue date, as with nonprepaid applications, the contestable period begins on the issue date; and
- if the effective date of insurance is earlier than the date of issue, as with backdated policies, the contestable period begins on the effective date.

Sometimes claim questions arise as to when the contestable period ends. For example, if the beginning date of a policy's two-year contestable period is June 5, 1987, and the insured dies on June 5, 1989, is the policy still contestable? The claim examiner's decision depends on the wording of the incontestable clause and on company practice. Some companies do not count the first day of the contestable period in computing the duration of the contestability period, whereas other companies do. If, using the previous example, the company's practice is to count the first day of the contestable period, then the contestable period expired at 12:01 a.m. on June 5, 1989, and the claim is not contestable.

In disability insurance, the contestability period may be suspended by the disability of the insured. For example, if the insured is disabled for four months during a contestable period of three years, the contestable period could be extended by those four months. In actuality, though, the contestability period is rarely extended because of an insured's disability.

Internal Replacements

Sometimes a policyowner chooses to surrender one life insurance policy in order to purchase another one that is issued by the same insurer. Replacements such as these are called *internal replacements*. When a life insurance claim is received on a policy that is an internal replacement and the new policy's contestable period has not expired, the claim examiner must thoroughly review the circumstances surrounding the issuance of the replacement policy before determining if the policy's contestable period is still enforceable.

In situations where a replacement policy is issued under a contractual right offered in another policy, the contestable period for the replacement policy usually runs from the issue date of the original policy. Courts generally consider the replacement policy to be merely a continuance of the original policy. However, when a new policy is issued in place of one being surrendered and no contractual right to conversion was contained in the original policy, a decision as to whether the replacement policy can be treated as having a new contestable period beginning at the time of replacement may depend upon the answers to a variety of questions. If all of the following questions are answered positively, then a claim examiner can assume that the contestable period runs from the issue date of the replacement policy and not from the issue date of the original policy:

- *Are there substantial differences between the original contract and the replacement contract?* Courts have found substantial differences to include (1) an increase in the face amount, (2) the imposition of new underwriting requirements, (3) a changed issue age, (4) a different premium rate, or (5) the addition of policy riders.
- *Did the policyowner intend to replace the original contract?* Whether or not there are substantial differences between the two contracts, courts look at the contractual intent of the policyowner in determining whether a contract is a new contract or a continuation of an earlier contract.
- *Was the policyowner warned that a new policy might result in a new contestable period?* The majority of states have enacted regulations governing the replacement of life insurance policies. These regulations specify that insurers must warn policyowners who are considering replacing a policy that a new contestable period may be imposed. If an insurer fails to disclose the required information, and if the policyowner's replacement policy is subsequently found to contain misrepresentations, then courts may not allow insurers to use the misrepresentations as a basis for rescission of the policy.

Failure to Attach Copy of Application

Another potential statutory barrier to the defense of misrepresentation is the requirement that a copy of the application be attached to the policy. Such statutory requirements are called "entire contract" provisions and typically read as follows: "This policy and the application, a copy of which is attached, when issued, constitute the entire contract." Entire contract provisions ensure that the applicant has an opportunity to review his or her statements made in the application and to have any errors corrected. Entire contract provisions also prevent the insurer from making alterations in the contract after policy issue. Court rulings have held that an entire contract provision requires all of the following elements:

- a copy of the application must be physically attached to the policy;
- the copy of the application must be legible; and
- the copy of the application must be complete, containing all questions asked of the applicant and all answers as recorded, along with the applicant's signature.

The entire contract provision establishes that failure to attach a copy of the application to the policy will prevent the insurer from successfully contesting a policy.

Involvement of Company Representatives

Sometimes when an insurer seeks to rescind a policy, a claimant will allege that a company representative such as an agent, medical examiner, or broker knew of the false information at the time the policy was written. If the claimant's allegations are true, the company may be prevented from successfully contesting a policy.

Agent's Knowledge

According to agency law, the knowledge of an agent is considered to be the knowledge of the person or organization for whom the agent is acting. If a soliciting agent was aware of a misrepresentation but did not record the true information on the application, then the insurer may not be able to claim reliance on the insured's statements. However, if there has been collusion between the insured and the agent, and if the insured is found to have known that the agent would not advise the company of the truth, then the insurer will probably be allowed to rescind the policy.

Some companies have made efforts to modify application forms by including a statement that notice to the agent or knowledge of the agent is not necessarily the knowledge of the company unless the information is recorded on the application. To strengthen further the insurer's position, the company may state limitations on the authority of the agent on application forms, denying the agent any authority to waive or alter any conditions of the application. However, court decisions are in conflict on the validity of such limitations.

When a claim examiner is faced with an allegation that the agent had knowledge of material information not recorded in the application, the examiner must carefully investigate all available information before deciding whether to contest the policy. Disappointed, angry, or embarrassed claimants sometimes allege that an agent was at fault in recording information on the application. Such an allegation may, of course, be the truth. On the other hand, the claimant's allegation may be an attempt to avoid admitting that he or she was not truthful on the application.

As a first step in the process of investigating an allegation against an agent, claim examiners ask the claimant to sign a written statement containing the details of the allegation. If the claimant refuses to prepare such a statement, the claim examiner may write a report based on information supplied by the claimant along with information contained in the policy file relating to the initial sale and underwriting of the policy. The claim examiner should note in the investigation file the claimant's expressed reason for refusing to write or sign a statement.

Next, the examiner should obtain full information from the agent. The agent should be informed in advance of the allegation and then should be asked to explain in either an interview or a written statement his or her position toward the charges. Any questions directed to the agent should be phrased objectively, so as to avoid coercing or leading the agent. The agent then should sign the statement.

As a third step, the examiner should review all facts in light of the charges and responses. If there are witnesses who might corroborate one side or the other, they should be identified and, if appropriate, be interviewed. Additional investigation to resolve other disputes of fact, such as times and places of meetings between agent and insured, might be appropriate. Evidence relating to the integrity of the agent and the claimant may also be appropriate to document.

If an investigation of an agent shows collusion between the agent and the insured, most companies will rescind the policy. In the absence of such collusion, the claim decision depends on several factors, including state law, application language concerning agent's knowledge, the company's claim philosophy, and the circumstances of the particular case.

Broker's Knowledge

Some policies are sold through the services of a broker rather than through a company agent. In cases in which a broker is alleged to have acted improperly, the legal position of the broker is not always clear. By one view, the broker is the agent of the insured, not of the company; hence, the knowledge of the broker cannot be imputed to the insurer. By the opposite view, the broker serves in the company's behalf by soliciting the application. In disputes involving brokers, the investigation may proceed along the same lines as that involving a company agent. However, a final decision on rescission must consider the law of agency in the jurisdiction, as well as the facts of the case.

Examining Physician's Knowledge

Claimants sometimes allege that an examining physician was responsible for excluding the correct admissions of the insured from the application. In such a situation, the company is likely to have a difficult time contesting the policy, even if the application contains a misrepresentation about the insured's medical history. The examining physician is assumed to have an appreciation of the significance of the insured's medical history and condition, and, thus, the company may be legally estopped (prevented) from raising the defense of misrepresentation.

In cases involving such allegations, claim examiners usually must prove fraud on the part of the examining physician before the company will be able to rescind the policy. In fact, the statutes of two states—Iowa and Wisconsin—provide that, in any case in which a medical examiner has certified the soundness of the medical risk, collusion between the applicant and the physician must be proved before the insurer can rescind the policy because of a medical misrepresentation.

Failure to Inquire

If an application for insurance contains unanswered questions or incomplete answers to questions, the insurer has a duty to inquire further to obtain the complete facts. Courts usually find that an unanswered or incompletely answered question on an insurance application constitutes a "Yes" response to the question. An insurer that accepts an unanswered or incompletely answered question is, in effect, saying that the answer to the question is immaterial to its acceptance of the risk. Such an insurer will be estopped from using the incomplete application as grounds for misrepresentation in court.

A similar situation exists when a company receives ambiguous or conflicting answers on an application. If an insurer had evidence that would put a prudent person on notice to conduct a further inquiry, then failure to make such an inquiry may pose a barrier to rescission of the contract for misrepresentation. For example, a proposed insured who indicates that his blood pressure is controlled by a prescription medication, and yet answers "None" to a question about the identity of his personal physician, should probably be investigated thoroughly during the underwriting process since he may be concealing a medical problem. If, during the underwriting of the policy, no investigation is made into the proposed insured's medical history, the company will find it difficult later to raise the defense of misrepresentation.

Delay by Company

In order to ensure its right of rescission, an insurance company must take prompt action once it discovers a misrepresentation in an application. If the company, knowing of the misrepresentation, treats the policy as continuing in-force, or if the company fails to object within a reasonable length of time, the company may be waiving its right of rescission.

Insurers may become aware of a misrepresentation in an application by any number of means, including the following:

- The insured under a still-contestable life insurance policy may file a claim under a health insurance policy issued by the same company; the claim may indicate a medical history that had not been disclosed in the application for life insurance.
- The soliciting agent may learn of hospitalization that had not been disclosed by the applicant/insured.
- The insured, who suspects he or she may have a medical problem, may apply for additional policies of comparatively small face values, thereby avoiding a medical examination which would otherwise be required if applying for a single large policy.

In each of these cases, the company can gain knowledge that it did not have at the time of initial underwriting—knowledge that might indicate misrepresentation in the original application. To avoid losing the right of rescission, the company should investigate such a case immediately, even though no claim has as yet been received on the contestable policy. Delaying investigation until a claim is received could establish a barrier to the defense of misrepresentation.

INVESTIGATION OF CONTESTABLE POLICIES

The investigation of a contestable policy requires particular tact. In many such cases, death or disability has occurred. Persons close to the insured may be emotionally upset and hostile to an investigation that might lead to the avoidance of the policy. Nonetheless, contestable investigations are essential for the protection of the company and its other policyowners.

Determining Claims to be Investigated

Most insurers, as a matter of practice, routinely investigate all death or disability claims arising during the contestable period. A uniform practice of investigating all contestable claims reduces the possibility that a policyowner might file charges of discrimination against an insurer. However, some insurers evaluate all contestable claims against established criteria before deciding which claims to investigate further. Evaluation criteria used by claim examiners in such analysis may include

- *amount of liability*—The larger the amount of liability, the greater the justification for investigation. With a death claim, the amount of liability is known immediately: it is the death benefit of the policy, plus any additional benefits, such as those for accidental death, less any policy loans or unpaid premiums. However, with a disability claim, the total long-term liability may be much higher than the amount of the initial claim, because of future medical, hospital, or disability benefits under the policy. Therefore, claim examiners looking at the amount of liability must carefully consider both the immediate and the long-term costs.
- *cause of loss*—If the loss is caused by a chronic condition, such as heart or circulatory disease, there is a higher probability that the condition predated the loss than if the cause resulted from an accident or from an acute condition, such as meningitis. Accordingly, claim losses occasioned by chronic conditions may involve a higher proportion of misrepresentations.
- *underwriting basis*—If an application has been underwritten on a medical basis, there is less likelihood of uncovering misrepresentations than if it had been written nonmedically.
- *record of the producer*—If the agent or broker who sold the policy has developed a record of careful attention to completion of policy applications, a claim examiner may decide to forgo investigation of borderline cases. On the other hand, if the sales agent is new to the business, that agent's contestable claims might be scrutinized more thoroughly.

Investigation Guidelines

The purpose of investigating claims during the contestable period is to establish whether any information was falsified or omitted in the application for insurance. If the initial investigation indicates that information crucial to acceptance of the risk was misrepresented or omitted, the investigation is then continued to obtain proof to be used as a legal basis for contesting the policy.

An investigation should not stop when one instance of misrepresentation has been found. An investigation should look into all areas of possible misrepresentation and also into any other factors that might have a bearing on the company's liability. For example, if investigation reveals that a claim involves both material misrepresentation and death by suicide within the suicide exclusion period, then both defenses should be documented. Such a careful and detailed approach strengthens the insurer's position in any legal action that might arise. Failure to document an apparent misrepresentation at the time of discovery may waive the insurer's right to use that misrepresentation later if needed.

During the course of an investigation, persons being contacted for information should be told frankly and briefly the reason for the investigation. The explanation should state that a claim for insurance had been submitted during the contestable period and that certain questions need to be answered before the claim processing can be completed and the coverage confirmed. The explanation should not divulge the nature of the death or disability since such information is protected by privacy laws.

The first step in the investigation should be a thorough review of the application and the claim file. Most of the misrepresentations in life insurance applications relate to the applicant's medical history or medical condition. The possibilities for misrepresentation in disability insurance applications are far greater than in life insurance applications and include misrepresentations about the applicant's occupation, income, or over-insurance.

Investigating Contestable Life Insurance Claims

Since many deaths are preceded by some period of hospitalization, most death claim investigations begin with a review of the records of each hospital where the claimant received medical treatment. Even treatments that occurred after the date of the policy application should be checked since they may provide information about unadmitted medical treatment prior to the application date. Identification of hospitals may be found in the claim or application file. In some cases, claim examiners make routine checks of hospitals near the locations the insured lived and worked to determine whether there was an unadmitted record of hospitalization. Additional leads indicating the names of hospitals where the insured may have gone for treatment can come from his or her social affiliations.

A thorough examiner who is investigating a contestable death claim will contact each physician known to have attended the insured, before or after the date of the application, in order to establish if there was unadmitted medical treatment that was material to acceptance of the risk. The names of attending or consulting physicians may be noted from any of several sources, including

- the claim statement,
- hospital records,
- the policy application,
- a death certificate,
- records of other insurance companies,
- prescription drug records, or
- records of other physicians.

In addition, physicians who have treated the insured sometimes are identified by interviews with friends, neighbors, employers, or coworkers of the insured, or from interviews with other local physicians or pharmacists.

A contestable death claim investigation also usually includes interviews with the claimant, close family members, business associates, and friends of the deceased. These individuals may provide important information about the insured's health and about activities in which the insured was engaged. A courteous investigator may elicit information that, on the one hand, could support the conclusion that there was no misrepresentation, or, on the other hand, could identify misrepresentations in the application.

Investigating Contestable Health Insurance Claims

As with investigations of contestable life insurance claims, investigations of contestable health insurance claims usually begin with a review of the insured's medical records. Claim examiners or investigators contact attending physicians to obtain verification of information about the insured's condition, diagnosis, suggested treatment, and proposed medications. In addition, for disability claims, investigators contact the insured's employer to determine or verify, among other things,

- that the insured is, in fact, not working;
- what the insured's job duties were before disability; and
- the insured's gross income.

Claim examiners also look closely at contestable group health claims for indications of overinsurance, which can occur when an applicant either fails to indicate other coverages in force or overstates income. If an issuing company discovers an applicant's overinsurance during the contestable period, the company may be able to successfully contest the policy on the basis of misrepresentation.

In 1980, the Disability Insurance Record System (DIRS) was developed by the Health Insurance Association of America to address the overinsurance problem in disability insurance. Administered by the Medical Information Bureau (MIB), the DIRS is a computer system that keeps track of all disability insurance policies issued by participating companies in the last five years. From the DIRS, the claim investigator can learn the full extent of the insured's coverage and can obtain—with proper authorization—specific information about an issued policy from the reporting insurance company.

In 1988, the MIB introduced the Health Claim Index (HCI), which is a computerized system for tracking all claims submitted by participating disability insurers. The HCI is designed to assist insurers in identifying claims that may involve overinsurance and fraud. The HCI allows authorized claim personnel to determine exactly how much disability income the insured is receiving. In addition, claim personnel can discover if an insured has a history of dropping coverages after maximum policy benefits have been collected.

The insured is one source of information available to the health claim investigator that is not available to the life claim investigator. Often during the course of an investigation, discrepancies occur between information reported on an application and information discovered. In such situations, a telephone call from the investigator to the insured may well clarify the discrepancy. Field representative support can also be used to detail and document the claimant's description of events and to gain insight into the nature and extent of the claimant's disability status.

POLICY RESCISSION

The decision to rescind a policy contract and to deny a claim because of material misrepresentation can be one of the most difficult judgments made by a claim examiner. A decision to rescind should be based on an appraisal of (1) state law and court decisions, (2) insurance department regulations, (3) the claim philosophy of the company, and (4) the facts of the specific case.

Rescission of a policy cannot be accomplished solely by the insurer. The other party of interest—the insured, if living, or the beneficiary—must agree to the rescission. In the absence of such agreement, the insurer may be forced into court to seek a declaratory judgment for rescission. In either event, the procedure for rescission is important, both to protect the feelings of the insured or beneficiary and to enable the company to preserve its legal rights.

Rescinding a Policy

In some companies, the claim area handles all rescissions, including those that are not related to claims. In other companies, rescission may be handled by the underwriting area, by the legal area, or by field personnel. Regardless of which area administers the rescission of a policy, one of the first steps is to notify the insured or claimant in writing of the company's decision to rescind the policy. The facts developed in the prior stages of investigation serve as the basis for the rescission letter. A sample rescission letter is shown in Figure 5–1. The essential elements of a rescission letter include

- basic identifying information regarding the insured and the policy contract—name of the insured, contract number, date of issue, face amount, plan of insurance, and riders, if any;
- a copy of the signed application, clearly identifying sections and questions from the application that are material to the underwriting process—instances where information has been falsified in or omitted from the policy application;
- an explanation of the materiality of the information misrepresented to the risk-selection process—a statement that the policy would not have been issued had all the facts been known;
- an outline of the specific findings of the investigation—names, dates, and all other information that supports the insurer's decision to rescind;
- the amount of premiums to be refunded and an explanation of the premium refund process; and
- a good-faith statement, soliciting any pertinent information from the claimant that might be unknown to the insurer and indicating the insurer's willingness to reassess the matter on the basis of new information.

In addition, some states require insurers to include specific information informing the insured or claimant that the state's insurance department is available for consultation. Also, some insurers include a statement in the rescission letter reserving the right to use other defenses.

Company practice dictates the way that delivery of the rescission letter is accomplished. Some companies prefer to send a company representative to hand-deliver the rescission letter and the premium refund, whereas other companies send the rescission letter and premium refund through registered mail.

Refunding the Premium

The usual practice of insurers is to refund all premiums paid in connection with a rescinded policy. For health insurance policies, some companies deduct the amount of any claims already paid from the premium refund.

February 2, 1989

Elizabeth R. Williams
Attorney at Law
Williams, Williams & Donald
1 Main Street
Smithvile, N.J. 08201

Insured: Robert Jones
Policy: 02 345 678

Dear Ms. Williams:

We have concluded our review of the claim for death benefits filed by your client, Susan Jones.

Policy 02 345 678 was issued April 15, 1988, on the life of Robert Jones, as a whole life contract in the amount of $25,000.

The contract states that it cannot be contested after it has been in force for two years during the Insured's lifetime. Since Mr. Jones' death occurred within the first two contract years, it was necessary for us to conduct inquiries to determine our liability.

These inquiries disclosed that Mr. Jones had been treated at Family Clinic since 1983; that he had a history of chest pain and hypertension. Further, Mr. Jones was hospitalized on October 27, 1985 and was determined to have suffered a myocardial infarction. Since then he has been treated regularly by Dr. J. Block for follow-up care and occasional angina attacks.

This information was not admitted on the application for insurance dated February 25, 1988. Had he admitted this medical history in response to questions 5, 7a, 7b, 8a, and 9b of the application, this contract would not have been issued.

It is the Company's position that the contract is void because of material misrepresentation in the application and that its liability is limited to the return of all premiums paid, $559.20, plus legal interest, $108.80, for total refund of $668.00.

This letter is written without prejudice to the Company's rights or defenses.

Sincerely,

Thomas L. White
Claim Consultant
Policy Claims Division

Figure 5-1. Sample rescission letter.

Other companies do not deduct the amount of claims already paid, on the basis that their legal position is stronger if all premiums are refunded.

Interest is sometimes added to the amount of the refund. If interest is included, the interest rate is the legal rate for the jurisdiction in which the refund is made. Those companies adding interest to the refund do so on the basis that interest is necessary in order to make the premium payor "whole"—that is, to return that person, as far as possible, to the position he or she would be in if the policy had not been issued. Companies that do not add interest to refunds refer to their own expenses (selling, underwriting, issue, and policy service) as justification.

An insurer should not assume that rescission is complete merely because the premium refund check is cashed. Mutual agreement is needed to effect a legal rescission. In order to substantiate the mutual agreement, some companies require a signed release from the insured or beneficiary, specifically setting forth the terms of the policy rescission. Other companies put the release directly on the check over the endorsement space for the payee of the check.

In the vast majority of health insurance policy rescissions, the insured is still alive and is able to sign a valid release for the premium refund. However, when the case involves a refund of life insurance policy premiums after the insured has died, the issue becomes more complex.

It might seem that the refund should be made to the estate of the insured, through the executor or the administrator. However, this approach is usually not practical for the following reasons:

- A legal representative may not have been appointed for the estate of the insured.
- If appointed, the representative may not be interested in the usually small amount of the refund or may be uncertain as to his or her authority to agree to rescission.
- It is actually the beneficiary, not the estate, who has an interest in the policy benefit and who must be satisfied by the rescission action.

For these reasons, in the case of rescission following death of the insured, most companies will return the premiums to the beneficiary. Some companies will also require the beneficiary to sign a release for all claims to the policy.

Court Action

If a policyowner or beneficiary does not accept the company's decision to rescind a policy and refuses to accept the premium refund, the policy claim should be referred to legal counsel for institution of legal proceedings to rescind the policy. An insurer must seek rescission action before the contestable period expires; otherwise, the insurance company may not be able to exercise some of its rights under the policy. Whether a company will initiate court action to have the policy rescinded depends on several factors: the strength of its case; the amount at risk, both immediately and potentially in the future; the advice of its legal counsel; and the specific facts of the case.

SPECIAL MISREPRESENTATION SITUATIONS

Fraud in the Application

In some cases, a claim examiner may believe that a misrepresentation was made with fraudulent intent. One example would be a physician who denied any medical problems in an insurance application but who actually had been treating himself for diabetes for four years before the application date. If such fraud is discovered while the policy is still contestable, the company may, of course, move to rescind the policy. But what if the fraud is discovered after the contestable period has expired?

As mentioned earlier, Canadian law permits insurance companies to contest a contract at any time, even after the contestable period has expired, when statements made in the application are fraudulent and can be proven to have been made with an intent to deceive the insurer. In the United States, however, in the absence of a policy provision specifically mentioning fraud as a basis for rescission after the expiration of the contestable period, fraud is generally held to be no different than any other form of misrepresentation and is thus subject to incontestability provisions.

Adjustments on the Basis of Age or Sex

In most states and in Canada, life insurance contracts are required by law to contain a **misstatement of age provision** that allows insurers to make adjustments in the policy's death benefit should the insurer or the policyowner discover that the age of the insured is incorrect as stated in the policy. Misstatement of age provisions sometimes also provide for adjustments to the policy's death benefit if the insured's sex has been misstated in the policy. In making adjustments to policy benefits because of a misstatement of an insured's age or sex, the insurer is not challenging the validity of the contract, but is, in fact, carrying out its terms. Therefore, a misstatement of age or sex by an applicant is not cause for an insurer to void a policy, even if the misstatement is discovered during the contestable period. Such adjustments are permitted throughout the life of the policy and are not affected by the incontestable clause. Adjustments on the basis of age or sex are discussed further in Chapter 9.

Smoking Misrepresentations

Most life insurance contracts do not contain provisions that specify that insurers will adjust policy benefits to correct for misstatements made in an application about a proposed insured's smoking habits. Instead, each company's policy dictates whether a smoking misrepresentation will be treated as a material misrepresentation or whether the company will attempt through a compromise agreement to adjust the benefit amount to that which the premium paid would have purchased at smokers' rates.

Much uncertainty currently exists within the insurance industry about the proper method of handling smoking misrepresentations. Companies that attempt to compromise and make downward adjustments in policy benefits risk the possibility that courts will construe their actions as an admission that the contract is valid and, thus, a waiver of the right to rescind the policy later should the compromise fail. On the other hand, insurers who favor policy rescission for all policies involving a smoking misrepresentation are unsure if courts will support such actions.

Only a few court decisions have addressed the issue of smoking misrepresentation in insurance applications. In one 1987 Quebec case, *Quellet* vs. *The Industrial Life Insurance Company*, a superior court found that the insured had made false statements in the application with regard to his smoking habits and that the false statements were material to the insurer's evaluation of the risk. Thus, the court ruled in favor of the insurer's decision to rescind the policy because of smoking misrepresentations. In the 1988 case—*Mutual Benefit Life Insurance Company* vs. *JMR Electronics Corporation*—a U.S. Circuit Court also supported an insurer's right to rescind a policy because of a smoking misrepresentation. However, no other cases at this time in Canada or in the United States have been so conclusive.

If an insurer, after consulting the laws in the jurisdiction involved, decides to pursue the rescission of a policy because of a smoking misrepresentation, the misrepresentation should be treated in the same manner as any other type of misrepresentation. The claim examiner should obtain medical records, signed statements from attending physicians, or possibly records from organizations designed to assist individuals in stopping smoking that prove that the insured misrepresented his or her smoking status on the policy application.

An insurer should consider two other important points before proceeding with the rescission of a policy because of a smoking misrepresentation. First, the insurer should determine if its agent had knowledge of the misrepresentation at the time of policy application. Since the knowledge of the agent is generally imputed to be knowledge of the company, the possession of such knowledge might estop the company from asserting a smoking misrepresentation. Second, the company should ensure that the insurance contract contained all questions and answers upon which the smoking misrepresentation will be based. If this requirement is not met, the insurer may not be able to rescind the policy.

AIDS-Related Misrepresentations

In 1981, the first cases of Acquired Immune Deficiency Syndrome (AIDS) were identified in North America. AIDS is caused by the human immunodeficiency virus (HIV), which disables the immune system, leaving its victims vulnerable to other infections and diseases they could normally withstand with a healthy immune system. In 1986, United States and Canadian insurers were estimated to have paid between $200 million and $300 million in AIDS-related claims on life insurance policies, an amount that represents about one percent of all claims for that year.

Many AIDS-related claims are received within the contestable period of the policy. Studies estimate that 34 percent of the total *number* of AIDS-related death claims and 44 percent of the total benefit *amount* of AIDS-related death claims occur within the first two years after policy issue. Such claim statistics indicate substantial antiselection on the part of people who (1) know they are at high risk for AIDS, (2) suspect that they may already be infected with HIV, or (3) are already showing symptoms of AIDS or AIDS-related diseases.

Where allowed by law, insurers include a question or questions about AIDS in their life insurance applications. One example is

Have you been diagnosed by or received treatment from a member of the medical profession for AIDS (Acquired Immune Deficiency Syndrome) or ARC (Aids-Related Complex)?

An applicant must answer "No" to a question such as this one in order to be insurable. If an applicant incorrectly answers "No" and the misrepresentation is discovered during the policy's contestable period, a claim examiner can take steps to rescind the policy.

One problem that claim examiners face in investigating AIDS-related misrepresentations after the insured's death is that medical personnel, particularly in certain sections of the country, are reluctant to state that a patient had AIDS. The death certificate of an AIDS victim may list the cause of death as natural causes or may list one of the insured's final infections or diseases as the cause of death without indicating that the insured had AIDS or an AIDS-related condition.

A claim examiner needs to be aware of the variety of illnesses associated with AIDS so that he or she can recognize all AIDS-related medical conditions and deaths. Figure 5–2 lists the indicator diseases specified by the U.S. Centers for Disease Control that may indicate AIDS or AIDS-Related Complex. If an insured's medical records or autopsy report lists any of these indicator diseases, and the claim examiner suspects that the insured may have misrepresented AIDS-related information on the application, then further investigation is warranted.

In some states, the claim examiner must prove that the insured's intent was to deceive the insurer about his or her AIDS-related condition. In these states, psychological and counseling records may be invaluable in reflecting the amount of knowledge possessed by the applicant at the time of

A person can be diagnosed as having AIDS if his or her medical condition meets certain requirements specified by the U.S. Centers for Disease Control and/or if he or she has one or more of the following indicator diseases.

Opportunistic Infections

candidiasis; also called thrush
cryptococcosis
cryptosporidiosis
cytomegalovirus disease
herpes simplex infection
lymphoid interstitial pneumonia
pulmonary lymphoid hyperplasia
tuberculosis and some other mycobacterial
    infections
Pneumocystis carinii pneumonia; also called PCP
    pneumonia, pneumonystis, pneumonia, or
    AIDS pneumonia
toxoplasmosis
some types of bacterial infections caused by
    Haemophilus, *Streptococcus*, or other
    pyogenic bacteria
coccidioidomycosis
histoplasmosis
isosporiasis
Salmonella septicemia

Other Diseases

Kaposi's sarcoma
lymphoma of the brain
some other types of non-Hodgkin's lymphoma
progressive multifocal leukoencephalopathy
HIV encephalopathy; also called HIV dementia or
    subacute encephalitis due to HIV
HIV wasting syndrome; also called HIV emaciation

Source: U.S Centers for Disease Control. Revision of the CDC Surveillance Case Definition for Acquired Immunodeficiency Syndrome. Mortality and Morbidity Weekly Report 1987; 36 (supplement no. 1S).

Figure 5-2.   Indicator diseases for AIDS.

application. Although psychologists and counselors may be reluctant to release the insured's records, the necessary material can usually be obtained if the authorization of medical information included in the application clearly includes records for psychological and emotional counseling.

Another difficult AIDS-related issue can arise when an insurer is documenting and explaining to a claimant the reasons for a policy rescission. In a significant number of AIDS-related rescissions, the claimant may not be aware that the insured was an AIDS patient. Although the insurer has a social responsibility to protect the privacy of the individual, the insurer cannot pay a claim if the initial contract was invalid because medical history was misrepresented in order to secure insurance. In some jurisdictions, the insurer can list the deceased's medical care providers in a rescission letter to the beneficiary and state that copies of the medical records can be obtained from either the insurer or the medical care provider. In other jurisdictions, the rescission letter itself must include the insured's full and complete medical history.

Third-Party Applicants

A substantial amount of insurance is issued to third-party applicants. A *third-party applicant* is one who applies for insurance on the life of another person. A business, for example, may purchase a life insurance policy covering a key employee. Most application forms require that the proposed insured sign the application. If a misrepresentation is later found, the third-party—presumably the beneficiary—might argue against rescission on the ground that he or she had no knowledge of the misrepresentation and so should not be penalized by loss of policy benefits. However, most application forms indicate that an applicant other than the proposed insured is bound by the representations made in the application. Hence, the innocence of the third-party applicant does not bar an insurer from seeking a rescission based on misrepresentations by the insured.

GROUP INSURANCE

Misrepresentation can occur in group policies just as in individual policies. However, the contest of an individual policy is a contest of the coverage of the insured; the contest of a group insurance policy, on the other hand, may be a contest of either the validity of the group policy itself or the validity of an individual insured's coverage under the group policy.

Contests of a group policy contract are quite rare. One possible basis for a group policy contest might be the failure of a group to meet a minimum size requirement. If the insurer could prove that the group policyholder misrepresented the size of the group, and that if the insurer had known the true size of the group that it would not have issued the policy, then the group policy could probably be rescinded.

In reality, most group policy rescission actions contest the coverage of one of the persons insured under a group contract. Typically, individuals eligible for coverage under a group policy do not have to complete medical examinations or answer any medical questions in order to be covered by the group policy. Nevertheless, there are two exceptions: late enrollees in the plan and persons seeking an amount of insurance higher than the amount provided on a nonmedical basis are both required to present evidence of their insurability. If there are misstatements in the information presented by an individual to prove his or her insurability, the misstatements can be used by the insurer to contest the individual insured's coverage.

An individual's coverage may also be contested if there is a question as to the eligibility of the individual for coverage in the group. For example, assume that a company listed a part-time employee as an employee eligible for group coverage. A certificate was issued to the employee, and the company paid the premiums for the employee's coverage. Five years later, the employee died. An investigation by the insurer revealed the fact that the employee had never been a full-time employee, as defined in the policy. Since the contestable period has expired, can the claim for the part-time employee still be denied? A claim examiner in such a situation would have to consider both the wording of the incontestable clause in the policy and the court rulings in the jurisdiction involved.

Legal decisions in similar cases have been split. The rulings of some jurisdictions have held that insurance on an employee ineligible for coverage was never valid and that to apply the two-year limit on contestability would force the insurer to cover someone it had never intended to insure. These jurisdictions regard as decisive the fact of ineligibility, not the representations that had been made concerning initial eligibility.

Other jurisdictions take an opposite approach and prohibit rescission after the incontestable period, even on the basis of initial ineligibility. Courts that follow this approach reason that if the insurer had investigated at the time of application, it could have discovered the ineligibility at that time rather than after the claim was filed. New York courts follow this approach, which is called the "Simpson rule." However, other courts have rejected the "Simpson rule" holding that it places an unrealistic burden on the insurer and tends to undermine the self-administered group concept, under which the policyholder maintains records of individual participants. The 1980 Group Life Model Act attempts to address this judicial uncertainty by requiring all group life policies to include the following provision: no incontestable provision "shall preclude the assertion at any time of defenses based upon provisions in the policy which relate to eligibility for coverage."

Investigations of contestable claims under group policies draw data from several sources to determine the eligibility of the insured. The insured's occupation that is listed on the death certificate is one source. Another source is the policyholder, usually an employer, who may provide detailed work or attendance records, wage and salary withholding forms, Workers' Compensation payments, and records of union dues withheld. If doubt still persists, interviews with coworkers and acquaintances may be necessary to determine whether the insured was a bona fide member of the group.

References

Bailey, Richard. *Medical Underwriting: Syllabus and Readings.* Atlanta, GA: LOMA, 1988.

Christian, Robert E. "Causal Relationship in Misrepresentation," *1986 ICA Life Insurance Workshop Notes,* 1–9.

Hebron, Robert J. "Replacement and Rollover: Reliance on New Contestable Periods," *1987 ICA Life Insurance Workshop Notes,* 145–154.

Maurer, A. J. "A Review of Underwriting-Related Claim Problems," *1987 ICA Life Insurance Workshop Notes,* 113–114.

Maurer, A. J. "Misrepresentations About Smoking," *1986 ICA Life Insurance Workshop Notes,* 84–89.

McRea, Kenneth L. and Young, Robert E. "AIDS-Underwriting and Claim Factors," *1986 ICA Life Insurance Workshop Notes,* 38–45.

Misrepresentation in Application: Report of the Law Committee. International Claim Association, 1986.

"Misrepresentation in Non-smoker Application," *ICA News,* 1989 (Vol 30, No. 4), 18.

Peterson, Vonna S. "AIDS Education—It is Imperative to Life," *1987 ICA Life Insurance Workshop Notes,* 67–68.

Rose, Kenneth S. "Overinsurance—Problems and Cures," *1981 ICA Individual Health Insurance Workshop Notes,* 68–75.

Sabia, William J. "Smoker vs. Non-smoker Actual Case Law," *1988 ICA Life Insurance Workshop Notes,* 68–71.

Soule, Charles E. *Disability Income Insurance: The Unique Risk.* Homewood, IL: Dow Jones-Irwin, 1984.

Sweet, Russell L. "The Rescission Decision," *1987 ICA Life Insurance Workshop Notes,* 69–78.

6

Determining When Coverage Ends

In Chapter 4, we described the importance to the claim approval process of determining when insurance coverage begins. This chapter continues the discussion of the coverage period by focusing on the process of determining when insurance coverage ends. In this chapter, we describe the termination of individual insurance coverage because of (1) failure on the part of a policyowner to make the required premium payments, (2) the surrender of a policy for its cash value by a policyowner, (3) failure of the policyowner to repay a policy loan, or (4) failure on the part of a policyowner to reinstate a policy. We also address termination issues for group life and group health insurance coverage.

POLICY LAPSES

A policyowner's failure to make a premium payment can result in termination of the policy's coverage. A **policy lapse** occurs when a policy is terminated because of nonpayment of premiums. In determining whether a policy has lapsed, a claim examiner must look for any factor that might have extended the period of coverage under the policy. The most common factor that extends coverage is the grace period provision.

Grace Period

Most individual life and health insurance policies contain a provision granting the policyowner a **grace period**, which is a specified period of time after a premium is due, within which the premium may be paid without penalty. All coverage remains in force during the grace period. If a covered loss occurs during this time, the company is liable for the claim. However, the amount of the overdue premium, or a prorata portion of it, may be deducted from the benefits paid. A typical grace period provision included in life and health insurance policies is as follows:

> We will allow a period of 31 days after the premium due date for payment of each premium, excluding the initial premium payment, during which period this policy will continue in force.

Life insurance policies usually provide for a grace period of 31 days. The length of the grace period in health insurance policies varies depending upon the frequency of the premium payments. When premiums for a health insurance policy are paid on a weekly basis, the minimum grace period is seven days; for those with premiums paid monthly, 10 days is the minimum grace period; for all others, the minimum grace period is 31 days. If the last day of a grace period falls on a Saturday, a Sunday, or a legal holiday, the grace period is frequently extended—by either statute or company practice—until midnight of the next business day.

Payment of a premium within the grace period is not considered a late payment. A late payment is one made beyond the expiration of the grace period. Many companies accept payments post-marked during the grace period even though the payments are not received within that period.

Extenuating Circumstances

Even if a policy's grace period has expired without payment of the required premium, extenuating circumstances might extend an insured's coverage beyond the grace period. Such circumstances include (1) statutory requirements for premium renewal notices, (2) actions of the agent, and (3) a company practice of accepting late premium payments.

Statutory Requirements for Premium Renewal Notices. In some jurisdictions, statutory requirements forbid an insurer from lapsing a policy for nonpayment of premium unless a renewal notice has been sent to the policyowner. In these jurisdictions, if the insurer fails to send a renewal notice by the end of the grace period, the insurer is prevented from lapsing the policy for a specified period, such as six months or one year after premium default; the insurer is also responsible for a covered loss occurring during that period. The burden of proof is on the insurer to show that

a premium renewal notice was sent to the policyowner. An insurer can usually satisfy this burden of proof by showing that other policyowners who had a premium due on the same date were mailed their renewal notices.

Agent's Actions.   In some situations, an insurer, through its representatives, may have contributed to a policy lapse. For example, an agent may have established a routine of calling upon a policyowner near the end of the grace period in order to collect a monthly premium but then stopped doing so. Before denying a claim for policy benefits in a situation such as this, the claim examiner must consider whether the actions of the agent contributed to the policy lapse. The policyowner may be able to show that the agent's actions established a pattern upon which the policyowner relied to his or her detriment. In such a case, the insurer may be estopped from denying policy coverage because of the actions of the insurer's agent.

Company Practice of Accepting Late Premium Payments.
As was stated earlier, many companies accept late premium payments made within a short period of time, a week to 15 days, beyond the expiration of the grace period. Insurers who make a practice of accepting late premium payments sometimes encounter problems with claims that arise shortly after the expiration of the grace period. A company that accepts isolated late payments does not necessarily establish a custom upon which a policyowner may rely. However, regular acceptance of late payments may have the effect of extending the grace period and may legally prevent the company from denying benefits for claims arising during that extended time.

A similar situation exists when an agent has regularly accepted premiums after the end of the grace period without requiring reinstatement applications. If late acceptance of premiums by an agent is repeated often enough to establish a custom, the policyowner may reasonably expect late payments not to affect his or her insurance coverage. An extended pattern of late acceptance can usually be established by reviewing the premium receipt book, the agent's collection and deposit records, or possibly the premium payer's own record of canceled checks. If such a late acceptance pattern exists, then the insurer may be legally estopped from denying a claim because of policy lapse.

POLICY SURRENDERS

As mentioned earlier, individual whole life insurance policies accumulate a cash value after they have been in force for a couple of years. The owner of such a policy with a cash value may request that the policy be surrendered for its cash value. If the insured dies before payment of the cash value has been accomplished, the claim examiner must determine whether the insurer is liable for the cash surrender value or the death benefit of the policy. As usual, companies' practices vary considerably according to company philosophy and the legal rulings in the jurisdiction in which the company operates.

The claim philosophy at some companies holds that the cash surrender feature is a continuing offer by an insurer and when that offer is accepted by a policyowner, as evidenced by a letter, then the company's liability is limited to a return of the cash surrender value of the policy. Companies following such a claim philosophy may proceed to issue a check for the surrender value on the strength of a letter from the policyowner without any formal surrender documents. Other companies following this same philosophy may require a surrender application which contains a discharge of the company's liability under the policy before processing the request for a surrender.

A number of companies, however, have established quite a different claim philosophy with respect to cash surrender transactions. These companies hold that surrender of a policy is not complete, regardless of whether an application or discharge has been signed, until the check for the surrender value is delivered to the policyowner. Some companies consider the transaction complete when the check is cashed by the policyowner. At these companies, a policy would be reinstated upon the return of an uncashed check for the surrender value, and the death benefit of the policy would be payable if a claim were submitted.

REINSTATEMENTS

Even after a policy lapses, the policyowner may still be entitled to restore insurance coverage. Throughout Canada and the United States, life and health insurance policies include **reinstatement provisions** that permit a policyowner to restore a lapsed policy to in-force status by meeting certain requirements. Reinstatement requirements typically are as follows:

- provision of evidence of insurability satisfactory to the insurer;
- payment of all premiums in default, with interest, from the premium due date to the reinstatement date;
- payment or reinstatement of any policy loan (life insurance policies only); and
- submission of the reinstatement request in writing within a time period specified in the policy.

Reinstatements offer benefits to both parties to the policy. Ordinarily, the insured is able to restore full coverage more easily by reinstatement than would be possible in applying for a new policy, and the insurer is able to conserve business on which it has already absorbed initial costs for sales and underwriting. Nonetheless, reinstatements can raise rather unique contestability questions; thus, claims arising on reinstated policies often merit special attention.

Life Insurance Reinstatements

In the United States, life insurance contracts usually specify that a policyowner has the right to apply for reinstatement of a lapsed policy within three to five years from the date the premium is in default. In Canada, the law allows insurers to specify a maximum period of two years for reinstatement. However, some insurers impose no time limits on a policyowner's right to apply for reinstatement.

The three basic procedures by which an insured may reinstate a life insurance policy are as follows: (1) accepting a late remittance offer made by the insurer, (2) submitting a short-form reinstatement application to the insurer, or (3) submitting a long-form reinstatement application to the insurer. The choice of which reinstatement procedure a policyowner will use depends upon individual company practice and how long the premium payment has been in default.

Late Remittance Offers

A *late remittance offer* is a letter to the owner of a lapsed life insurance policy specifying that the company will accept an overdue premium after the expiration of the grace period. If the policyowner accepts the offer, the company will reinstate the policy without requiring the completion of a reinstatement application or the submission of evidence of insurability. The letter usually specifies that the remittance must be received by a specified date—such as 30 to 90 days after the end of the grace period— and it may further state that the insured must be living when the payment is made. Figure 6–1 shows a sample late remittance offer letter.

However, if an insurer has established a pattern of accepting overdue premium payments in connection with late remittance offers, the company may be found liable for claims that arise during the late remittance period regardless of whether the premium is received within the specified period or whether the insured is still living. For example, assume that an insurer regularly makes 15-day late remittance offers to its policyowners, and one insured consistently takes advantage of those offers. If that policyowner dies 14 days after the end of the grace period without paying the overdue premium, the insured may be legally estopped from denying policy benefits because of policy lapse. The reason is that the company had habitually accepted the insured's premiums beyond the grace period, leading the insured to expect that the late premium would be accepted.

ABC Life Insurance Company
123 Street
Anywhere, U.S.A.

February 27, 1989

Policy No: S-456778

Insured: Mary Kay Brown
      #2 Court
      Any Town, U.S.A.

The premium payment for your policy was due on January 25, 1989. The premium payment Grace Period for your policy expired on February 26, 1989, and your coverage lapsed as of that date.

If you submit your premium payment by March 26, 1989, your coverage will be reinstated as of the date your remittance is received. After March 26, 1989, you will be required to submit satisfactory evidence of good health in order to reinstate the coverage under this policy. This voluntary offer to waive evidence of insurability is a special offer and will not apply to any future premium payment.

Manager
Policyowner Communications

Figure 6–1. Sample late remittance offer.

Short-form Reinstatements

Insurance companies use short-form reinstatement applications to guard against reinstatements by insureds whose condition has changed drastically since the premium due date. A *short-form reinstatement application*, which must be completed within a comparatively short period such as 30 to 90 days after the end of the grace period, requires the insured to answer a few health questions that focus on any changes in his or her condition since the due date of the unpaid premium. An insured generally would not be declined reinstatement if there had been no change in insurability during the lapse period. To illustrate consider the following example:

Eric Lightcap, the insured under a lapsed life insurance policy, has requested that his policy be reinstated. On the short-form reinstatement application, Eric states that he began regular treatment for diabetes while his policy was in force.

A claim examiner probably would not decline a reinstatement such as this one because there has been no change of insurability during the lapse period.

The objective of short-form reinstatements is to decline those cases in which, after the expiration of the grace period, the insured has

- developed, or first become aware of, an impairment of underwriting significance;
- had a worsening or a complication of a previous impairment of underwriting significance; or
- had a change of diagnosis of a previous impairment that is of underwriting significance.

Long-form Reinstatements

Typically, if more than six months have passed since the policy lapsed, then insurers will require a long-form reinstatement application. A *long-form reinstatement application* resembles a policy application in that both address the complete health history of the insured. The extent of the underwriting required for a long-form reinstatement depends on several factors:

- the length of time since the policy has lapsed,
- the type and amount of coverage, and
- the risk classification of the insured at the time the policy was issued.

Underwriters treat the reinstatement application as if it were a new policy application and require current evidence of insurability. Some insurers, however, may underwrite somewhat more liberally if the policy had been in force for several years before lapsing. If the insured does not present evidence of insurability that satisfies the company's underwriting standards, then the company has the right to decline to reinstate the policy or can rewrite the policy at a higher premium rate.

The Effect of Reinstatement upon Contract Provisions

Whether reinstatement of a life insurance policy legally results in a continuation of the original contract or in the creation of a new contract is of utmost importance to a claim examiner, since the answer may affect such policy provisions as the incontestable provision and the suicide clause.

Incontestable Provisions.   In Canada and in the vast majority of jurisdictions in the United States, for purposes of contestability, reinstatement marks the beginning of a new agreement between the insurer and the insured. Thus, the incontestable provision begins to run again from the date of reinstatement. Therefore, if the insured made a material misstatement in the reinstatement application, the company can void the reinstated policy within two years of the date of the reinstatement.

Suicide Provisions. In most jurisdictions in the United States, a policy's suicide provision dates from the original date of policy issue and not from the date of reinstatement. Therefore, if a reinstated policy's suicide provision has expired and the insured commits suicide, the insurer cannot deny policy benefits because of the suicide exclusion.

However, in Canada, a policy's suicide provision begins to run again from the date of reinstatement. Thus, if an insured commits suicide within the reinstated policy's suicide exclusion period (one or two years from the date of reinstatement), the insurer may properly decline a claim for benefits.

Claims Arising during Reinstatement

Occasionally the owner of a lapsed life insurance policy dies while in the process of attempting to reinstate the policy. Claims that arise under such policies can present a variety of problems for the claim examiner. In some instances, the policyowner submits the premium and the reinstatement form to the insurer but dies before the insurer formally approves the reinstatement application. In such cases, the question of claim liability is similar to that of liability under prepayment receipts requiring approval by the insurer before coverage commences. Consider the following example:

> The insured, Dawn Davis, completed a reinstatement application and mailed it to the insurer, together with the amount of premium in arrears. Before the reinstatement application could be approved by the insurer, Dawn died. The reinstatement application contained a provision that a reinstatement is not complete until it has been approved by the company.

Faced with a situation like the one above, a company could rely upon strict interpretation of the reinstatement wording and deny claim liability. However, the insurer might face the same legal challenges as were discussed under prepayment receipts. A court might find that the insurer's acceptance of the premium amount in arrears created a reasonable expectation on the part of the insured that insurance coverage was in effect. As an alternative, the insurer could proceed with *post mortem* reinstatement, provided the following conditions were met:

- the insured's attempt to reinstate had been made in good faith, *and*

- the insured's health was such that the application would have been approved, *or*
- any additional information that would have been required for approval of the application can still be obtained. Such information might be a hospital record or an Attending Physician's Statement. However, if the company would have required a physical examination, this condition could not be met.

If an insurer decides to evaluate a reinstatement application on a *post mortem* basis, it must do so in a timely manner. As a general rule, courts have found that an unreasonable delay in acting on a reinstatement application constitutes a waiver of the insurer's right to decline to reinstate the policy.

In addition, when a reinstatement is pending at the death of a former insured, the insurer should advise the beneficiary of the lapsed policy and should note that (1) the insurer will hold any premiums paid by the former insured until a reinstatement decision is made or (2) the insurer will return such premiums if the beneficiary so requests, thereby terminating the reinstatement application. Unconditional acceptance or retention of premiums by a company can legally lead to reinstatement.

Extended Insurance Options

As discussed in Chapter 2, when a whole life insurance policy that contains a cash value is surrendered, the policyowner can use the net cash value of the policy to purchase extended term insurance for the amount of coverage available under the original policy but for a period of time less than that provided by the original policy. The extended term insurance option is the automatic nonforfeiture option for whole life insurance policies issued on a standard basis in the United States.

Sometimes companies encounter cases in which a person insured under a reinstated policy dies during a period when (1) the reinstatement is contestable and (2) the insured would have been covered under extended term insurance if the policy had been allowed to lapse. In such situations, the claim processing procedure depends upon what other term riders or benefits are included under the original policy.

If no accidental death benefits or other additional benefits are involved, either because they are not included in the policy or because they are not applicable to the cause of death, and if the amount of extended insurance is approximately the same as if the policy were processed on a fully inforce basis, then there is no need for a claim examiner to investigate the reinstatement application. The policy's full face amount would be payable under either the reinstated policy or the extended insurance coverage.

The situation is different, however, if the insured's death was due to an accident, and the policy has an accidental death benefit provision. Since extended term insurance coverage rarely provides for an accidental death benefit, a close examination of the reinstatement application is warranted. If the claim examiner can show that the reinstatement is void because of material misrepresentation in the reinstated application, then the claim is payable only under the extended insurance option, and only the face amount of the policy is payable. A claim examiner should consider investigating any claim under a reinstated policy for which there is an increase in an insurer's liability due to a provision in the original policy, such as the use of dividend accumulations to increase the amount of insurance.

Undated Reinstatements

Occasionally an insurer accepts an undated reinstatement application because of an error by company personnel or because the company finds it more economical to accept undated reinstatement applications than to return such applications for dating. An undated reinstatement application may create a claim problem if the insurer raises a defense of material misrepresentation and if the condition allegedly misrepresented arose about the time the reinstatement application was completed. The lack of a date raises a substantial question of fact in the defense. Stamping each application with the date received may be helpful to the defense but is not necessarily conclusive evidence in a legal proceeding.

Agent's Actions

Sometimes a case arises in which an insured informs an agent of a desire to reinstate a policy, pays the premium in arrears, but does not complete a reinstatement application form because the agent does not have one. If the insured then dies before completing the application, there are three possible claim decisions:

- denial of liability, based on strict interpretation of the requirements of reinstatement;
- *post mortem* processing of the case, obtaining whatever information is available and applying standard reinstatement criteria to determine whether the policy would have been reinstated; and
- acceptance of liability, on the theory that responsibility for the missing application lies with the company, through its agent, and not with the insured.

A strong case can be made for this last decision. However, actual acceptance or denial of liability will depend on both the legal jurisdiction involved and the claim philosophy of the company.

Health Insurance Reinstatements

Individual health insurance policies contain a reinstatement provision that allows the owner of a lapsed policy to reinstate the policy if certain conditions are met. Individual health insurance policies are typically reinstated in the following ways: (1) by a policyowner's acceptance of an insurer's late remittance offer, or (2) by an insurer's acceptance of a past due premium and approval of the reinstatement application.

Late Remittance Offers

Health insurance late remittance offers are similar to life insurance late remittance offers. The insurer informs the policyowner by letter that the policy can be reinstated automatically without a reinstatement application if the policyowner will submit the overdue premium payment within a specified time period, usually 10 to 30 days after the expiration of the grace period. If the policyowner accepts the insurer's late remittance offer and submits the overdue premium, the reinstatement cannot be declined. Usually, coverage under the policy continues as though the policy had not lapsed.

Sometimes an agent, duly authorized by an insurer, accepts a past due premium within a short period of time, such as 10 to 30 days after the expiration of the grace period. In these situations, the acceptance of the past due premium results in automatic reinstatement of the policy. Even if the company is not aware of such a practice by an agent, the agent is acting for the company, and, thus, the reinstatement is automatic.

Conditional Premium Receipt and Underwriting of the Reinstatement Application

If more than 30 days have passed since the expiration of the grace period, the insurer usually requires a policyowner to submit a reinstatement application along with the past due premium payment. In such cases, the reinstatement application is subject to an underwriting review, and the company has the right to impose limitations, such as adding exclusions or eliminating riders on the policy, or to decline reinstatement of the policy. If the company declines the reinstatement application, then the premium is returned to the former policyowner. If the company approves the reinstatement application, then the policy is reinstated as of the date of the approval, subject to any coverage restrictions specified in the reinstated policy. If the application has not been declined or approved by the 45th day (30th day in New Mexico) following the date of the conditional premium receipt, the policy becomes reinstated automatically.

Claim Restrictions Following Reinstatement. To guard against antiselection, health insurance reinstatements often include time limits that restrict the time when coverage begins again under the reinstated policy. According to the standard time limits included in the NAIC's Uniform Policy Provisions, a reinstated policy covers sickness only if the sickness began more than ten days after the date of reinstatement. Accidental injuries are covered immediately upon reinstatement.

GROUP INSURANCE

Determining when coverage ends under a group insurance policy can be somewhat more complex than determining when coverage ends under an individual policy because the claim examiner may have to consider questions about several matters, such as (1) the lapse of the group policy, (2) the termination of an individual's coverage under the group policy contract, or (3) the termination of the group insurance contract itself. In this chapter, we describe only the termination of the group policy because of policy lapse. In later chapters, we discuss the other topics.

Policy Lapses

All group insurance policies contain a 31-day grace period. If an overdue premium has not been paid by the end of the grace period, the policy lapses for nonpayment of premium. Unless a group policyholder sends written notice to the insurer discontinuing the policy's coverage before the end of the grace period, the insurer is liable for any claims incurred during the grace period. However, if coverage is in force during any part of the grace period, the group policyholder is contractually responsible for payment of the grace period premium or for a pro rata portion of the premium for the time the policy was in force during the grace period.

Although no legislation in Canada nor the United States requires group policies to contain a reinstatement provision, group insurers usually send a premium notice to the policyholder at the end of the grace period, or within a few days thereafter, stating that the past due premium along with the current premium due may be remitted in what amounts to an automatic reinstatement of the policy. Claims that occur after the grace period will be covered if the policyowner remits the premium due within the time specified by the premium notice.

References

Walker, Dennis. "Life Claims and Policies in Transition," *1987 ICA Life Insurance Workshop Notes*, 189–195.

Life Claim Administration

7

Examining Life Insurance Claims

Twenty-five years ago, the examination of life insurance claims was a relatively simple process. Whole life and term life insurance with average face amounts of $25,000 or less constituted the bulk of an insurer's life insurance claims. Paying life insurance claims was a manual process accomplished with the assistance of an adding machine. Fair claim practices legislation had yet to be enacted. In rare cases in which rejected claims were litigated, claim examiners did not generally have to worry about sympathetic juries awarding extracontractual damages to beneficiaries, since such awards were almost unheard of 25 years ago.

Today, the process of examining life claims is entirely different. Substantial changes have taken place in the product lines of insurance companies. As we discussed in Chapter 2, companies still sell whole life and term life insurance products, but they have added an array of other insurance products such as universal life insurance and variable life insurance. Claim examiners today must be knowledgeable about new insurance products, and they must be able to adjust rapidly to new plan provisions and to new types of benefits. In addition, today's claim examiners must be able to manipulate a computerized data base or a computerized system file containing insurance master records. Moreover, claim processing decisions today are affected by a proliferation of state, provincial, and federal laws and regulations, by educated consumers who demand faster and more accurate service, by a litigious society in which litigation and the award of extracontractual damages are commonplace, and by the ever-increasing potential for and occurrence of insurance fraud.

In this chapter, we describe the examination of basic life insurance claims. Chapter 8 looks at claim examination for supplementary life insurance benefits. Chapters 9 and 10 discuss the payment of life insurance and supplemental insurance proceeds.

VERIFYING THE LOSS

The process of examining both individual and group life insurance claims begins when claim department personnel receive notification of the death of an insured. The claim department may receive notification of death from the beneficiary, the policyowner, an agent of the company, or the company's policyowner service department.

After the claim examiner has verified that the coverage is in force, that the insured is covered, and that there is no misrepresentation in the application, then the examiner seeks proof that a loss did occur, along with sufficient detail to describe the exact nature of the loss.

The claim department sends the beneficiary a claim form or claimant's statement to complete and return. As shown in Figure 7–1, the claim form requests basic information about the insured and the insured's death.

Along with the completed claim form, the beneficiary is asked to submit proof of the insured's death. In the absence of a contract or statutory provision to the contrary, sufficient proof of death is any form of evidence that is substantial and trustworthy enough for the insurer to form an intelligent determination of the company's liabilities. An insurer decides whether proof is sufficient. However, if the sufficiency of proof is disputed, the sufficiency becomes a question of law to be determined by the courts.

Death Certificates

A death certificate is the generally accepted proof of death in both Canada and the United States. A death certificate can be either an original, bearing the seal or signature of the official having authority to issue death certificates, or a copy of an original certified by the proper officials as being a "true copy."

Insurers have traditionally refused to accept a copy of a death certificate that has been produced by an unauthorized individual. Authorized persons usually include the Registrar of Vital Statistics, deputies, and local registrars, but do not include undertakers. Although the statutes of states

INDIVIDUAL LIFE CLAIMS

CLAIMANT'S STATEMENT **ABC Life Assurance Company of America**

NOTE: The Company and its Agents are prepared to assist in the completion of Proofs of Claims, and settlement can readily be obtained by direct communication with the Company or its nearest local representatives.

This form is to be completed by the person or persons to whom the policy is legally payable as beneficiary. If the beneficiary is the insured's estate, the statement should be completed by the executor or administrator and a certified copy of the appointment issued by the proper court and bearing the clerk's signature must be furnished. If the beneficiary is not of legal age, a guardian should complete the form and submit a certified copy of the appointment issued by the proper court and bearing the clerk's signature.

A certified copy of the Official Certificate of Death, certified by the issuing agency, must be furnished the Company.

If the beneficiary is entitled to receive and desires settlement under an optional mode of settlement a form 1400 should be completed. If the proceeds are to be paid as a life income, proof of age of the beneficiary must be furnished.

For policies with a CHILDREN'S RIDER or FAMILY and PARENT AND CHILDREN policies, see instructions on Supplemental Statement 123.

If death occurred within the two year period following the date of issue of the policy, form 34(a), Death Claim Medical History form, executed by the insured's next of kin, must be furnished.

1. POLICY NOS.				
2. NAME OF DECEASED		3. RELATIONSHIP TO INSURED (IF OTHER THAN INSURED)	4. RESIDENCE AT TIME OF DEATH	
5. CAUSE OF DEATH		6. PLACE OF DEATH	7. DATE OF DEATH	
8. DATE OF BIRTH		9. PLACE OF BIRTH	10. EMPLOYER	

FRAUD STATEMENT REQUIRED BY SOME STATES

Any person who knowingly and with intent to defraud any insurance company or other person files a statement of claim containing any materially false information, or conceals for the purpose of misleading, information concerning any fact material thereto, commits a fraudulent insurance act, which is a crime.

BENEFICIARY'S TAX IDENTIFICATION NUMBER*
(see explanation on reverse side)

Under penalties of perjury, I certify:
That the number shown on this form is my correct taxpayer identification number; and
☐ Check box if you are NOT subject to backup withholding under the provisions of section 3406 (a) (1) (C) of the Internal Revenue Code.
FAILURE TO CHECK BOX WILL RESULT IN COMPANY WITHHOLDING 20% OF INTEREST PAYMENT ON LUMP SUM PROCEEDS.

AUTHORIZATION TO OBTAIN INFORMATION

Name of Deceased _____
                                    (Please print)

To all doctors; medical professionals; hospitals; clinics; other health care providers; insurers; insurance support organizations; and other persons who have information about the patient.

I authorize you to give the ABC Life Assurance Company of America and/or the ABC Life Assurance Company its reinsurers or its agents: (a) all information you have as to illness, injury, medical history, diagnosis, treatment and prognosis with respect to any physical or mental condition of the patient; and (b) any non-medical information about the patient which the Company believes it needs to perform the business functions described below.

The information obtained will be used to determine if the patient is eligible: (a) for insurance; or (b) for benefits under a Company policy. It will also be used for any other purpose which relates to the insurance or benefits.

This form will be valid for the duration of the claim. I know that I may request a copy of it. I agree that a copy is as valid as the original.

DATE SIGNED	SIGNATURE OF BENEFICIARY
	RELATIONSHIP TO DECEASED

*
BENEFICIARY'S TAX ACCOUNT NO. (SOCIAL SECURITY NO.)	ADDRESS (NO. & STREET, CITY & STATE)

Figure 7-1.   Sample life insurance claim form.

and provinces do not preclude an insurer's accepting photocopies made by an undertaker as satisfactory proof of death, they do suggest that the making of official death certificates by persons other than public officials violates local public policy. Further, if litigation becomes necessary, a copy made by an undertaker might not be admissible as evidence in court in some jurisdictions.

Of more immediate concern to the claim examiner is the possibility of fraud. Changes that are almost impossible to detect on a photocopy might be made on the original death certificate in such areas as cause of death, age, or identity of the deceased. Occasionally, insurers will accept noncertified copies of death certificates for very small policy claims. However, in such cases, the insurer usually will require the beneficiary to submit corroborating evidence, such as newspaper clippings, or will require the attending physician, undertaker, or coroner to verify the death of the insured.

Other Accepted Proofs of Loss

As an alternative to a certified death certificate, most companies will accept an Attending Physician's Statement (APS), a coroner's certificate, or a hospital's certificate of death. When the insurer has reason to question the cause of death, the insurer may also request an autopsy report.

Sometimes a beneficiary refuses to submit proof of death in any of the acceptable forms. In the absence of a policy provision specifying the kind of proof the claimant must furnish, the claimant's duty is to furnish *prima facie* evidence of death. **Prima facie** evidence is a set of facts that, in the absence of evidence to dispute them, will entitle the bearer to whatever he or she seeks. Some courts hold that a person with knowledge of the facts can submit a document that attests to and certifies the death of the insured. In some jurisdictions, including New York, such a document has been deemed to be sufficient proof of death. In those jurisdictions, the company may have to accept the proof as offered and then obtain a copy of the official death record at its own expense.

Death of Insured Outside of North America

Deaths occurring outside of North America can create unique problems for a claim examiner seeking proof that a loss did take place. Perhaps the most obvious problem arises when proof of death is presented in a language that is foreign to the examiner, who then must find a qualified translator. Further complicating the claim process is the unpredictability of the mail service in many countries.

In addition to these types of procedural problems, statistics indicate that claims originating outside of North America are much more likely to involve fraud than claims originating within North America. Formalities and procedures for registration of death in other countries are not always as stringent as those in North America. For example, in some countries, if two people make a statement to authorities that a death has occurred, a death certificate will be issued without an investigation into the truth of the statements.

A claim examiner who suspects that the proof submitted by a claimant about a foreign death may be fraudulent may contact that country's embassy or consulate to verify that the form received is the official death certificate of that country. Contact can be made by telephone or letter. The embassy or consulate may be helpful in attesting to the authenticity of documents and may help in obtaining the services of a translator.

In addition, a claim examiner may wish to verify passport or immigration information on a decedent. In the United States or Canada, the immigration/passport authorities will have records pertaining to entry into, residence in, or departure from the country. Many other countries maintain similar entry and exit controls. From immigration information, a claim examiner may be able to prove that the person was not within a particular country at the time at which the death was said to have occurred.

In some cases, a claim examiner may wish to initiate an overseas investigation of an insured's death. Commercial private investigators that specialize in foreign claim investigations either will have agents established in particular countries or will agree to send an agent to a particular country or area to obtain the necessary information. Alternatively, the claim examiner may contact other insurance companies that have a substantial volume of business in a given country. These companies may have contacts or resources that can be used to provide information about an insured's death.

Disappearance

In some life insurance claims, the death of the insured cannot be proven; rather, it must be presumed from the person's disappearance. Cases involving the disappearance of the insured present particularly complicated claim problems. Disappearance claims fall into two categories: those in which the disappearance can be explained and those in which it is mysterious.

Explainable Disappearance

Explainable disappearance occurs when an insured has been exposed to a specific peril that can reasonably account for his or her disappearance. A typical example is as follows:

> The insured, Gloria Swenson, purchases a ticket for an airplane flight from Atlanta to Toronto and is seen boarding the craft by relatives.

An hour later, before making any landing, the plane crashes. There are no survivors, and Gloria's body is not found.

In a case such as this, the failure of Gloria to appear is reasonably explained by what is known as a "specific peril," in this case, the airplane crash. This case is sufficiently clear-cut to warrant payment of benefits on the life of Gloria. But suppose, in the example above, that the plane had made a stop in Detroit before the crash. Even though Gloria's destination might have been Toronto, there is the possibility that she left the plane in Detroit, before the crash. Such a situation might warrant further investigation to determine whether Gloria had any reason to disappear.

Mysterious Disappearance

In other claim situations, the claim examiner receives no immediate explanation for the disappearance of the insured. All that is known is that the insured has not been seen or heard from for a considerable period of time. Cases of mysterious disappearance require more investigation, as a rule, than do cases of explainable disappearance, since payment of the death benefit is based only on a presumption of the insured's death.

Presumption of Death. All states and provinces recognize that a presumption of death arises after an unexplained absence of a number of years. In most jurisdictions, an insured must have been continuously absent for seven years. Recently, the statutes of some states have been amended to lower this requirement to five consecutive years, and in one state, Minnesota, it has been lowered to four consecutive years.

However, a presumption of death does not arise automatically after the required period of time has passed. Instead, a reasonable search must have been made for the missing person, and the search must have continued for some time. What constitutes a reasonable search can be determined only from a review of the case law of the jurisdiction involved.

In most cases of mysterious disappearance, the claimant will ask a court to establish a legal presumption of death. Sometimes, however, a claimant will wait the required period of time and then ask an insurer to pay the death benefit without such a presumption. Some insurers, in such cases, will investigate to determine if payment can be made. Most insurers, though, will not pay a death benefit without a legal presumption of death.

Date of Death. If a court issues a presumption of death, the court will also set a legal date of death. The general rule is that the death of the insured occurred at the end of the presumptive period. A small minority of courts hold that death occurred at the time the insured first became absent and that the running of the statutory or common law period merely confirms that death. In either case, the life insurance policy must still be in force when the presumption of death is established. Many times, life insurance policies lapse for nonpayment of premiums before the presumption of death arises. In such cases, the beneficiary must prove that the insured actually died prior to the date of policy lapse, or no benefits will be payable.

Investigating Disappearance Claims

The first step in investigating a disappearance is to determine whether the missing person is dead or alive. If the insured is found to be actually or presumably dead, then the investigator may try to establish the time of death. The investigative procedures used depend upon the nature of the disappearance.

Investigating Explainable Disappearances.   The investigation of explainable disappearances involves claims in which the insured was subject to some known peril, such as a boating accident, fire, plane crash, or storm, and is thought to have died, even though the body has not been recovered and the usual death certificate has not been issued. Investigations of this type of claim usually require a detailed tracing of the insured's actions prior to the event that is alleged to have caused death.

Interviews with the last persons to see the insured, as well as with persons who witnessed the event, are an important part of such an investigation. Also important are reports of official investigative agencies, such as the police, fire department, Coast Guard, or Federal Aviation Administration.

If a body was recovered, it may be necessary to establish its identity as that of the insured. In establishing such identity, the claim examiner will find that the following steps are usually helpful:

- Determine the insured's physical characteristics, including height, weight, color of eyes and hair, any physical impairments, birthmarks or tattoos, and dental characteristics. This data may be obtained from the claimant, from the insured's medical or dental records, or from the insured's employment records.
- Determine what the insured was wearing at the time of the event in question, including a description of clothing, jewelry, watch, and religious or other medals.
- If possible, obtain the most recent photograph of the insured.

This information can be compared with information developed about the body by the police, coroner, or medical examiner. The investigation also should consider the possibility of suicide by the insured.

Investigating Mysterious Disappearances. An investigation of a mysterious disappearance usually begins with the development of a personal profile of the insured. The personal profile should include the following information:

- the last time the insured was seen or heard from,
- aliases or nicknames the insured used,
- organizations to which the insured belonged,
- arrest or prison records of the insured,
- military experience of the insured,
- medical treatment of the insured prior to the disappearance,
- previous residences of the insured,
- sources of non-earned income, (pensions, dividends, interest, and royalties),
- the work performance record of the insured, and
- the marital status of the insured.

As a next step, the claim examiner will want to study the circumstances surrounding the insured's disappearance. The examiner should note inconsistencies in the accounts given by witnesses and should determine the probability of the events' occurring as described. How probable was it for the insured to die and the body to disappear? Was it physically possible for the insured to have taken part in the described actions?

Finally, the claim examiner should determine if the insured had a motive for wishing to disappear. What was happening in the insured's life just prior to the disappearance? Was the insured experiencing a personal crisis? Was the insured worth more financially dead than alive?

If the investigation reveals that the insured may still be alive, the investigation should then focus on finding the missing person. Phone books, city directories, credit bureaus, telephone records, post office change of address records, driving records, police records, medical records, local travel agency records, passport information, and Social Security information are all sources that can be used to verify the existence of the insured.

Discovery of the Missing Insured. In some claim cases, the absent insured is located but does not want his or her whereabouts disclosed. There are several forms of evidence the insurer can obtain to support denial of the claim, without revealing where the insured resides. One form is the insured's notarized signature beneath a statement providing identifying details such as place and date of birth, name of father, maiden name of mother, maiden name of wife, and names of children. The statement should be signed and dated by the insured.

Another form of evidence is a photograph of the insured together with the investigator; a current issue of a magazine or newspaper in the photograph will provide further evidence of the date of their meeting. The insured should then make a signed statement in writing on the back of the photograph, attesting to his or her identity, the date of the photograph, and the circumstances under which it was taken.

The insured's wishes for confidentiality should be respected. However, the insurer should inform the insured that, according to law, the information may be disclosed in court proceedings or upon proper request of an appropriate government agency.

VERIFYING POLICY COVERAGE OF THE LOSS

After a claim examiner has verified the circumstances surrounding an insured's death, the insurance contract must be checked to ensure that the death was not excluded from coverage by a contract limitation or exclusion. The most common life insurance contract exclusions are for suicide, aviation accidents, and war hazards. In addition, insurers sometimes place avocation exclusions in life insurance policies.

Suicide Exclusion

The average person is likely to think of suicide as an aberration—an event occasionally heard of but rarely encountered. However, suicide is much more prevalent than is ordinarily assumed. In 1985, two percent of all deaths in the United States resulted from suicide. Suicide is the eighth leading cause of death for adults in the United States and the third leading cause of death for teenagers.

Insurance companies seek to protect the interests of existing policyowners from the claims of an individual who secures insurance for his or her dependents while contemplating suicide. Insurers effect this protection by placing a suicide exclusion in life insurance policies. A typical suicide exclusion reads as follows:

> Death from suicide within two years from the date of issue, whether the insured is sane or insane, shall limit the liability of the company to the return of the amount of premiums paid.

Length of Suicide Exclusion Period

The period during which death by suicide can be excluded varies according to the jurisdiction involved. Most state and provincial statutes provide that suicide within two years from the date of policy issue is excluded from coverage. However, some states such as Colorado and North Dakota provide for only a one-year exclusion period; in Missouri, suicide can be used as a defense to deny benefits only if the insurer can show that the insured was contemplating suicide at the time of the application. In the United States, the suicide exclusion period generally dates from the original policy issue date regardless of whether the life insurance policy has been reinstated. In Canada, a policy's suicide exclusion period begins to run again from the date of a reinstatement.

Application of the Suicide Exclusion to an Insane Person

If a suicide exclusion clause excludes risk of death by suicide while an insured is sane or insane, then suicide by an insane insured will not ordinarily be covered during the exclusion period. Nonetheless, the courts in several states have held that the suicide clause cannot be applied to an insane person, regardless of the wording of the policy exclusion, because such a person cannot comprehend the physical nature and consequences of the act. In such jurisdictions, suicide while insane results in payment of the regular death benefit. In addition, if there are accidental death benefits involved, the laws in these states provide that suicide while insane constitutes an accident and should result in payment of the accidental death benefit.

Burden of Proof

The suicide exclusion is one of the most difficult defenses for an insurer to uphold in court. Since suicide generally is held to be against human instinct, the burden is upon the insurer to prove in a court of law that an insured's death was a result of suicide. Even in cases in which all facts strongly indicate suicide, if there is any possibility that death was caused by means other than suicide, the death will generally be ruled as nonsuicidal. However, in a claim for accidental death benefits, the burden of proof shifts to the beneficiary—aided by the presumption against suicide—to prove that the cause of death was accidental.

Payment of a Limited Benefit

When the suicide clause is invoked, the insurer returns the premiums paid for the policy to the beneficiary. It might appear that invoking the suicide clause is similar to rescinding a policy since both actions are accompanied by a return of premiums. However, when the suicide exclusion is invoked, payment of the premiums is not a refund, but is the payment of the limited benefit that was contractually agreed upon at the time the policy was applied for and issued. Therefore, invoking the suicide clause does not involve contesting the policy. To the contrary, the contract's validity is being affirmed by the application of the provision under which a limited benefit is payable to the beneficiary named in the contract.

Suicide Investigations

In many claims, the insured's death by suicide may appear to be relatively clear. In such cases, the claim examiner may be inclined to pay the limited benefit to the beneficiary without extensive investigation. Nonetheless, quick payment of a claim without a thorough investigation may result in legal problems later and possibly charges of unfair claim practices. As stated previously, the insurer may have to prove to a jury that the beneficiary is not entitled to the full policy benefit. If a thorough investigation is not completed before a claim decision is made, the insurer may find it impossible months or years later to prove its position in court. In addition, in California, insurers are required by state law to investigate thoroughly and completely every possible circumstance tending to establish liability. Failure to do so may constitute "bad faith" on the part of the insurer.

General Guidelines for Suicide Investigations

Suicide implies a direct connection among three factors: intention, action, and result. That is, the deceased must have intended to commit suicide, must have committed some self-destructive action, and must have died from that action. The phrase *equivocal suicide* describes cases in which there is doubt about one or more of these three factors and which may require investigation in order to decide whether death was suicide or whether it resulted from natural, accidental, or homicidal causes.

Equivocal suicides, such as those resulting from a gunshot, a drug overdose, or carbon monoxide poisoning, often raise the question of suicide versus accidental death. Specific guidelines for investigating accidental death cases are discussed in Chapter 8. In this section, we cover investigation guidelines that can be applied to all cases of equivocal suicide, regardless of the means of death.

When the possibility of suicide is an issue, an insurer's investigation focuses on both the physical aspects of the death and also on the psychological state of the deceased immediately preceding death. Because of the legal presumption against suicide, the company usually must be able to show that the insured had some motive or reason for suicide. The classical motives for committing suicide are economic, domestic, or health problems that may appear to the insured to be insurmountable.

In some cases, the insured may leave a suicide note or tell friends or relatives about his or her decision to commit suicide. If a suicide note was left, the investigation should uncover all information concerning it: its contents, when and where it was found, by whom it was found, and who currently is in possession of the note. A date on the note is especially important to rebut possible allegations that it was old or that the insured constantly left such notes without actually intending to carry out the suicide.

If the suicide note is unambiguous in its language, is written in the handwriting of the insured, bears the signature of the insured, and is dated, such facts would be sufficient in most cases to demonstrate that the death was a suicide. However, if any of those elements are missing or doubtful, further investigation will be necessary to learn of a possible motive.

Interviews with relatives and friends may disclose family problems or some seriously embarrassing or humiliating event recently experienced by the insured. The investigation also should seek to determine whether the insured had

- been involved in criminal activity,
- been subpoenaed to appear before any investigative body,
- been known to associate with persons of questionable reputation,
- been in poor mental or physical health,
- been experiencing any personal financial problems,
- previously attempted or threatened suicide, or
- any family history of suicide.

In some cases of violent death, the insured may have been murdered, with the death made to appear an accident or a suicide. Any information suggesting this possibility, such as reported threats against the life of the insured, should be included in the investigation report.

If the evidence of motivation for suicide is weak, the insurer may obtain a ruling of suicide if the physical facts of the death clearly rule out the possibility of an accident. Sources of information include police reports, coroner's records, autopsy reports, and pertinent newspaper articles. Figure 7-2 provides a checklist for a claim examiner to follow in an investigation of a possible suicide.

During investigation of a suicide, the claim examiner must recognize the particularly sensitive nature of the question being decided. Grieving relatives or friends are often unwilling to admit that the insured committed suicide. Witnesses and informants sometimes seek to disguise a suicide through evasion, denial, concealment, and even direct suppression of evidence. For example, family members may destroy a suicide note. In a few cases, especially those involving prominent individuals, local officials may be reluctant to mention the existence of a suicide note or to reveal its contents.

Nonetheless, a prompt and thorough suicide investigation has many advantages for the beneficiary. Often, the beneficiary is not aware of the health or other problems that precipitated the suicide. The findings of the investigation may be therapeutic by reducing the guilt of the survivors and making it easier for them to accept the death of the victim. In addition, an investigation may reveal that a claim is payable even when the death appeared to be the result of a suicide.

(Basic questions: Policy in force? Contestable? Loss Covered?)

I. Identification of insured
Name and address
Marital status
Occupation
Religion
Age

II. Insured's medical background
Medical history of insured
General physical condition
Recent medical treatment
Hospitalization
Psychotherapy
Family death history
Suicides
Ages at death
Cancer/heart disease/other illnesses?

III. Personality of insured
Basic personality—relaxed, or tense?
Did the insured have many friends?
Interests or hobbies?
Religiously active?
Any history of prior violence?
Any prior suicide attempts?

IV. Life-style of insured
Employed—if so, any recent changes at work?
If not employed—How long was the insured unemployed? Was
  insured fired or laid off?
Retired—if so, what was reaction to retirement?
Any evidence of substance abuse?
Recent losses or deaths?
Recent changes in home environment—separation or divorce?
Recent accidents or injuries?
Financial difficulties?
Any evidence of compulsive gambling?

V. Details of death
Place and time
Manner
Any witnesses
Police/coroner reports
Ambulance/medical/hospital records
Newspaper accounts
Location of body
How was body clothed?

VI. Final behavior of insured
Who were the last persons to see or talk with the insured?
Was there a suicide note?
Why was the insured at the place of death?
Was the insured under the influence of alcohol or drugs?
What was the emotional and physical state of the insured imme-
  diately preceding death? Tired? Emotionally or physically
  stressed? Angry?

Figure 7-2.   A checklist for investigating a possible suicide.

Aviation Exclusion

Today, aviation exclusion clauses are not commonly included in basic life insurance policies because of the aviation industry's overall good safety record. Instead, insurers usually charge an extra premium if an insured's aviation activities constitute a special risk. However, aviation exclusions are still common in accidental death policies or riders. Since the majority of claim questions relating to the aviation exclusion involve accident benefits rather than basic death benefits, we present specific guidelines for evaluating and investigating aviation claims in Chapter 8.

War Hazard Exclusion

The hazards posed by war present special considerations both in underwriting and in claim administration. Insurers generally are unwilling to accept the liability for deaths occurring during times of war because of the companies' inability to (1) predict accurately the number of war deaths and (2) establish appropriate premium rates based on that number. In times of war or when war seems imminent, insurers include a provision in life insurance policies that limits the amount of liability for deaths resulting from acts of war. Most insurers in North America do not include war hazard exclusions in policies issued today because war has not been imminent for the United States or for Canada during recent years. However, war hazard exclusions are commonly included in accidental death policies or riders. Therefore, we discuss war hazard exclusions in more detail in Chapter 8. We should note, however, that many life insurance policies that are still in force contain a war exclusion; if circumstances change so that applicants are subject to the special hazards of war, life insurance policies would again be issued with war hazard exclusion clauses.

Avocation or Sports Exclusions

United States and Canadian citizens fill an increasing amount of leisure time with a variety of sports and hobbies. Mountain climbing, sports car racing, and scuba diving are just a few of the hazardous activities that many people engage in during leisure hours. Avocation or sports exclusions allow insurers to exclude from coverage death resulting from an applicant's higher-risk activities.

As with other types of exclusions, the specificity of the exclusion will determine its effectiveness if it is challenged in court. The wording of the exclusion must not be ambiguous because, in the event of any ambiguity, the courts will find in favor of the claimant. In addition, the exclusion must be sufficiently narrow so that a determination can be made as to exactly what is being excluded. For example, to exclude coverage "from or while engaged in mountain climbing" would be far too general in a determination of what constitutes mountain climbing. A more definitive approach would be to specify a height limit for the insured's mountain climbing activity or to localize the mountain climbing activity to a specific region. However, even very specific exclusions may be difficult for an insurer to uphold in court.

References

Bailey, Richard. *Underwriting in Life and Health Insurance Companies*. Atlanta, GA: LOMA, 1985.

Homer, Charles T. "The Claim Examiner: Past, Present, and Future," *1986 ICA Life Insurance Workshop Notes*, 26–32.

"Investigative Resources," *ICA Claim Investigation*, 1/10.

MacArthur, R. M. "Avocations and Exclusions," *1987 ICA Life Insurance Workshop Notes*, 134–135.

Ruppenthal, Harry. "Disappearance Claims," *1984 ICA Life Insurance Workshop Notes*, 35–37.

Shields, Richard J. "Suicide." *1987 ICA Life Insurance Workshop Notes*, 157–167.

Suicide as a Defense: Report of the Law Committee. International Claim Association, 1982.

Walker, Dennis. "Life Claims and Policies in Transition," *1987 ICA Life Insurance Workshop Notes*, 189–195.

8

Examining Claims
for Supplemental
Life Insurance Benefits

To increase the basic coverage offered under life insurance plans, a policyowner may purchase supplemental insurance coverages. Accidental death coverage and spouse and children's insurance coverage are two of the most common types of supplemental coverage sold by insurance companies. In this chapter, we describe the claim processing for these two types of supplemental benefits.

ACCIDENTAL DEATH BENEFITS

As discussed in Chapter 2, an **accidental death benefit (ADB)** typically provides that, upon the accidental death of the insured, a benefit amount in addition to the death benefit of the policy will be paid to the beneficiary. An accidental death benefit rider, shown in Figure 8–1, is commonly offered in conjunction with life insurance. However, accidental death benefits are also available through (1) limited accident policies designed to cover only specific types of accidents, such as aviation or traffic accidents; (2) disability income policies; and (3) separate stand-alone accident policies.

Accidental death benefits may provide for additional benefits for

Rider for Insured's Accidental Death Benefit

Benefit—We will pay the amount of this Benefit that we show on the Contract Data page(s) for the Insured's accidental loss of life. But our payment is subject to all the provisions of the Benefit and of the rest of this contract.

Manner of Payment—We will include in the proceeds of this contract any payment under this benefit.

Conditions—Both of these conditions must be met: (1) We must receive due proof that the Insured's death was the direct result, independent of all other causes, of accidental bodily injury that occurred on or after the contract date. (2) The death must occur (a) no more than 90 days after the injury; and (b) while the contract is in force.

Exclusions—We will not pay under this Benefit for death caused or contributed to by: (1) suicide or attempted suicide while sane or insane; or (2) infirmity or disease of mind or body or treatment for it; or (3) any infection other than one caused by an accidental cut or wound.

Even if death is caused by accidental bodily injury, we will not pay for it under this Benefit if it is caused or contributed to by: (1) service in the armed forces of any country(ies) at war; or (2) war or any act of war; or (3) travel by, or descent from, any aircraft if the insured had any duties or acted in any capacity other than as a passenger at any time during the flight. But we will ignore (3) if all these statements are true of the aircraft: (a) It has fixed wings and a permitted gross takeoff weight of at least 75,000 pounds. (b) It is operated by an air carrier that is certificated under the laws of the United States or Canada to carry passengers to or from places in those countries. (c) It is not being operated for any armed forces for training or other purposes. As used here, the word aircraft includes rocket craft or any other vehicle for flight in or beyond the earth's atmosphere. The word war means declared or undeclared war and includes resistance to armed aggression.

Benefit Premiums—We show the premium for this Benefit on the Contract Data page(s).

Termination—This Benefit will end on the earlier of:
1. The date the contract is surrendered under its Cash Value Option; and
2. the date the contract ends for any other reason.

This Supplementary Benefit rider attached to this contract on the Contract Date

Figure 8-1. A sample accidental death benefit rider.

dismemberment, in which case the benefit is called an ***accidental death and dismemberment (AD&D) benefit***. AD&D benefits specify that the full benefit amount will be paid if the insured loses any two limbs or the sight in both eyes as a result of an accident. In many cases, a smaller amount, such as half the accidental death benefit amount, will be payable if the insured loses one limb or the use of one eye. The loss of a limb may be defined as either the actual physical loss of the limb or as the loss of the use of the limb.

Claims for accidental death benefits are some of the most difficult and most interesting claims that a claim examiner administers. Evidence supporting a claim for accidental death benefits may not always be clear cut; for example, what initially appears to be a suicide or murder may in fact be an accidental death. Further complicating the claim situation are varying court interpretations of policy provisions and policy exclusions relative to accidental death benefits. Finally, advances in technology have inadvertently resulted in many new and sometimes bizarre ways in which a person can be accidentally killed. For example, claims for accidental death benefits have been filed on behalf of insureds who died from being struck by a submarine or being hit by a low-flying airplane. For all of these reasons, this chapter can only touch on the subject of claims for accidental death benefits.

Accidental Death Benefit Provisions

A basic understanding of some of the claim difficulties that accompany accidental death claims must begin with a discussion of accidental death benefit provisions. The type of accidental death benefit provision usually included in life insurance policies today is called an accidental result provision because the result of the event must be accidental. An **accidental result provision** states that accidental death benefits are payable:

> Upon receipt of due proof that the death of the insured on or after the effective date of this provision was the result, directly and independently of all other causes, of accidental bodily injury.

Traditionally, accidental death provisions specified that benefits would be payable:

> Upon receipt of due proof that the death of the insured occurred, while this benefit is in effect, as the result, directly and independently of all other causes, of bodily injury caused solely by external, violent, and accidental means.

This second type of accidental death provision is called an ***accidental***

means provision because the death of the insured must have been caused by accidental means.

At first glance, the wording of these two provisions is deceptively similar. However, consider the following case, *United States Mutual Accident Association* vs. *Barry*, which illustrates the complex differences between the two provisions.

> The insured, a doctor, jumped four or five feet off a platform to the ground. Two of his companions also jumped; they landed safely. But the insured suffered a ruptured duodenum when he landed, an injury from which he died nine days later. The insured's accidental death policy included the *accidental means* provision.

In the *Barry* case, the U.S. Supreme Court held that because the insured jumped in the way he had intended, there were no accidental means. Thus, even though the result had been accidental, the policy requirements for accidental means had not been fulfilled and no accident benefits were payable. Assume, however, in the preceding case, that the insured's policy had included an accidental *result* provision. In such a case, benefits would have been payable because the insured certainly did not anticipate that jumping four or five feet would result in his death.

The Supreme Court's decision in the *Barry* case has been the subject of much criticism. Probably the most influential criticism was that of Justice Cardozo in *Landress* vs. *Phoenix Mutual*, which involved the death of a golfer by sunstroke. Again, the Supreme Court ruled that the death was not by accidental means because the golfer's voluntary exposure to the sun was intentional. In his dissenting opinion, Justice Cardozo said, "The attempted distinction between accidental results and accidental means will plunge this branch of the law into a Serbonian bog."[1]

Justice Cardozo's opinion reflects a general public sentiment that it is improper for insurers to deny accidental death claims because of technical wording that is beyond the comprehension of the general public. Since the Landress case, most insurers have revised the wording of their accidental death benefit provisions to include the accidental result clause. In addition, many state courts have abolished the distinction between accidental means and accidental result clauses in their jurisdictions and treat accidental means clauses as if they were accidental result clauses. Other courts have held that the accidental means provision in a policy will be given effect, but that if there is a close question as to whether a death was caused by accidental means, the decision will be made in favor of the beneficiary.

---

[1] John Milton in *Paradise Lost* referred to Lake Serbonis in Egypt in which entire armies were engulfed.

Policy Conditions

In addition to determining whether a policy has an accidental means or accidental result clause, a claim examiner must ascertain the conditions under which death will be considered accidental as stated in the policy and the effect of any exceptions listed in the policy.

Age Limitations

Age limitations specify that the accident benefit is not payable prior to, or later than, a stated age. For example, a policy may state that the accidental death benefit is not payable before the insured reaches age 5 or after the insured reaches age 65. Age limitation provisions are included because of the high incidence of accidents at these low and high ages and because claim examiners often are not able to determine whether the death of a very young or very old person was due to natural causes or to an accident.

Time Limitations

Most accidental death provisions specify a time limit, measured from the date that the injury occurred, within which death must occur if the death is to be considered as accidental. A time limitation of 90 days from the date of injury is common in many policies. However, some policies issued in recent years have liberalized this limitation to 120 or even 365 days from the date of injury. The reason for the inclusion of time limitations is to reduce questions that may arise about whether the injury was the true cause of death when there is an intervening period between injury and death. Although time limitations are an attempt to simplify the claim decision, they have resulted in complicated claim questions as well.

For example, it is not uncommon for a person injured in an accident to lie in a coma for several months before dying. With advances in medical technology, this situation occurs more and more frequently. If medical skill alone prolongs the insured's life, the insurer may or may not deny benefits because of the time limitation; practice differs among companies and according to the laws of the jurisdiction involved.

A notable case in this area is the case of *Burne* vs. *Franklin Life Insurance Company*. In this case, the Supreme Court of Pennsylvania held that enforcement of a 90-day time limit without regard to causation was arbitrary, because the state of medical science has grown to the point that it is often capable of prolonging life indefinitely. This ruling has been interpreted to mean that all arbitrary time limitations on accidental death benefits are against public policy and hence are not enforceable in Pennsylvania. Courts in two other states have also held time limits to be arbitrary when the cause of death was clearly the result of an accident. However, courts in other states, including Florida, have supported time limitations.

Proximate Cause Limitations

Accidental death policies usually specify that the accidental death benefit is payable only if an accident is the proximate cause of death. The term *proximate cause of death* is defined as the event that is directly responsible for the death or the event that initiates an unbroken chain of events that lead to death. In general, if an accident results in an injury which in turn causes a disease, and that disease results in death, the accident is considered to be the actual cause of the death. For example:

> The insured, Raoul Gerrard, while lifting a 50 pound object, ruptures a duodenal ulcer and a few weeks later dies from pneumonia that develops as a complication from the ruptured ulcer.

Although the pneumonia was the actual cause of death, the perforated ulcer set in motion the chain of events that resulted in death. Thus, the accident was the proximate cause of death, and the accidental death benefit probably would be payable.

Policy Exclusions

Just as certain risks are excluded from basic life insurance coverage, insurers usually exclude certain risks from accidental death benefit coverage. Some exclusions—such as those based on war and military service—are made because the risk is deemed too high for coverage. Other exclusions—such as those involving drugs, poisoning, and inhalation of gas—are made because of the difficulty in determining whether the death was accidental or suicidal. Although exclusions vary from insurance company to insurance company, here we discuss the exclusions that are most commonly included in accidental death coverages.

Contribution of Disease Exclusion

Deaths resulting from bodily or mental infirmities or disease often are excluded from accidental death coverage. A typical policy provision excludes accident benefits when death results

> Directly or indirectly from bodily or mental infirmity or disease or directly or indirectly from medical or surgical treatment therefor.

A claim examiner seeking to apply a contribution of disease exclusion must thoroughly review the claim and any relative case law of the involved jurisdiction to determine if the insured's condition can be considered a disease, and if so, to what degree the disease actually contributed to the death of the insured.

Definition of "Disease." Courts in most jurisdictions generally find that the term "disease" as used in policy provisions is limited to a condition which is so considerable or significant that it would be characterized as a disease in the common speech of men. In Ohio, however, *disease* is that which is recognized as such by medical authorities. Other courts have found that disease is a condition that is of a serious nature, or that is progressive, or that may be expected to have serious consequences.

Conditions that are normal with advancing age often are discounted as diseases, particularly if they developed while the policy was in force. For example, assume that an insured, who is 64 years old and suffering from severe arthritis, stumbles while walking down a street and skins his knee. The insured's leg becomes infected, and he dies from complications associated with the infection. In a case such as this one, most insurers probably would pay the accidental death benefit. Although arthritis certainly contributed to the insured's injury and resulting death, a court probably would not find arthritis to be an active disease for purposes of the exclusionary clause.

Alcoholism and drug addiction may or may not be considered diseases under a court's interpretation of an exclusionary clause, even though both conditions are increasingly considered to be diseases in the common speech of men. Two recent cases illustrate the diversity in court decisions in this area. In a 1982 Florida case—*Williams* vs. *New England Mutual*—an appeals court found that the term "disease" was highly ambiguous and that there was conflicting medical testimony as to whether alcoholism should be considered a disease. Since ambiguity in an insurance contract is resolved against the insurance company, the court ruled that the beneficiary was entitled to the accidental death benefit. However, in sharp contrast, a 1984 Arizona court decision—*Kelly* vs. *Republican National Life Insurance*—cited a number of authorities to support its ruling that alcoholism is a disease within the exclusionary language of the accidental death benefit provision.

Extent to which Disease Contributes to an Insured's Death.
Since both disease and accidental injury are present in many accidental death claims, a claim examiner must often decide to what degree disease contributed to an insured's death. Court cases involving this question have been classified into three general categories. There is considerable unanimity among court decisions in the first two categories of cases, but considerable diversity is present in the third category of cases.

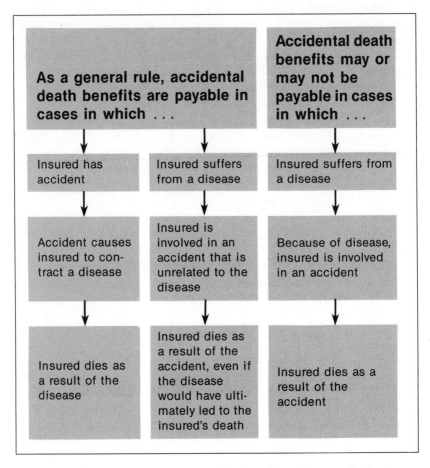

Figure 8-2.   Accidental death benefits payable when disease is a contributing factor in the insured's death.

The first category consists of cases in which an accident causes a disease or condition which, together with the accident, results in an insured's death. As discussed in connection with the topic of proximate cause, the general rule in both the United States and Canada is that the accident alone is considered to be the cause of the insured's death.

The second category consists of cases in which the insured was suffering from a disease or condition at the time of a fatal accident, but the disease or condition had no causal connection with the insured's death. Again, the general rule in both Canada and the United States is that the accident is considered the sole cause of death.

The third category consists of cases in which, at the time of the accident, the insured had a disease or condition that, together with the accident, resulted in the death of the insured. In some instances, the disease or condition was dormant and was activated by the accident. In other cases, the disease or condition was active at the time of the accident. Court decisions in this type of case have been mixed. Some courts follow the policy language and hold that no accidental death benefit is payable because the accident cannot be considered the sole cause of death. But other courts follow the theory of proximate cause, allowing recovery of the accidental death benefit if the accident is found to be the immediate or proximate cause of death, with the disease or condition being only a remote cause.

Other Claim Considerations. The portion of the contribution of disease provision pertaining to death resulting from medical or surgical treatment can also present claim questions. For example, some accidental death claims have listed a malfunctioning internal pacemaker or an improperly filled kidney dialysis machine as the cause of death. Accidents involving medical devices may occur during or after the course of medical treatment. If failure occurs during treatment—for example, a heart-lung machine malfunctions during surgery—a resulting death might properly be excluded from accidental death coverage under the contribution of disease exception. However, in two actual cases involving a pacemaker and a kidney dialysis machine, two different insurers considered the malfunctions to be "supervening mishaps," that is, malfunctions that took place after the basic treatment had been completed. Accidental death benefits were paid in each case.

Occasionally the question of medical malpractice arises in connection with accident benefit claims. If there is a clear case of malpractice that results in the death of the insured, the claim examiner must determine whether the death was an accident for which accidental death benefits should be paid. Cases of this sort are often difficult to decide. If the insured had a disease or condition that would eventually result in death, then payment of the accidental death benefit might properly be denied because of the contribution of disease exclusion, even though medical malpractice may have contributed to the actual death of the insured. Far more difficult to decide is a case in which there was in fact no such disease or condition, but in which an improper diagnosis or treatment by a physician led to the death of the insured. Such a case might have to be considered as accidental within the terms of the policy.

Suicide Exclusion

In the strictest sense, a suicide exclusion should not be necessary in an

accidental death rider or policy because suicide is self-inflicted, not accidental. Nonetheless, most accident coverages do include a suicide exclusion.
Suicide exclusions and guidelines for investigating suicides were discussed
in Chapter 7. In this chapter, we describe only the ways in which accidental death benefit suicide exclusions differ from suicide exclusions in basic
life insurance policies.

The wording of a typical suicide exclusion in an accidental death benefit
provision is similar to the typical suicide exclusion found in life insurance
policies and is as follows:

> No payment shall be made under this benefit for any loss caused
> or contributed to by suicide or any attempt thereat, whether the
> insured is sane or insane.

As mentioned previously, when a claim is made for basic life insurance
benefits, the burden of proving that an insured committed suicide is upon
the insurer. However, accidental death benefit claims require the beneficiary
to prove that the insured's death was accident-related rather than suicide.
If the claimant furnishes a death certificate that describes the cause of death
as accidental or that indicates a violent death, the claimant has met the
requirement. If the insurer wishes to enforce any policy exclusion, such
as the suicide exclusion, the burden of proof returns to the insurer. The
presumption of the law is against suicide. Therefore, using the guidelines
set forth in Chapter 7, the claim examiner should assemble a strong set
of facts before denying claim liability because of suicide.

War Hazard Exclusion

As mentioned in Chapter 7, deaths from war or acts of war generally
are not excluded from regular death benefit provisions. However, such
deaths are commonly excluded from payment of accidental death benefits.
It is not uncommon for a death to be covered by the regular death benefit
but to be excluded from the accidental death benefit provision because
of a war hazard exclusion. A typical war hazard exclusion clause reads
as follows:

> The liability under this policy shall be limited to the greater of (1)
> the net premiums paid on this policy or (2) the net reserve under
> this policy, if the insured should die as a result of an act of war,
> declared or undeclared.

The first war exclusion clauses did not cover any death that occurred
while the insured was in military service during time of war, regardless
of the cause of death. Such war exclusion clauses are referred to as **status**

clauses because an insured's military status during time of war triggers the exclusion clause regardless of the way in which the insured dies. For example, assume that Susan Mullen, on leave from the Navy during a period of war, dies in a commercial airline crash. The ADB rider of Susan's life insurance policy contains a status type of exclusion clause. Susan's beneficiary will, therefore, receive the basic death benefit from the life insurance policy, but only the amount of premiums paid for the ADB rider or the policy reserve, whichever is greater.

Status clauses were viewed by the general public as too restrictive. Several state insurance departments even took action to prevent the inclusion of status clauses in policies. Therefore, many insurers began using a *result clause*, which specifies that only deaths resulting from acts of war will be excluded from coverage. If Susan's policy had used a *result* type of exclusion clause, accidental death benefits would have been payable in her case. Some insurers are now administering existing status clauses as if they were result clauses.

The war hazard exclusion clause, whether of the status or result type, has raised difficult claim questions over the years. For the most part, these questions have involved definitions of the terms *war* and *act of war*.

War.   Not all acts of violence between countries constitute war. Obviously, if there has been a formal declaration of war, the question is decided immediately. However, in recent history there have been several major U.S. military actions—such as the Korean and Vietnam conflicts, for example—in which there was no formal declaration of war.

Undeclared wars such as these led to changes in the wording of the war clause. One particularly significant change is the inclusion of the phrase "declared or undeclared" to modify "war" in the war hazard exclusion. This phrase clarifies the right of the company to apply the war clause in those cases in which war exists in all but the formal definition. In attempting to decide whether a specific hostility constitutes war, the claim examiner may consider several points:

- whether the acts of violence were performed by groups of nationals or by unorganized individuals,
- whether the acts of violence were planned by one nation as an attack upon—or as an insult to—the sovereignty of the defending nation,
- whether the attacks were sporadic or sustained,
- the length of time during which the attacks continued,
- the number of persons involved in the attacks,
- the severity of the attacks,
- the degree of mobilization and economic organization for war in the attacking country, and
- the existence of a serious basis for a national dispute.

The question of determining whether, in fact, a war has begun has its converse side: determining when a war has ended. Casualties may occur between the end of large-scale hostilities and the time a peace treaty is signed. In the few cases on the subject, the courts have regarded the ending of mass hostilities as being the end of the war. The inclination of these courts has seemed to be toward not considering occasional subsequent acts of violence as acts of war.

Act of War.   Deaths of service personnel occasionally result from warlike acts in the absence of war itself. Recent examples of such deaths include the following:

- On October 23, 1983, the United States embassy in Lebanon was bombed, resulting in the deaths of 241 Marines.[2]
- On October 25, 1983, the United States invaded the island of Grenada, resulting in the deaths of 18 Americans.[3]

As a general guideline for the claim examiner, it seems that the courts are reluctant to apply "act of war" language to limit or exclude an insurer's liability for such claims unless a state of war already exists or was inevitable when the act occurred.

Proof of Death in War.   The armed forces supply an official Report of Casualty for most claims arising from the death of a service person in a war area. The long-form report usually shows whether death was "battle" or "nonbattle" related and gives a brief description of the circumstances.

Sometimes service personnel are listed as missing-in-action. In such cases, the military command often certifies death within a few days. But if the insured is truly missing-in-action, rather than being one whose death cannot immediately be determined, the missing-in-action status continues. At one time the practice of the military authorities was to review each missing-in-action case at the end of one year to determine whether the person should be declared dead. Now that review is not automatically scheduled but rather is performed as circumstances warrant.

Aviation Exclusion

Accidental death coverages commonly exclude deaths from certain high-risk aviation activities. A typical policy provision excludes deaths resulting

---

[2] *Facts on File*, December 23, 1983, p. 958.
[3] *Facts on File*, December 16, 1983, p. 944.

directly or indirectly from travel or flight in, or descent from, any kind of aircraft, if the insured

- is a pilot or crew member or has any duties aboard the aircraft,
- is giving or receiving any kind of training or instruction aboard the aircraft, or
- is being flown for the purpose of descent from the aircraft while in flight.

Thus, the typical aviation exclusion does not apply to persons who are fare-paying passengers on an aircraft. Courts typically find that persons who are aboard an aircraft to pilot it, to provide navigation services, or to attend the passengers are excluded from accidental death coverage. However, claims have been filed for other individuals who were working aboard an aircraft. For example, claims have been filed for a Federal Aviation Administration representative who was aboard an aircraft to check the flight performance, for a wild game census-taker who was in an airplane and counting game on the ground, and for an aerial photographer. Courts generally find that individuals in occupations such as these have "duties aboard an aircraft" in that these individuals have a greater exposure to the aviation hazard than mere commercial passengers do, even though the duties do not deal with the actual operation of the aircraft.

To determine an insured's status aboard an aircraft, a claim examiner can check the following sources of information:

- the flight log book,
- the federal agency that investigated the accident,
- the airport at which the plane was usually hangared,
- the last airport from which the plane departed,
- flight schools and flight instructors,
- detailed documentation of any crash scene and the position of the body or bodies, and
- in cases involving military aircraft, Public Information Officers.

Although a claim investigation may reveal that an insured had duties aboard an aircraft, the accidental death benefit may still be payable. Under most aviation exclusions, the fact that the loss occurs in connection with an aircraft is not sufficient reason to apply the aviation exclusion; rather, the loss must result from the aviation hazard. The following examples illustrate the difficulties that claim examiners can encounter in processing this type of claim:

An airplane crashes into a lake within a short distance of the shore. The pilot tries to swim to shore and drowns.

An airplane makes an emergency landing in a meadow. The pilot walks for help and is gored to death by a bull.

An airplane lands safely at an airport and then, while taxiing to the hangar, strikes an obstruction and overturns, killing a pilot.

A typical aviation exclusion would not exclude the death of an insured in situations similar to those in the first two examples above because the insured's death in these examples was not a result of an aviation hazard. However, most aviation exclusions do specifically exclude aviation accidents that occur in the airplane on the ground, as well as those that occur in the air. Therefore, the death of an insured in a situation similar to the third example probably would not be covered. However, some aviation exclusions might provide coverage. Thus, policy wording and legal precedents influence the claim decision in such cases.

One of the most complicated legal questions that has arisen in recent years is whether an aviation exclusion applies to hang gliding and parachuting. With respect to hang gliding, a U.S. Superior Court found in *Fielder* vs. *Farmers' New World* that an insured operating a hang glider is a pilot for purposes of the aviation exclusion and that a hang glider constitutes a vehicle or device for aerial navigation within the purview of a policy's aviation exclusion. A Canadian court in *Gowen* vs. *North American Life Assurance* also found that aerial flight is commonly defined as "moving or flying in or through the air." Therefore, since a kite or glider leaves the earth, it is in "aerial flight" of a kind, and the person on it is making an "aerial flight."

Generally, if a parachutist leaps from a plane and dies during the fall or as a result of the landing, the recovery of accidental death benefits will be governed by his or her status aboard the plane. If the parachutist was a crew member attempting to escape from a plane about to crash, the accidental death benefit would likely not be payable. If the parachutist was merely a passenger in the plane, accidental death benefits might or might not be available. The aviation exclusion cited at the beginning of this section would deny accidental death benefits because it excludes death that occurs while the insured is being flown for the purpose of descent from the aircraft. Other policies, without such specific wording, however, would pay accidental death benefits in such a case. Once again, the specific wording of the exclusion is most important in determining whether an aviation activity is excluded.

Other Risks Excluded from Coverage

In addition to the previous exclusions, accidental death benefit coverages may exclude from coverage the accidental death of an insured whose death results directly or indirectly from infection, drugs, gas inhalation, poison, or criminal offense.

Infection.   Accidental death benefits are not payable if the injury or death results from any infection, other than a pyogenic (that is, pus-producing) infection occurring through and at the time of an accidental cut or wound. The infection exclusion is designed to eliminate situations where an insured's infection, such as bacterial meningitis, may have existed before an accident and be in no way related to the accident.

Drugs.   Determining whether a drug overdose was intentional or accidental is often difficult. Therefore, many policies specifically exclude from accidental death coverage deaths from drugs unless such drugs were taken as prescribed for the insured by a physician. If a policy contains a drug exclusion, and if the death is related to drugs, the claim examiner should obtain an autopsy and toxicological report to determine the exact cause of death.

Sometimes an insured will die from a synergistic reaction. A ***synergistic reaction*** occurs when a person ingests two or more drugs at the same time, and the resulting combination produces death. The effect of the drugs acting independently might not cause death, but the same quantity taken together is fatal. The most common example of death due to a synergistic reaction occurs when a person consumes a small amount of alcohol in conjunction with drugs. In such cases, the circumstances surrounding the death of the insured must be investigated thoroughly in order to determine if the insured's death resulted from suicide or an accident.

Poison and Gas Inhalation.   Many policies specifically exclude from accidental death coverage deaths from any gas, fumes, poison, or any poisonous substance. An investigation of a death involving poison or gas inhalation should include a diagram of the room in which the death occurred, showing all dimensions and ventilation features. The weather at the time of death should also be recorded to determine if the insured's failure to provide proper ventilation was a result of severe weather. Weather information can be obtained from a local newspaper or from the local weather bureau.

Criminal Offenses.   In some claim cases, the insured has been killed while committing a crime. The insured may have been killed by the intended victim or by the police. Most accidental death policies contain a provision excluding such deaths from payment of accidental death benefits.

Generally speaking, in order for the criminal offense exclusion to apply, the crime must be a felony. Minor crimes, such as traffic violations, disturbing the peace, and drunkenness, are insufficient as a basis for denying accidental death benefits. Also, there must be an important connection between the commission of the crime and the death of the insured. Consider the following example:

> After robbing a store, Carl Jackson escapes in an automobile driven by Darlene LaBelle. When the car goes off the road at a high rate of speed, both Carl and Darlene are killed.

In the case of Carl, the question of time becomes important. If the crash occurred just a few minutes following the robbery, there was a connection between the crime and the death. Accident benefits might be denied. But if the crash occurred several hours later, when the escape had been successfully completed, the connection would have been broken. In that event, accident benefits might be payable. The fact that an insured has once committed a crime does not preclude the award of accident benefits forever thereafter. An ADB claim on the death of Darlene will depend on whether Darlene was a part of the robbery. If Darlene was an active participant in the crime, an ADB claim would follow the same rules as those for Carl. But if Darlene was merely an innocent companion of Carl, accidental death benefits probably would be payable to Darlene's beneficiary.

In a growing number of cases, the violation of law at the time of death involves the illegal use of drugs by the insured. As noted earlier in this chapter, many policies exclude from accidental death coverages all deaths resulting from the use of drugs. However, in the absence of a drug exclusion clause, ADB liability may be denied if the use of drugs was in violation of the law. Generally, a denial is more likely when stronger drugs—such as heroin, morphine, or cocaine—are involved. A New Mexico Supreme Court decision in *Vallejos* vs. *Colonial Life and Accident* upheld denial of ADB liability in such a case, but not all other jurisdictions have followed that course. The possession of milder drugs, although illegal, is frequently not a felony and hence does not serve by itself as a basis for denial of ADB liability.

The claim examiner should be aware that the courts have, in general, become increasingly liberal in deciding whether the ADB should be paid for death resulting from the commission of a felony. Often the view of a court is that the insured, although committing a felony, did not intend to die as a result of that action. In addition, if the argument that one should not profit from an unlawful act is raised, the courts have sometimes found that the insured is dead and cannot reap any profit from the crime. The beneficiary, however, may have had nothing to do with the crime; he or she may be a parent with children to support. Such reasoning was followed in a Pennsylvania Supreme Court decision—*Mohn* vs. *American Casualty*

Company—that required the ADB to be paid for an insured who was shot and killed by the police as he attempted to escape the scene of a burglary he had committed.

Nonetheless, Canadian courts have applied the criminal offense exclusion fairly strictly in one area—motor vehicle deaths. Courts in Canada usually rule that the criminal offense exclusion applies in motor vehicle accident deaths in which the blood alcohol level of the insured driver exceeds the local legal limit.

Accidental Death Investigations

The term *accident* covers a wide range of mishaps that can befall a person. In the preceding section, we described several types of accidental deaths that insurers often exclude from accidental death coverage. Many guidelines for investigating these types of deaths have already been mentioned. In this section, we will describe general investigation guidelines for accidental death claims and mention some specific guidelines for investigating particular types of accidental deaths. Guidelines for the claim examiner to use when evaluating most types of accidental death claims are presented in the Appendix at the end of this textbook.

General Investigation Guidelines

Government authorities such as the police and fire-fighting personnel customarily investigate violent deaths. These authorities document their findings in reports that can serve as an important starting point in an accidental death investigation.

Autopsy reports also provide valuable information on the cause and nature of death. Although some accidental death benefit provisions give the insurer the right to exhume the body of a deceased insured for an autopsy, it is usually preferable for the family of the deceased to request an autopsy before burial takes place.

Ambulance personnel keep records that document any treatment rendered to the insured following an accident. If the insured was conscious after the accident, the claim examiner may be able to find out what the insured said about the accident. In addition, medical records may show any treatment or medication given to the insured before his or her death.

Newspaper accounts of an accident sometimes provide information not contained in official records. However, such information should be verified if it is to be used as the basis for the claim decision. Eyewitnesses to an accident may also provide vital information, but their accounts are often unreliable. The eyewitnesses may be stunned by the accident or may have reasons to modify or withhold some information. Therefore, an insurer's case is strengthened if several corroborating witnesses can be found. In recording an eyewitness statement, the examiner should document:

- the exact location of the witness at the time of the accident;
- whether the witness had a clear view or an obstructed view of the accident;
- whether the witness has impaired vision or hearing;
- whether the witness knew, or was related to, the insured;
- whether the witness knew, or was related to, anyone else involved in the accident; and
- where the witness had been shortly before the accident.

A witness' responses to these questions can have a bearing on his or her reliability. For example, if the witness knew or was related to the insured, then the testimony is not as valuable as that of a disinterested bystander. Further, if a witness had been in a bar shortly before the accident, then the claim examiner must consider if the witness' perceptions of the accident were influenced by alcohol.

Drowning.   In cases in which death was caused by drowning, the investigation is usually directed at ruling out the possibilities of suicide or the contribution of disease. In some cases in which the body has been submerged for a lengthy period, there also may be a question of positive identification of the body. In reviewing the report of the coroner or medical examiner, the claim examiner should be aware that drowning can occur simply from asphyxiation, leaving little or no water in the lungs.

Drugs.   Investigation of cases involving death caused by drug overdose is sometimes necessary in order to decide whether the death resulted from suicide or from an accident. The number of such cases has risen sharply in recent years, an inevitable result of the growing use of both prescription and nonprescription drugs. As noted earlier, many companies exclude all drug-related deaths from accidental death coverage.

Drug cases, particularly those involving a barbiturate, sometimes raise the issue of automatism. *Automatism* refers to a condition in which the drug user takes repeated doses of a drug without realizing that the drug is being taken and without the intention of taking a lethal dosage. For example, a person may take a normal dosage of two sleeping pills. A few hours later, while in a semi-conscious state, the person takes two more pills. A few hours later still, the person repeats the dosage. Upon awakening—if he or she does—the person will have no recollection of taking any overdose. Automatism is sometimes raised by a claimant to support a contention of accidental death rather than suicide. However, there is little confirmed medical opinion to support the concept of automatism.

Falls or Jumps.   Death following a relatively minor fall is not uncommon for older people or for those who are physically disabled. The usual question is whether the death was attributable to the fall or whether the fall was only incidental to a death or injury that was caused by other means. It is important to remember that liability for accidental death benefits is not ruled out solely because the insured was physically infirm or because the fall was attributable to the weakness or unsteadiness of advanced age.

Sometimes a person suffers a fall from such a height that, if the fall were intentional, it could be regarded as suicidal. In such cases, the statements of any witnesses may be a deciding factor. Details of the scene of the fall also are very important as a means of distinguishing an accident from a suicide. A lengthy treatise on the trajectories of humans in falls and in jumps appeared in the July 1942 issue of the *Journal of Applied Physics* and can be useful in distinguishing between the two actions.

Fires.   In cases involving death by fire, the most common question is whether the insured died from the fire or from a natural cause, such as a stroke or heart attack, with the fire occurring thereafter. There also may be a possibility that death resulted from natural causes or from suicide and that the fire was set deliberately in order to make the circumstances appear accidental. The report of the fire department is often a source of important information in fire investigations.

Gunshot Wounds.   Investigations of deaths involving gunshot wounds are usually made to determine who fired the gun and whether the firing was criminal, accidental, or suicidal. If it is established that the insured was shot by someone else, the investigation should determine whether the aggressiveness of the insured was a factor. (We discuss aggressorship in greater detail in a subsequent section.) If it appears that the beneficiary inflicted the fatal wound, details of that conclusion should be developed because laws preclude payment of policy proceeds to someone who purposefully caused the insured's death. If the injury was self-inflicted, the policy is in the suicide period, and the policy contains an accidental death benefit suicide exclusion, then the investigation should establish whether the death was accidental. The investigation should include a diagram and description of the shooting scene.

Traffic Accidents.   In contemporary society, traffic accidents are a particularly common hazard simply because of the widespread use of the automobile. Death resulting from a traffic accident normally is covered

by standard accidental death provisions. In addition, many policies offer
a "traffic accident benefit." A typical version reads:

> If an Accidental Death Benefit is payable . . . and if the required
> due proof shows that the injury resulting in the accidental death
> was sustained by the Insured
>
> (a) while driving or riding in a private automobile not in use for
>   commercial or occupational purposes by the Insured, or
> (b) as a result of being struck by a motor vehicle while not himself
>   or herself driving or riding in a motor vehicle, or
> (c) while riding as a passenger in or upon a public conveyance pro-
>   vided by a common carrier for passenger service,
>
> the Company will pay, in addition to all other benefits provided by
> the policy, a benefit equal to the face amount.

In a claim filed under such a traffic accident benefit, questions can arise
over any part of the provision. Basically, part (a) of the policy wording is
intended to cover drivers and passengers in private cars. Part (b) is intended
to cover pedestrians struck by motor vehicles. Part (c) is intended to cover
fare-paying passengers in common carriers such as taxis, buses, trains,
airplanes, and steamships. In administering claims under this type of
coverage, an examiner may encounter any number of situations that require interpretation of the policy wording. For example, the type of vehicle involved in the accident may or may not be included in the policy wording. Benefits have been paid in cases in which the vehicle was a Jeep, a
camper coach, a drag racer, or a converted hearse used to transport Little
League ballplayers. Claims have been rejected when the vehicle was a fire
engine, motorcycle, motor scooter, or golf cart.

In some cases involving traffic accident benefits, the element of proximate cause may be a consideration. For example:

> The insured, Joseph Hilburn, is covered by traffic accident coverage
> as described by the foregoing policy wording. While Joseph is walk-
> ing on the sidewalk, an automobile goes out of control and strikes
> a nearby utility pole. The utility pole snaps and falls on Joseph, caus-
> ing his death.

In such a case, the death of Joseph probably would come under part
(b) of the policy language because of the element of proximate cause.
Although Joseph was not struck by the automobile, the crash of the car
into the utility pole was the proximate cause of Joseph's death.

In an investigation of a traffic accident claim, suicide may be considered,
especially if the insured was driving alone at the time of the accident. The

contribution-of-disease factor also may be considered. Any investigation of a traffic accident should include a drawing of the scene, showing all the essential physical facts.

Special Legal Considerations

The various laws and court rulings that influence a claim examiner's decision to pay or deny accidental death benefits have been mentioned throughout this chapter. In this section, we will describe two other areas of law that have a strong impact on the administration of accidental death claims.

Natural Death Legislation

The advances of medical science in prolonging the life of a person by life-support procedures have given rise to a movement to recognize the right of the individual to withhold or withdraw the use of such procedures. Natural death legislation has been enacted in many jurisdictions to "recognize the right of an adult person to make a written directive instructing [the] physician to withhold or withdraw life-sustaining procedures in the event of a terminal condition."

Natural death legislation usually states that the withholding or withdrawal of life-sustaining procedures does not constitute a suicide. For purposes of insurance, then, the withholding or withdrawal of life-sustaining procedures is not itself to be considered as the cause of death. Instead, to determine whether the cause of death is natural, accidental, or suicidal, the claim examiner must turn to whatever caused the insured to be placed under, or considered for, the life-sustaining procedures. That cause determines the type of death, not the action taken with regard to the life-sustaining procedure.

Foreseeability

Sometimes people intentionally place themselves in dangerous situations. Claims have been filed for insureds who have died as a result of riding on the top of a car, from lying on a highway, or from diving 139 feet off the top of a dam. Such acts lead to the question of whether the insurer should be liable for accident benefits, given the fact that the insured accepted voluntary exposure to a known danger.

A chief thread running through all court definitions of the term *accident* is the element of the unexpectedness of the event. If a natural and probable consequence of a person's voluntary act is the harm that results, there is no accident regardless of what the insured otherwise intended. The principle of insurance law that supports this contention is called foreseeability, or voluntary exposure to a known hazard. As used in accidental death cases, **foreseeability** literally means the ability of the insured to reasonably anticipate that harm or injury would be a likely result of a certain act or an omitted act.

If an insured voluntarily performs or omits an act that in all probability would result in his or her injury or death, and if that injury or death does occur without the intervention of any other event or cause, then such injury or death is regarded as being reasonably foreseeable. That being true, the act or omission is not covered by an accident provision. This determination is usually not based on an exclusion in the policy, but rather is based on the definition of what constitutes an accident. If a denial of ADB benefits is based on a voluntary exposure exclusion in the policy, the burden of proof rests with the insurer. In contrast, if the ADB provision does not contain a voluntary exposure exclusion, the insurer may introduce the fact of voluntary exposure as a defense to a claim of accidental injury, leaving the claimant with the burden of proof.

In some states, notably Pennsylvania, it is very difficult for an insurer to establish a defense of foreseeability. A leading Pennsylvania case is that of *Beckham* vs. *Travelers Insurance Company*, in which the insured died as a result of a self-administered overdose of narcotics. The insurer paid the regular death benefit under the policy but denied liability for accidental death benefits. The Pennsylvania Supreme Court ruled that the accidental death benefit was payable, holding that there was no basis in the record for concluding that the insured was unduly exposing himself to the risk of death by his action.

Foreseeability is also an issue in cases involving aggressorship. **Aggressorship** occurs in a situation in which the insured makes an attack on another person in such a way as to invite deadly resistance from the other person. If an insured is killed by the resisting person, the death probably cannot be regarded as accidental, since the insured voluntarily put his or her life at stake.

An ADB investigation that involves aggressorship on the part of the insured should look at the degree of foreseeability that may be attributed to the insured. If an insured attacks another person with a deadly weapon, he or she should reasonably expect the other person to respond with equal force and with an equally deadly weapon. For example, assume that an insured enters into a violent argument with another person and rushes at that person with a knife. If the attacked person pulls out a hidden pistol and kills the insured, the death probably cannot be attributable to an accident. On the other hand, if a small, nonathletic person punches a professional football player who then pulls out a gun and kills his attacker, then the degree of the football player's response to the aggressive behavior is unwarranted. In a case such as this one, accidental death benefits would probably be payable.

A few companies have included in their accidental death benefit provisions an "assault" exclusion, specifying that if the insured dies while participating in an assault, accident benefits are not payable. Such an exclusion probably would preclude payment of accidental death benefits in either of the preceding examples.

SPOUSE AND CHILDREN'S INSURANCE

A person buying individual life insurance often wishes to purchase life insurance on a spouse and children. A *spouse and children's insurance rider* can be added to any type of permanent life insurance policy. Insurance companies sometimes market such insurance as a separate family policy that covers all family members. In either case, the coverage provided for the principal insured is permanent insurance, and the coverage provided for the spouse and children is term insurance of a substantially smaller amount than that provided for the principal insured. Evidence of insurability is required for all family members who are proposed for insurance in the application. After the policy is issued, children added to the family by birth, legal adoption, or remarriage usually are covered automatically.

Several benefits commonly included in family policies and spouse and children's insurance riders are

- the privilege to convert the term part of the contract to permanent insurance at specified ages or dates,
- a feature providing that the insurance on the dependents will become paid-up when the primary insured dies, and
- a decrease in the premium and/or automatic increase in the amount of insurance on the primary insured if the spouse dies first.

Verifying Policy Coverage

Verifying coverage under this type of rider or policy can present numerous problems for the claim examiner. As mentioned earlier, if additional children are born, adopted, or gained by marriage after the coverage is purchased, the children are included automatically at no extra premium and without meeting any standards of insurability. The guidelines for determining coverage of children depend upon how the rider or policy defines a dependent child. A typical definition of a dependent child is as follows:

Only a child, stepchild, or legally adopted child of the Insured, who has reached the day 15 days after his or her date of birth but who has not yet reached the policy anniversary immediately following his or her 25th birthday and who either (1) is named in the application for this policy and on the date of such application had not yet reached his or her 18th birthday, or (2) is acquired by the Insured after the date of such application but before such child's 18th birthday.

From this definition—which, although typical, may not always apply exactly to every policy—a claim examiner can assume the following about the coverage of an insured's dependents:

- A child born on or after the effective date of the policy is automatically covered at age 15 days.
- A stepchild within the age limits is covered the moment the principal insured marries the child's parent. Should the principal insured later divorce the child's parent, the previously acquired stepchildren remain covered.
- A child born in or out of wedlock is eligible for coverage.
- Once covered, a child remains covered until reaching the limiting age, which usually ranges from 18 to 25.
- A child that does not meet an insurer's standards of insurability at the time of application but who later becomes insurable can add coverage after presenting satisfactory evidence of insurability.
- A foster child does not meet the policy definition of a dependent child and so is not eligible for coverage.

Some insurance companies have been particularly concerned about the possibility of fraud in connection with death claims submitted on children who are added after policy issue. Insurers are afraid that claims may be submitted on children who are not related to the policyowner. Consequently, when a claim is received for a child added after policy issue, companies usually require submission of either a long-form birth certificate or a long-form death certificate, both of which list the names of the child's parents.

Contestability and Misrepresentation

Applying the standard incontestable provision to multiple coverages can raise many claim questions. What happens if the misrepresentation does not involve the principal insured but involves the spouse or children? Is the entire policy contestable or only the portion covering the spouse or dependent?

To some extent the question of whether a spouse or child's coverage can be severed from the principal insured's coverage because of misrepresentation depends upon the manner in which premiums are charged. If a separate premium is charged for each person insured under the policy, there is a greater likelihood that the contract will be held to be severable than if a single premium is charged for the entire family. However, some insurers take the position that if there are misrepresentations concerning any member of the family, then the entire contract is suspect and should be rescinded. Nonetheless, if litigation ensues, the courts might well react sympathetically to the policyowner's wish to continue coverage on the other members of the family. Aside from the legal aspects, an insurance company is in business to provide insurance, and thus it might prefer to provide the insurance on the other family members as a matter of company policy.

Suicides

The permanent insurance coverage on the principal insured contains a suicide provision. In most cases, the suicide provision applies only to the principal insured so that a suicide by a spouse or child, even within the suicide exclusion period, warrants payment of the full benefit amount to the principal insured.

If the principal insured dies by suicide within the suicide exclusion period, many family policies and riders specify that the policy becomes void and the company's liability is limited to a return of the policy's premiums. Therefore, in most cases, the company would not be responsible for providing the spouse and children with paid-up insurance nor with the opportunity to convert coverage. However, at least one state requires that the spouse and children be given a conversion privilege if the principal insured dies of suicide during the policy's suicide exclusion period.

In some cases in which the suicide exclusion period is still in effect, the principal insured mortally wounds the spouse and then commits suicide. In determining benefits, the order of death governs. If the spouse dies before the principal insured, the company would be liable for the spouse's benefits and, because of the suicide, would return the premiums paid for coverage of the principal insured. But if the principal insured dies first, liability would be limited to the return of premiums and the contract would be void.

Simultaneous Deaths

Sometimes claims are submitted for two or more persons who are covered under a single policy and who apparently have died simultaneously. If there is not sufficient evidence that any of the insureds died other than simultaneously, the insurer can apply presumption of simultaneous death legislation, which is described in detail in Chapter 9, and distribute the policy proceeds as though each insured person survived his or her beneficiary.

Special Administrative Considerations

There are several special administrative considerations that pertain to family life policies and spouse and children's riders.

Policy Loans

Provisions regarding the deduction of a policy loan from death benefits vary from policy to policy. Some policies provide that loans are deducted only when the principal insured dies; others specify that loans will be deducted, to the maximum amount possible, from any death claims arising under a policy. If there is a comparatively large loan outstanding against a policy, this latter provision can result in a very small benefit payment's being made upon the death of a spouse and, particularly, upon the death of a child. Of course, deducting the amount of the loan from the policy proceeds reduces or cancels the indebtedness. The principal insured is then able to take out a new policy loan. Thus, on a strictly practical level, deducting the amount of the loan is often a relatively unimportant matter.

Paid-up Insurance on Survivors

As mentioned previously, many family life policies and spouse and children's insurance riders provide that the insurance on the lives of the spouse and children becomes paid-up after the death of the principal insured. Some companies have the surviving spouse complete a paid-up insurance form at the time that the claim on the death of the principal insured is being processed. This form lists the names and dates of birth of the surviving spouse and children, including any children added after policy issue whose names may not appear elsewhere in the insurer's records. Some companies then issue certificates of paid-up insurance; others endorse the policy as paid-up for the insurance on the spouse and children; other companies leave the policy in the possession of the spouse, on the basis that the policy provisions state that the insurance is paid-up.

Policy Returns

Life insurance policies covering a single life typically provide that the policy be returned to the company upon the filing of a death claim. However, family life policies and spouse and children's riders usually do not contain this provision because the death of any one covered person does not necessarily terminate coverage of the other insureds. However, there are times when a request for a return of the policy is reasonable and proper: for example, when the last of all persons insured under the policy dies; when the contract is rescinded for misrepresentation; or when the principal insured commits suicide during the suicide period and premiums are being returned by the company.

Retention of Claim Data

Unlike individual life insurance policies, the filing of a death claim under a family policy or under a spouse or children's rider is not a singular event. Information received as part of one claim may be important later in evaluating other claims. For this reason, claim personnel should retain claim papers for possible future reference. One way is to file them with the insurance application, which is usually kept indefinitely.

Second Insured Riders

Many insurance companies have begun marketing a second insured rider, also called an optional insured rider, that can be added to any permanent insurance policy. A company may offer a second insured rider in place of offering spouse and children's insurance riders. In this way, the same rider can be used to provide coverage either on a spouse or on an individual who is not related to the insured. Companies that offer the second insured rider also generally offer a separate children's insurance rider that provides coverage only to an insured's children.

References

Beckham vs. *Travelers Insurance Company*, 424 Pa., 107, A2d 532, 7 L.C. 2nd, 368 (1987).
"Beneficiary Recovers Proceeds After Shooting of Insured," *Bests Review*, January, 1987, 105.
Burne vs. *Franklin Life Insurance Company*, 451 Pa. 218 (1973).
Claims Related to the Use of Drugs: Report of the Law Committee. International Claim Association, 1970.
Disease and the Accidental Death Benefit: Report of the ICA Law Committee. International Claim Association, 1976.
Fielder vs. *Farmers' New World Life Insurance Company*, 435 F. Supp. 912 (1977).
Gowen vs. *North American Life Assurance Company*, Court of Appeal, (1985).
Kelly vs. *Republican National Life Insurance Company*, 1984 Life Cases 677 (Az. Ct. App. 1983).
Landress vs. *Phoenix Mutual Life Insurance Company*, 291 U.S. 491 (1934).
MacArthur, R.M. "Avocations and Exclusions," *1987 ICA Life Insurance Workshop Notes*, 124-139.
Meyerholz, John P. "Drugs, Death, and Disability—A Further Serbonian Bog." *ICA Continuing Education Manual*, 1971, 1-29.
Mohn vs. *American Casualty Company of Reading, Pennsylvania*, 326 A2d 346 (1974).
United States Mutual Accident Association vs. *Barry*, 131 U.S. 100 (1889).
Vallejos vs. *Colonial Life & Accident Insurance Company*, (N.M.S.Ct. 1977) 571 P2d 404.

Voluntary Assumption of a Known Risk and Liability for Accidental Death Benefits: Report of the Law Committee. International Claim Association, (1969).

Williams vs. *New England Mutual Life Insurance Company*, 419 So. 2d 766 (Fla. App. 1982).

9

Paying Life Insurance Benefits— Part I

After the examination of a life insurance claim is complete, the claim examiner should be in a position either to pay the insurance benefits or challenge the claim. Payment of life insurance benefits involves three major steps: (1) calculating the amount of benefits payable, (2) determining to whom the benefits will be paid, and (3) determining in what manner the benefits will be distributed.

In this chapter, we describe the first two steps in the payment process. Distribution of the benefits is the subject of Chapter 10.

CALCULATING THE BENEFIT AMOUNT

A life insurance contract is not a contract of indemnity because the beneficiary does not have to prove the amount of loss in order to collect benefits. Instead, upon verification of loss, an insurer is liable for payment of the full death benefit plus any additions to the policy benefit or minus any deductions from the policy benefit.

Amounts that are typically *added* to the death benefit include

- accidental death benefits,
- policy dividends currently payable but not yet paid,

- policy dividends that were left on deposit with the company to accrue interest,
- paid-up additional insurance that has been purchased by the policyowner,
- excess premiums paid in advance for coverage extending beyond the date of the insured's death, and
- interest paid on delayed claims.

Deducted from the death benefit are the amounts of any

- outstanding policy loans,
- accrued policy loan interest, and
- premiums due but unpaid if death occurs during the grace period.

Adjustments for Age or Sex Misstatements

As we described in Chapter 5, life insurance policy proceeds are sometimes increased or decreased if the insured's age or sex is incorrect in the policy. Age or sex misstatements require specific proofs and careful claim investigation.

Age Discrepancies

A proposed insured's age is one of several factors that insurers consider when establishing a premium rate. The accuracy of the premium rate depends upon the insurer's knowing the actual age of the insured. For this reason, the insurer must have some protection against a proposed insured's misstatement of age. This protection is afforded by the misstatement of age provision included in life insurance policies. A typical misstatement of age provision reads as follows:

> If the age of the insured has been misstated, the amount payable and every benefit accruing under this policy shall be such as the premiums paid would have purchased at the correct age according to the company's published rates at date of issue.

Since the incontestable clause does not apply to the misstatement of age provision, age adjustments may be made at any time, even after the contestable period has expired. Most age discrepancies are uncovered when claim examiners compare the age shown in the policy records with the age shown in the claim forms. However, the discrepancy may come to light in various other ways. For example, the claim examiner may in the course of investigating a life insurance claim discover that the

- insured retired at an apparently early age,
- insured was receiving government-provided old age benefits when the age on insurance records indicated the insured would not have been eligible for such benefits,
- ages of the insured's children seem inconsistent with the age of the insured, or
- cause of death seems inconsistent with the age of the insured.

The result of an age adjustment may be either an increase or a decrease in the benefit payable under a life insurance policy. In addition, the age adjustment may make the insured ineligible for some benefits that are limited by the insured's age. For example, in many policies, the accidental death benefit terminates when the insured reaches a specified age, such as 65 or 70. Therefore, if a person insured under a policy that includes accidental death benefits dies in an accident but had misstated his or her age on the insurance application and was actually 72 years old at the time of death, then the insurer would probably not be liable for the accidental death benefit.

Insurance companies are particularly sensitive to the need for prompt payment of death benefits. If an investigation of an insured's age is deemed desirable and is likely to cause delay in payment of the proceeds, some companies will make a partial payment using the age in the policy record. Upon receipt of authoritative proof of an insured's age, the company will either pay an additional amount to the beneficiary or initiate an action to recover part of the proceeds.

As a general rule, if the insurer believes that benefits should be reduced because the insured was older than the policy age, the burden of proving that the insured was older falls upon the company. If the claimant believes that benefits should be increased because the insured was younger than the policy age, the burden of proving that the insured was younger is upon the claimant.

Proof that can be used to establish the correct age of an insured may be either primary or secondary proof. Any single primary proof of age is usually accepted by an insurer as adequate proof to establish the actual age of an insured. Primary proofs include

- a copy of the birth record, issued by a bureau of vital statistics and recorded within a few days of the date of birth;
- a baptismal certificate showing a specific date of birth and attesting that baptism occurred within a few years of birth; and
- a record in a family Bible which was published before the birth

of the insured and in which the appearance of the writing and the position of the entry (in order of date) suggest authenticity.

If none of the primary proofs is available, a company may turn to secondary proofs. Companies usually require two or three such proofs to establish actual age. The sources of secondary proofs include

- school records,
- record of religious confirmation,
- marriage records,
- naturalization records,
- passport information,
- official census records,
- medical records,
- employment records,
- military service records,
- occupational licenses,
- police records,
- other insurance policies,
- bank records,
- social welfare records,
- trade union and fraternal societies' records,
- undertakers' and cemetery records,
- unemployment compensation records,
- voting registration records,
- Workers' Compensation records, and
- motor vehicle records.

Sex Discrepancies

Sometimes during the completion or processing of a life insurance application, the sex of the proposed insured will be misstated: a male will be listed as a female or vice versa. Some insurers have modified their misstatement of age provisions to allow for corrections to misstatements about an insured's sex. Insurers who have such provisions in their policies adjust policy benefits for a misstatement of sex in a manner similar to that of adjusting policy benefits for a misstatement of age.

DETERMINING THE PROPER PAYEE

In the majority of life insurance claims, the proper payee is readily identifiable and can be paid at once. Nonetheless, a variety of problems can arise in connection with a beneficiary designation and with the various types of beneficiaries. Thus, although the percentage of cases with complicating factors may be small, the claim examiner must be alert for those complications so that the rights of all beneficiaries will be honored.

Beneficiary Designations

The owner of an individual life insurance policy (who may or may not be the insured), or the insured under a group life insurance policy, has the right to designate the beneficiary of the policy when the insurance is issued. The **beneficiary** is the person or entity who will receive the life insurance benefits payable upon the death of the insured. Sometimes a *contingent*, or alternate, *beneficiary* is designated to receive the benefits if the first, or primary, beneficiary predeceases the insured. If a primary beneficiary is living when the insured dies, then the contingent beneficiary's interest in the policy's proceeds ends. A policyowner (under an individual policy) or an insured (under a group policy) generally can name anyone or any legal entity as beneficiary. However, laws in both Canada and the United States usually prohibit a person insured under an employer-employee group life insurance plan from naming the employer as beneficiary.

If a beneficiary is not specifically named, the policy proceeds are generally payable to the estate of the policyowner/insured. Some policies provide for predesignated classes of beneficiaries who become eligible for policy proceeds when the policyowner/insured has not named a beneficiary or when there is no surviving named beneficiary.

Change of Beneficiary Procedures

Problems resulting from changes in a policy's beneficiary can complicate the payment of benefits. Most life insurance policies issued today in both Canada and the United States allow the policyowner (under an individual policy) or an insured (under a group insurance policy) to change the beneficiary designation as often as desired. The right to change the beneficiary designation is usually granted in a policy provision that specifies the procedure for making an effective policy change.

There are two ways to change beneficiaries: the endorsement method and the recording method. Under the **endorsement method**, a beneficiary change becomes effective when the policyowner submits the policy to the insurer and the insurer changes the name of the beneficiary on the policy. Under the more commonly used **recording method**, the beneficiary change becomes effective when the company receives written notification of the policyowner's desire to change the beneficiary designation from one person to another person. Most companies, using the recording method, require that the policyowner file a change of beneficiary form with the insurer. A change made by either of these methods can result in claim questions regarding whether a change of beneficiary was complete at the time an insured died.

Substantial Compliance. The view of the majority of courts is that a beneficiary change can be considered effective without strict or complete compliance with the requirements of the policy. If a policyowner has substantially complied with policy requirements, as viewed by a court, then the proposed change is considered to be complete. However, courts are not entirely predictable in their rulings as to what constitutes substantial compliance.

Courts have found that a policyowner does not actually have to endorse a beneficiary change on a policy even if the policy specifies the endorsement method of beneficiary change. The policyowner may have lost the policy, or the policy may be in the possession of the current beneficiary, who will not relinquish it. Thus, most insurers currently either specify in their policies the recording method for changing beneficiary designations or, if the endorsement method is specified, waive the requirement that the policy be returned for endorsement to effect a beneficiary change.

Generally, courts find that the mere expression of an insured's intent to make a change will not constitute substantial compliance with beneficiary change requirements. For example, a policyowner may write to an insurance company and request a change of beneficiary form, but may die before receiving the form. In such a case, courts usually have found that there is no substantial compliance and, therefore, no beneficiary change is effective. However, if the policyowner's written request for a change of beneficiary form were couched in more decisive language, such as, "I desire a change of beneficiary form so that I may change my beneficiary from X to Y," then some courts might find that the request substantially complies with policy requirements.

Incompetence of Policyowner/Insured. A claim problem that may arise in connection with beneficiary changes and the distribution of proceeds involves the mental competency of the policyowner or the insured. A mentally incompetent person cannot make a legally effective beneficiary change. Nonetheless, an insurer, with no reason to question the mental capacity of the policyowner, is not responsible for verifying the mental competency of the policyowner at the time a beneficiary change is made. Usually, an insurer who pays the policy proceeds in good faith to the beneficiary named by the policyowner will be protected from having to pay the proceeds again should the incapacity of the policyowner be established later.

Sometimes, a person who has lost beneficiary status through a beneficiary change will contact the insurer to challenge the mental capacity of the policyowner. In such cases, the burden of proving incompetency is upon the party asserting the incompetency; the question in such a case is whether the policyowner understood the nature and effect of the beneficiary change. The opinion of the policyowner's attending physician is usually a critical factor. Other proofs can include hospital records, testimony of those in personal contact with the policyowner, and evidence of the policyowner's ability to handle other business transactions.

Limitations on a Policyowner's Right to Change Beneficiaries

A policyowner's right to change a beneficiary designation may be limited in some situations. Such limitations may affect how an insurer distributes a policy's proceeds.

Revocable and Irrevocable Beneficiaries.   The vast majority of designated beneficiaries are called **revocable beneficiaries** because their interest in a life insurance policy can be revoked at any time by a policyowner. A policyowner may, however, designate a beneficiary as an **irrevocable beneficiary** and, thus, give up the right to change the beneficiary. In the province of Quebec, the designation of a spouse is automatically considered irrevocable unless the policyowner indicates otherwise. An irrevocable beneficiary's interest in a policy terminates upon the death of or the completion of a signed release by the irrevocable beneficiary. Upon such a termination of interest, the policyowner is able to name another beneficiary.

Preferred Beneficiaries.   For Canadian policies issued prior to July 1, 1962, beneficiaries who were members of the life insured's family had special rights and were called **preferred beneficiaries**. The policyowner was not permitted to change the beneficiary to anyone outside the preferred class without the written consent of the designated preferred beneficiary. Further, such consent was also required for any policy loan, surrender, or assignment.

However, effective for policies issued on or after July 1, 1962, the legal concept of preferred beneficiaries was discontinued. Nonetheless, the rights of existing preferred beneficiaries are protected for as long as the designation remains intact. The designation ceases to be intact, and the preferred beneficiary's rights terminate, upon the preferred beneficiary's death, upon the divorce of a spouse-beneficiary, or upon the completion of a signed release by the preferred beneficiary.

Beneficiary Designations in Wills.   In the United States, a change of beneficiary in a will is not usually legally effective. However, in Canada, an insured may designate a revocable, but not an irrevocable, beneficiary in a will. If an insured in Canada does attempt to use a will to name an irrevocable beneficiary, the designation is treated as that of a valid revocable designation.

Types of Beneficiaries

Typically, the beneficiary of a life insurance policy is a specific person who is named in the application for insurance. However, a policyowner under an individual policy or an insured under a group policy may designate any of a number of different people or entities as beneficiaries. For example, a class of people such as "children," or an estate, or even a trust may receive the proceeds of a life insurance policy. A claim examiner must carefully consider the wording of the beneficiary designation to ensure that the claim is paid to the proper person, persons, or entity.

"Children" as Beneficiaries. A policyowner or insured may designate his or her "children" as beneficiaries. The primary advantage to the policyowner or insured of making such a designation is that children born or adopted after the issuance of a policy are automatically included as beneficiaries. A variety of problems may occur, however, in connection with claims under policies including this designation.

The death of the insured often takes place many years after the insured's children have attained adulthood and have moved from the family residence. In some cases, a child may have disappeared or may be dead. In order to settle a claim in which "children" are designated as the beneficiaries, the claim examiner must locate all of the insured's children because each, if living, has a right to a share of the proceeds. In a situation in which one of the children is dead, the claim examiner must receive verification of the child's death.

There may also be a problem in trying to determine exactly who is a child under the "children" designation. A designation of "children" as beneficiaries normally includes all legitimate children and all legally adopted children of the insured unless one or more is specifically excluded. For example, an insured may exclude children of a former marriage. In addition, a recent trend among courts is to include illegitimate children of the insured as "children" under the beneficiary designation.

Legally Incompetent Beneficiaries. To receive the proceeds of a policy, a beneficiary must sign a release. The release is the company's record which indicates that the company, in good faith, paid the proceeds under the policy to the person it believed was the named beneficiary. A signed release relieves the company of any future liability caused by the claim of a second claimant. Sometimes a beneficiary is a minor or is mentally incompetent and is thus unable to sign a valid release for payment of a claim. In such cases, a court can appoint someone to act for the beneficiary in the capacity of a legal representative. However, for a minor beneficiary, the insurer often holds the proceeds on deposit with interest accruing until the minor attains the age of majority.

If a court appoints a legal representative for an incompetent beneficiary, the appointed individual or corporation is generally called the **guardian** of the incompetent person's estate. A guardian can sign a valid release for a policy's benefits. Before a claim payment is made to a guardian, however, the claim examiner should ensure that the guardian is properly qualified. In most cases, a short-form court certificate of appointment is acceptable as proof of qualification. The claimant is responsible for obtaining the certificate of appointment. Claim payment checks are payable to the legal representative or representatives listed in the certificate of appointment.

In some cases, no guardian is appointed for a minor. Statutes in some states permit payment of a small amount of the proceeds, typically $2,000 to $5,000, to a minor of a specified age without a legally appointed guardian. Three types of such statutes exist in various states: facility of payment statutes, affidavit statutes, and payment to minor statutes.

- *Facility of payment statutes* provide that any person under a duty to pay or deliver money or personal property to a minor may pay or deliver the money or property to: (1) the minor if 18 or more years of age, or married; (2) any person having the care and custody of the minor; or (3) a financial institution to be placed in a state- or federally-insured savings account or certificate of deposit in the sole name of the minor with notice of the deposit to the minor.
- *Affidavit statutes* allow an insurer to pay a parent with whom the minor resides after the insurer receives an affidavit from the parent stating that the total estate of the minor does not exceed a specified amount and that no guardian is to be appointed.
- *Payment to minor statutes* provide that an insurer may pay limited amounts per year directly to older minors. The age at which payment to the minor can be made is usually 16, but in some states the minor must be at least 18 years old in order to receive payment.

An Estate as Beneficiary.   Insurance benefits are often paid to the estate of an insured or to the estate of a named beneficiary. Situations in which insurance benefits can become payable to an estate include those in which

- the insured's estate is designated as the beneficiary in the life insurance contract;
- the insured is not survived by a named beneficiary; or
- the insured is survived by a named beneficiary, but the named beneficiary dies before the insurance proceeds can be paid.

The claim examiner will follow the same general payment procedure regardless of whose estate is to be the recipient of the proceeds. Normally in this situation, payment would be made either to the **administrator** of the estate, in the case of a decedent without a valid will, or to an **executor** of the estate, in the case of a decedent with a valid will. The administrator or executor is appointed by a probate court and is responsible for managing the decedent's estate until all debts have been paid and the remaining assets in the estate have been distributed. The administrator or executor should furnish the insurer with a recently certified copy of the Letters Testamentary or Letters of Administration issued by the probate court before the insurer makes any claim payment.

Small Estates Statutes.   Sometimes the legal expenses of probate court are difficult for a small estate to pay. In such cases, the heirs of the decedent may seek to have claim payments made to them without the necessity of a formal probate proceeding and its attendant costs. Many states have enacted **small estates statutes** that enable an insurer to pay relatively small amounts of policy proceeds to an estate without involved court proceedings.

There are no small estates statutes in the provinces of Canada. However, some provinces such as Ontario provide that if an estate is a small one, a surrogate court, which has very specific responsibilities relating to the probate of wills, the settlement of estates, and the appointment of guardians, may prepare for a minimal fee all the necessary papers leading to a grant of probate.

There are basically two types of small estates statutes: summary statutes and affidavit statutes. Summary statutes require the claimant to apply to the local probate court but do not require the services of an attorney. Affidavit statutes merely require the claimant to complete an affidavit setting forth certain pertinent facts including the name, age, and date of death of the decedent, as well as the value of the entire estate less liens. Figure 9-1 is a sample small estates affidavit. Both types of statutes apply only to estates of a certain maximum value, and the maximum value amount varies according to the state involved. Most small estates statutes apply to estates valued in the $5,000 to $25,000 range.

STATE OF _____   **AFFIDAVIT FOR COLLECTION**
COUNTY OF _____   **OF PERSONAL PROPERTY**

   Affiant, _____, being first duly sworn,
deposes and states:

1. Affiant resides at _____
   _____;

2. _____ died at the age of _____ on
   _____, 19_____, and at the time of death, resided at
   _____,
   City of _____, County of _____,
   State of _____, having Social Security Number
   _____;

3. Affiant as _____ is the successor of
   the above identified decedent;

4. The value of the entire estate, wherever located, less liens and en-
   cumbrances, does not exceed $5,000.00;

5. Thirty (30) days have elapsed since the death of the decedent;

6. No application or petition for the appointment of a personal
   representative is pending or has been granted in any jurisdiction;

7. Affiant, the claiming successor, is entitled to payment or delivery
   of the following described property, to-wit: _____
   _____
   _____

   FURTHER AFFIANT SAYETH NOT.

Dated: _____

_____

Subscribed and sworn to before me this
_____ day of _____, 19_____
_____
Notary Public, _____ County.
My Commission expires _____.   (SEAL)

Figure 9–1. Sample small estates affidavit.

Many small estates statutes contain a **discharge provision** that releases from liability the person who makes the payment pursuant to the prescribed procedure to the same extent as if payment were being made to a court-appointed personal representative of the decedent. When such a discharge provision exists, the claim examiner should ensure that all of the information required by the affidavit or summary statute is complete, is in the correct form, and is signed by the proper person. Poorly drafted or incomplete forms could jeopardize the insurer's discharge from liability. Most statutes also specify that a certain period of time, such as 30 days, must elapse after the date of the decedent's death before any payments are made. After the claim examiner obtains a properly executed discharge, payment to the person listed in the affidavit or summary form is generally safe.

As mentioned previously, Canada and some states in the United States do not have small estates statutes. In these jurisdictions, when a claim is payable to a small estate, a claim examiner sometimes will pay a life insurance claim without the protection of a statutory procedure. In deciding whether to make such a claim payment, the claim examiner must weigh such factors as

- the amount of the insurance proceeds: usually the proceeds must be less than a stated amount, such as $15,000;
- whether a general agreement exists among the persons known to be interested in the estate as to how the insurance proceeds should be paid on behalf of the estate; and
- the availability and willingness of someone to claim the insurance proceeds on behalf of the estate and to sign whatever affidavit or indemnity agreement the insurer deems necessary.

Trusts. A **trust** is a legal arrangement whereby one person or corporation holds and administers property for the benefit of one or more other persons. The person or corporation responsible for administering the property is called the **trustee**. The person setting up the trust is called the **grantor**, **trustor**, or **donor**. The person benefiting from the trust is called the beneficiary or *cestui que trust*.[1]

In claim administration, trusts are generally encountered as beneficiaries of life insurance policies. The method of paying a life insurance claim to a trust varies somewhat depending upon the type of trust involved.

The type of trust to which life insurance proceeds are most often paid is called a **living**, or **inter vivos**, **trust** because the trust is created through a formal agreement to take effect during the life of the grantor/insured. If such a formal trust agreement exists when a trustee beneficiary designa-

---

[1] The person for whom the trust is established.

tion is made, the life insurance contract will be quite specific in the manner in which the trust is named a beneficiary. For example, the beneficiary designation may specify that benefits are payable to "John Doe and Richard Roe, Trustees under a Trust Agreement dated June 27, 1988." The beneficiary provision usually states that the insurer may pay the specified trustees without determining their specific authority to receive the proceeds and without inquiring into their intended use of the proceeds. If the trustees named as beneficiaries claim policy benefits, a claim examiner usually has little more to do than draw the check to their order as trustees. However, sometimes trustees die or resign from their position by the time the proceeds are payable. In such cases, the claim examiner should obtain proof that the trustees making the claim have authority to receive the proceeds. This information usually can be verified when the examiner obtains and reviews the terms of the trust agreement and verifies that the new, or successor, trustees have been properly appointed.

A **testamentary trust** is created by a provision in the will of a grantor/insured and does not become effective until the death of the grantor/insured. Neither the name of the trustee nor the date of the will are included in the beneficiary designation since either or both could be changed at any time prior to the grantor/insured's death. Instead, upon the death of the insured, the insurer must receive a true copy of the probated will and a copy of the letters testamentary. In addition, the following proofs are usually required:

- proof that the will is valid,
- proof that the person named in the will to be the trustee is qualified as trustee,
- proof that the trust gives the trustee the power to collect life insurance proceeds, and
- proof that the trustee's claim is being made within the time specified.

Because of the administrative difficulties involved with testamentary trusts, some insurers are reluctant to accept a testamentary trustee as beneficiary of a life insurance policy. When such a beneficiary provision is put into a policy, the estate of the insured is usually listed as the contingent beneficiary.

A **voluntary trust** is created informally by the terms of a beneficiary designation in an insurance contract. No separate written trust agreement exists. In a voluntary trust, the person for whom the trust arrangement will be created is a named beneficiary. The beneficiary designation specifies the name of the trustee who will receive payment of the proceeds on the beneficiary's behalf if the policy proceeds become payable while the

beneficiary is less than a stated age or while the beneficiary is incompetent. The advantage to this arrangement is that the funds are readily
available for the care of the beneficiary.

Payment of life insurance proceeds will be made under a voluntary trust
arrangement after an insurer receives proof of the beneficiary's age or
mental incapacity and proof that the trustee identified in the beneficiary
designation is the person filing for payment of the benefits. As a matter
of practice, insurers accompany the payment of the proceeds with a letter
informing the trustee that payment is made for the benefit of the beneficiary,
and that the trustee may need to consult an attorney to determine his or
her exact duties.

Other Payees

In addition to designated beneficiaries, other individuals or corporations
such as assignees, attorneys, and tax collectors may sometimes be entitled
to receive the proceeds from a life insurance policy.

Assignees

The owner of an individual life insurance policy has the right to transfer
some or all of the rights of ownership to another person or entity through
an *assignment*. In some instances, the insured under a group life insurance
policy also has this right. The person transferring policy rights is known
as the *assignor*. The person receiving those rights is known as the
assignee. A policy may be assigned to a single person, to a corporation,
to two or more parties jointly, or to two or more parties as tenants in common. *Tenants in common* share title and use of an estate, but have no
right of survivorship. A *right of survivorship* provides that if an assignee
dies, the assignee's survivors are entitled to his or her portion of the
assignment.

An *absolute assignment* is an irrevocable transfer of all of a policyowner's rights in a policy. An absolute assignment is usually made when
the policyowner wishes to make a gift of a policy to another person or
entity. A *collateral assignment* is a transfer of some of the ownership
rights in a policy. A collateral assignment is often used to secure a loan.
Once the loan is repaid, all transferred rights revert to the assignor.

Collateral Assignment Forms.   The American Bankers Association (ABA) developed a standard form of collateral assignment, the ABA
Form No. 10, Assignment of Life Insurance Policy as Collateral. For many
years, the ABA Form No. 10 was used by banks and other lending institutions when life insurance policies were assigned to them as security for
loans. However, this collateral assignment form is no longer under the purview of the ABA. Instead, the ABA recommends that lenders obtain a col-

lateral assignment form from a state's insurance department. Nonetheless, the collateral assignment forms currently being used incorporate most of the features of the ABA form, and in some states, the original ABA form is still being used. Under most collateral assignment forms, the assignee receives the right to

- collect the net proceeds of the policy upon either the death of the insured or the maturity of the policy;
- surrender the policy for cash;
- receive all dividends and exercise all dividend options;
- obtain a loan, either from the insurer or from some other lender, using the policy as security; and
- exercise all nonforfeiture options and receive all benefits.

However, these rights are granted subject to limitations. The assignee agrees not to surrender the policy unless there is a default in repaying the loan or a failure to pay a premium when due. Even then, the assignor must be given notice before the assignee may surrender the policy. The ABA form specified that the assignor receive 20 days' notice. Collateral assignment forms also provide that if the amount of policy proceeds exceeds the amount of the loan at the time of the insured's death, the assignee may collect the entire proceeds but must pay the excess amount to the person or persons who would have been entitled to the proceeds had there been no assignment.

Collateral assignment forms generally provide that the following rights remain with the assignor of the policy:

- the right to designate and change the beneficiary,
- the right to elect an optional settlement mode, and
- the right to collect any disability income benefits that may become payable under the policy.

Validity of Assignments.   Most insurers specify in their life insurance policies that they acknowledge assignments but assume no responsibility for the validity of assignments. Such a disclaimer is necessary because an insurer cannot look into the circumstances surrounding every policy assignment. Thus, when an insurer in good faith pays a policy's proceeds to an assignee, the insurer generally cannot be held liable for a second payment if the assignment is later challenged by another claimant. An exception might occur in a situation in which an insurer had information that should have put the insurer on notice that an assignment might not be valid. For example, an insurer waiving premium payments on a policy because of the total disability of the insured due to schizophrenia should be on notice that any assignments made by the insured while disabled might not be valid.

A question sometimes arises as to whether the policyowner may assign a policy without the consent of the beneficiary. The courts of most jurisdictions agree that if the policyowner has reserved the right to change the beneficiary, in other words, if the beneficiary is not an irrevocable beneficiary, then the policyowner may assign all policy rights without the consent of the beneficiary. However, courts in a minority of jurisdictions hold that all beneficiaries acquire a vested interest in the policy proceeds and that, without a policy provision to the contrary, the consent of such beneficiaries must be obtained. Most policies issued today include a statement that allows the policyowner to assign all rights without the consent of the beneficiary. However, when claims are made on older policies that have no such statement, the claim examiner may have to review the policy language and court rulings in the jurisdiction involved.

Unrecorded Assignments.   Life insurance policies often include a provision that requires an assignor to give the insurer notice of an assignment in order to make it legal. However, if there is no policy provision requiring notice of an assignment, the policy can be legally assigned without such notice. Thus, it is not uncommon for an insurer to learn of an assignment at the time a claim is filed for the policy proceeds.

In some cases, an insurer receives a claim from a person who bases his entitlement to the proceeds upon possession of the policy. The claimant contends that the policy had been assigned "by delivery" rather than by a formal assignment document. Assignment by delivery is recognized by a majority of courts as valid. Such an assignment may be made either as a gift or for a consideration. Before a payment can be made in such circumstances, the claim examiner will require some written agreement from the beneficiary listed in the life insurance contract. Without such an agreement, insurers generally let the courts decide to whom payment should be made.

Payment of the Proceeds.   Once an assignment is accepted as valid, the claim examiner must determine how the assignment affects payment of the policy proceeds. If a policy has been absolutely assigned, and if the assignment is not challenged by another claimant, then the policy's entire proceeds are usually paid directly to the assignee. However, some insurers, seeking to avoid situations in which a beneficiary might later challenge an assignment, issue a joint check made payable to both the beneficiary and the assignee. In addition, if the absolute assignment was executed for the purpose of securing a debt, the assignment will be treated as a collateral assignment so that a creditor will not realize more money from the proceeds of the policy than the principal and interest due on the loan.

In collateral assignments, the assignee, or creditor, is given the right to obtain reimbursement from the policy proceeds for a loan made to the assignor. If the assignment was to a bank, and if the bank used a standard collateral assignment form, then there should be no conflict between the beneficiary and the assignee. Most collateral assignment forms require the beneficiary to sign the form, thus indicating the beneficiary's consent to the terms of the assignment.

In collateral assignments not involving a bank, the insurer usually tries to obtain the beneficiary's consent before paying any of the proceeds to a creditor. Without such consent, the beneficiary might later seek to recover the amount paid to the assignee, either by attacking the validity of the assignment or by arguing that the amount paid to the creditor was more than the amount owed by the insured. To overcome the latter argument, the company might issue a joint check made payable to both the beneficiary and the assignee.

If an assignment was to tenants in common, the claim check should be drawn to them as such. As mentioned previously, tenants in common usually do not possess a right to survivorship. However, in some states, statutes do provide for survivorship rights. Therefore, a claim that involves an assignee as a tenant in common who predeceases the insured will require a review of the appropriate statutes to determine whether payment should be made to the estate of the assignee or to the surviving tenant or tenants in common.

Attorneys

A claimant is sometimes represented by an attorney even when a claim settlement involves no controversy. If an attorney notifies an insurer that he or she represents a claimant, payment of the policy's proceeds should be delivered to the attorney. An attorney, in such an instance, has a lien, either by common law or statute, against the proceeds of the claim. A *lien* is a charge, on real or personal property, that is established to satisfy a debt or an obligation. If the company pays the proceeds directly to a claimant who does not pay the legal fee, the attorney may take action against the company. Usually, it is acceptable for the insurer to draw the check to the order of the claimant, forwarding it to the attorney on behalf of the claimant. Some insurers, however, will make the check payable jointly to the insured and the insured's attorney.

Attorneys in Fact. Occasionally a claim is received from someone who purports to be a claimant's attorney in fact. An ***attorney in fact*** is a layperson acting with the claimant's power of attorney. The claim is usually accompanied by a document supporting the authority of the person regarding the financial affairs of the beneficiary.

There are at least two hazards confronting an insurer in dealing with an attorney in fact. First, the power of attorney may not actually extend to collecting policy proceeds and giving a valid release. Second, and unknown to the insurer, the power of attorney may have been revoked, either expressly by the beneficiary or as a matter of law upon the death or insanity of the beneficiary. Therefore, the insurer should take care to determine that the power of attorney is currently valid and that it includes authority to collect policy proceeds. To be safe, the insurer should authenticate any such power of attorney that is more than one year old. Even if the power of attorney is found to be authentic, the insurer should not make payment directly to the attorney in fact; instead, the check should be drawn to the order of the beneficiary and then be delivered to the attorney. This procedure recognizes the authority claimed by the attorney, but it also places responsibility upon the local bank for determining the validity of the power of attorney when the check is presented for payment.

Tax Collectors

In the United States, the cash value of an insured's life insurance policy is subject to federal income tax collection. If an insured has unpaid income taxes, a government revenue authority can impose a tax lien on the cash value of the policy. An insurer who is notified of a tax lien has ninety days in which to pay the amount of the lien from the policy's cash value to the appropriate government authority.

If a tax lien was attached to the cash surrender value of a policy during an insured's lifetime but was not paid before the insured's death, taxes can be collected after death to the extent of the cash surrender value. However, if a tax assessment was not made until after the insured's death, neither the insurance company nor the beneficiary is liable for any of the insured's back taxes, provided that life insurance proceeds are exempt from the claims of the insured's creditors in the jurisdiction in which the proceeds are paid.

Since a disputed claim of this sort involves complex questions of law, most insurers are not willing to determine the validity of competing claims of the beneficiary and the government. Instead, the insurer usually informs the parties at interest that the proceeds will be paid when those parties have settled their differences.

Disqualification of the Beneficiary

In a few claims, the beneficiary designation will be clear, but the beneficiary will be disqualified from receiving the proceeds because he or she was responsible for the death of the insured. Common law provides that no person should profit from a criminal act, and statutes in most jurisdictions confirm this rule. As a result, a beneficiary who intentionally and maliciously murders the insured will be disqualified from receiving insurance proceeds. Two questions arise in claims of this type. What is the liability of the company, if any? If there is liability, who is the proper recipient of the proceeds?

Determining Company Liability

If an insurer can show that a policy was taken out by the beneficiary with the intent to murder the insured, the company is responsible only for a return of the premiums paid with interest. In such cases, the insurance was issued for a purpose contrary to public policy; hence, the insurance contract was void from its inception. Cases of this sort are quite rare. More commonly, the policy is obtained in good faith. Thus, the insurer is liable for the full policy benefit. Nonetheless, a beneficiary who intentionally and maliciously murders the insured will be denied payment of the life insurance benefit. In cases involving the murder of the insured by the beneficiary, to whom should the life insurance benefit be paid?

Determining the Proper Payee

Life insurance claims involving the possible murder of the insured by the beneficiary are extremely complex to administer and require a detailed investigation into the circumstances surrounding the death of the insured in order to determine any involvement by the beneficiary. If an insurer, knowing that an insured's death was a homicide, pays the policy proceeds to a beneficiary without a thorough investigation, the insurer might be liable for a duplicate payment either to a contingent beneficiary or to the insured's estate if the beneficiary later is convicted of the insured's murder.

When the Beneficiary is a Suspect.   Sometimes a beneficiary is a suspect in the murder of an insured but there is not enough evidence to arrest the beneficiary. An insurer's investigation should focus on uncovering information that will either prove or disprove the beneficiary's involvement in the death of the insured. If conclusive information is not discovered, and if the police close their investigation of the case, then an insurer will normally pay the proceeds to the named beneficiary.

However, if the beneficiary is the primary suspect and the criminal investigation is not complete, an insurer will delay payment of the claim until the investigation is complete. If the investigation continues beyond a reasonable period, then the proceeds should be turned over to a court to decide upon their distribution. Although some states may impose time limits on how long an insurer may hold proceeds before they must be paid, in many states there are no firm rules as to what constitutes a reasonable period. Thus, an insurer's claim personnel must carefully consider how long the insurer can reasonably wait before disbursing proceeds.

In some cases, an indicted beneficiary may be willing to release his or her interest in the proceeds in favor of the contingent beneficiary or the estate of the insured—particularly if there are children of the indicted person who would benefit from the proceeds. In any such case, the claim examiner should explain the law to the beneficiary objectively without attempting to persuade the beneficiary to release the proceeds.

When the Beneficiary is Convicted or Acquitted in a Criminal Trial. In many states, a beneficiary's criminal conviction for first or second degree murder or voluntary manslaughter conclusively eliminates the beneficiary's rights to policy proceeds. In other states, a beneficiary's criminal conviction does not automatically disqualify the beneficiary. In these states, a civil trial is necessary to determine to whom the proceeds should be paid. In such a civil trial, the record of the criminal conviction may be introduced as evidence and may be sufficient to disqualify the beneficiary unless refuting evidence is offered. However, a few states have ruled that a conviction in a criminal trial has no bearing in any subsequent civil trial and that the issue of guilt must be retried in the civil case.

Regardless of whether a criminal conviction is conclusive of a beneficiary's disqualification, a beneficiary's acquittal does not usually affirm a beneficiary's rights to the policy proceeds. Thus, a criminal conviction often automatically disqualifies a beneficiary's rights to the proceeds, but an acquittal rarely affirms the indicted beneficiary's rights. A civil trial is often necessary to establish the beneficiary's rights to the proceeds.

Other Claim Considerations. Most policies specify that payment is to be made to the primary beneficiary, if living, otherwise to a contingent beneficiary if one is named. A beneficiary who is disqualified from receiving the policy proceeds because he or she is responsible for the death of the insured is, nonetheless, still living. Therefore, the contingency on which the contingent beneficiary's right is based has not happened. In some states, statutes specifically cover this type of situation and permit payment to the contingent beneficiary. In other states, payment must be made to the insured's estate.

Special Payee Considerations

Among the other factors for a claim examiner to consider when determining the payee for a life insurance claim are the simultaneous deaths of an insured and the insured's beneficiary, disclaimers of interest, and community property laws.

Simultaneous Deaths

When the insured and the primary beneficiary die simultaneously and there is no proof that either party survived the other, a claim examiner cannot determine the order of death. Legislation has been passed in the United States and Canada to specifically address the problem of simultaneous deaths. In the United States, the Uniform Simultaneous Death Act has been used as the model for such legislation. In all Canadian provinces except for Quebec, the Uniform Life Insurance Act is applied in simultaneous death situations. The Quebec Insurance Act covers simultaneous death situations in Quebec.

All such legislation provides that, in the absence of a policy provision to the contrary, in the event of simultaneous death, and if there is not sufficient evidence that the persons have died other than simultaneously, an insurer will presume that the insured survived the beneficiary. Therefore, in such cases, the policy proceeds are distributed as if the insured had survived the beneficiary.

From an insurer's perspective, there are two problems with simultaneous death legislation. First, an insurer often has difficulty deciding if there is sufficient evidence to support the simultaneous death presumption. Second, these laws do not protect a company from possible double liability if contradictory evidence is presented after payment of the claim. Therefore, the claim examiner must exercise care in determining the basis upon which the proceeds are paid. In many cases, the insurer may have to resort to interpleader, which will be described later in this chapter.

Policy Provisions. Simultaneous death legislation comes into effect when a policy contains no policy provision that provides for the contingency of simultaneous death. However, a policyowner can specify how proceeds are to be paid in a simultaneous death situation by including various provisions in a policy. Some policies, for example, contain a provision which, in effect, reverses the presumption of simultaneous death legislation. Such a provision states that, in the case of apparently simultaneous deaths and without sufficient evidence to the contrary, the proceeds will be distributed as if a beneficiary had survived the insured. In the United States, such a provision allows the estate of a beneficiary/spouse to take advantage of the marital deduction provided by federal estate law. The marital deduction, which is discussed in Chapter 10, applies only if the beneficiary survives the insured.

Other policies contain a **short-term survivorship provision**, which states that payment of proceeds to the beneficiary is dependent upon the beneficiary's being alive for a specified period such as 15 days or 30 days following the death of the insured. This type of provision is sometimes referred to as a *common disaster clause*, but that phrase is actually a misnomer because the insured and the beneficiary need not die in a common disaster for the provision to apply.

For example, the insured, Alvin Tobias, dies in a car accident on May 1. His beneficiary, Bernice Hall, dies of a heart attack on May 4. The policy contains a 10-day survivorship provision. Without the 10-day survivorship provision, the policy proceeds would be payable to the estate of Bernice. However, the inclusion of the short-term survivorship provision would result in the payment of the proceeds to Alvin's estate because Bernice would not have fulfilled the requirement of surviving Alvin by 10 days. In the United States, the short-term survivorship provision often prevents policy proceeds from being subjected to federal estate tax twice: once upon the death of the insured, and a second time upon the death of the beneficiary.

Qualified Disclaimers of Interest

A beneficiary may desire not to receive the proceeds of a life insurance policy. In the United States, Section 2518b of the Internal Revenue Code provides that an individual may refuse to accept an interest in property such as insurance proceeds by filing a qualified disclaimer of interest. Section 2518b of the Code defines a qualified disclaimer as "an irrevocable and unqualified refusal by a person to accept an interest in property," and it specifies four conditions that each transaction must fulfill:

- The refusal must be in writing.
- The refusal must be received by the transferor no more than nine months after the later of (1) the day on which the transfer creating the interest was made or (2) the day on which the person making the disclaimer reaches age 21. For insurance proceeds, the transferor is the insurer.
- The person making the disclaimer must not have accepted the interest or any of its benefits prior to the signing of the disclaimer. Acceptance of any consideration in return for making the disclaimer is treated as an acceptance of the benefits of the interest disclaimed.
- The property interest must pass to a person other than the person making the disclaimer. The person making the disclaimer cannot direct the redistribution of property.

Given the technical nature of this type of transaction, claim examiners may want to have each disclaimer reviewed by legal counsel for acceptability.

Community-Property Laws

Arizona, California, Idaho, Louisiana, Nevada, New Mexico, Texas, Wisconsin, and Washington are known as community-property states. In a *community-property state*, a spouse is entitled, by law, to an equal share of the income earned and, under most circumstances, to an equal share of the property acquired by the other during the period of marriage. However, property acquired during marriage by gift, bequest, or descent may be excepted from community-property laws. Upon the death of a spouse in a community-property state, half of all community property becomes the sole property of the survivor, while the other half passes in a manner directed by a will or by the laws of descent and distribution.

When an insured dies while a resident in a community-property state, the application of community-property laws could affect who is entitled to the proceeds. If the policy proceeds are payable to the surviving spouse, the question of community property does not arise because the surviving spouse receives all of the policy proceeds. However, if the proceeds of the deceased spouse are payable to someone other than the surviving spouse, the issue could be more complex. For example:

> A life insurance policy covered the insured, Anna Lockey, who was married to Sylvester Lockey. The sole designated beneficiary was Anna's mother, Beverly. The policy was purchased while Anna and Sylvester were living in Ohio, where they remained and continued to pay premiums from both their salaries for seven years. Then Anna and Sylvester moved to California where they remained for two years, and then they moved to Georgia. One year later, Anna died. The beneficiary designation had not been changed.

Strict application of the community-property laws would require the insurer to determine that 20 percent of the premiums on the policy (i.e., premiums paid during 2 of the 10 years of policy coverage) had been paid while Anna and Sylvester resided in a community-property state. If those premiums had been paid from community funds, then a proportionate share of the policy proceeds constitutes community property for purposes of distribution.

Obviously, this sort of situation imposes substantial burdens upon the insurer. Strict adherence to the concept of community property would require that the insurer determine whether a deceased person had ever come under the jurisdiction of community-property laws. Recognizing the inequity of that burden, all community-property states have passed *exculpatory statutes*, which allow an insurer to pay the proceeds of a life insurance policy in accordance with the terms of that policy without fear of double liability. Unless the insurer has received prior written notice of a conflicting claim, payment of a claim in accordance with the terms of a policy fully discharges the insurer from any other claims under the policy.

The exculpatory statutes have greatly simplified and expedited claim processing in community-property states. However, some legal uncertainty remains regarding these statutes because of what might be viewed as an invasion of a property right conferred by law on the spouse. Therefore, as an additional safeguard when proceeds exceed a stated limit, such as $10,000, some companies obtain a release from the surviving spouse before making payment to a nonspousal beneficiary.

Matrimonial Regimes

Instead of community-property statutes, the province of Quebec provides matrimonial regimes. A *matrimonial regime* is an arrangement selected by spouses or imposed by law that regulates the ownership and disposal of the property of the spouses during the course of their marriage. Matrimonial regimes do not prevent a spouse from naming a beneficiary under a life insurance policy nor do they in the ordinary course of events affect the distribution of life insurance proceeds. However, in situations in which no specific beneficiary has been named, matrimonial regimes could determine who will share in the life insurance proceeds under the policy.

Divorce

Divorce alone does not generally affect one spouse's beneficiary rights to the insurance of the other spouse. In all states except Michigan and Oklahoma, courts generally have found that when a divorced insured fails to change his or her beneficiary designation after a divorce, the ex-spouse designated as beneficiary is entitled to receive the proceeds. This rule also holds true for policies issued after 1962 in all Canadian provinces except Quebec.

In Michigan and Oklahoma, on the other hand, a spouse's interest as a beneficiary is cut off by divorce unless a provision to the contrary is included in the divorce decree. If a divorce decree does not address the issue of life insurance proceeds, the policy is payable to the estate of the deceased insured or to a contingent beneficiary if one was named. Likewise, in Quebec, divorce renders null and void any designation of the spouse as beneficiary, whether revocable, irrevocable, or as a contingent beneficiary.

In many instances, a divorce settlement may affect the manner in which proceeds are to be paid. A divorce settlement often specifies that the divorced insured must continue to pay insurance premiums and maintain his or her ex-spouse as beneficiary on some or all of his or her insurance. Nonetheless, the insured may designate someone other than the ex-spouse as beneficiary. An insurer who pays the policy proceeds to the beneficiary designated in the policy with no knowledge of a conflicting beneficiary will not generally be liable for payment a second time. However, an insurer would probably be liable if proceeds were paid after the insurer received notice of a divorce or of a rival claimant.

Adverse Claimants

Throughout this chapter, we have referred to a variety of situations in which there may be adverse claimants, or conflicting claimants, for a policy's benefits. Although the number of claims involving adverse claimants is very small, the improper disposition of the policy benefit in such cases could result in substantial costs to an insurance company. At a minimum, the insurer might have to pay the policy benefit twice. At a maximum, the insurer might have to pay the policy benefit twice, and also punitive damages to one or more of the adverse claimants. *Punitive damages* are assessed by a court and are designed to punish a company for its behavior. Thus, a claim examiner should always handle adverse claimants with extreme caution and should always work in conjunction with the insurer's law department.

When confronted with adverse claimants, a claim examiner notifies each of the adverse claimants of the other's claim. The role of the insurer in such proceedings must be carefully limited. Each of the claimants, and his or her lawyer, should be given the full facts as the company knows them: the beneficiary designations, assignments, policy provisions, and any other facts that are pertinent to the claim. The claim examiner should avoid interpreting any of the facts for the claimants.

Amicable Resolution

As a first step, the claim examiner may want to encourage the conflicting claimants to settle the question of distribution of proceeds among themselves. Such an amicable resolution avoids the time and expense of subsequent legal action. If the involved parties can agree in writing as to how the policy's proceeds should be distributed, then the insurer can safely pay the policy's proceeds without fear of any additional liability. However, if the adverse claimants are unable to reach an agreement, then interpleader will have to be initiated.

Interpleader

Interpleader is an action at law whereby a party—here, the insurer—holding property belonging to someone else submits to a court the question of who is rightfully entitled to the property. In brief, when an insurer admits liability for a policy's proceeds but is unable to determine to whom the proceeds should be paid, a bill of interpleader is filed with a court, and the proceeds are deposited with a court. The court then decides among the various claimants and disburses the property to the appropriate person or persons.

In some cases involving adverse claimants, the insurer does not initiate an action of interpleader, but rather waits in the hope that the claimants can agree among themselves. If one of the adverse claimants sues to recover the policy proceeds, the company then responds with interpleader in order to settle the claim and to discharge the company's liability.

Interpleader can be a valuable procedure to an insurer faced with potential double liability over payment of policy proceeds. However, the legal expenses of this approach can be costly. In general, insurance companies consider interpleader to be a last resort after all reasonable efforts to resolve a case have been unsuccessful. Almost all companies endeavor to recover their expenses involved in such an action when such recovery is allowed by law.

Indemnity Bonds and Agreements

As an alternative to interpleader, and when an amicable resolution has not been reached, some companies use an indemnity bond. According to the terms of an indemnity bond, the bonding company will reimburse the insurer in the event that the policy proceeds must be paid a second time to another claimant. If a claimant appears to be entitled to the benefits and is anxious to receive the money, he or she may pay the cost of the indemnity bond. In other cases, the company may be willing to incur the cost of the bond in order to settle the claim.

If the amount of proceeds is comparatively small, the company may accept a hold harmless release from a payee. A **hold harmless release** states that the payee will reimburse the company in the event that a subsequent claimant successfully challenges the disbursement of the proceeds. However, the value of such an agreement depends on the resources and willingness of the payee—rather than on a bonding company—and so is generally considered to provide less protection to the insurer.

Unclaimed Property Statutes

Insurance companies and other firms, such as banks, that hold funds due to another person are sometimes unable to locate the person to whom the funds should be paid. Funds that cannot be disbursed to the rightful payees are referred to as **unclaimed property** and become subject to the unclaimed property statute of the state of the beneficiary's last address. When unclaimed funds are paid to a state, the funds are said to **escheat** to the state. Thus, unclaimed property statutes are sometimes referred to as *escheat laws*.

Many of the states have adopted, sometimes with variations, the

Uniform Disposition of Unclaimed Property Act. These laws provide that abandoned property that has not been claimed within a certain number of years, typically seven, must be paid to the state to hold for the rightful owner. Should the owner of the property appear at some later date and wish to reclaim his or her property, then he or she may petition the state for the property.

In all of the Canadian provinces except Quebec, an insurer who cannot locate a payee can deposit the amount payable with a court of law through an interpleader action. The question of proper distribution of the proceeds is then determined by the court. In Quebec, unclaimed sums are administered by a public curator. A **public curator** is the public officer authorized by the government to administer the property of persons who have disappeared.

References

Bernier, J. P. *Legal Aspects of Life Insurance in Quebec.* Toronto, Canada: Canadian Life and Health Insurance Association, 1982.

Cooper, John W. "Payee Problems," *1984 ICA Life Insurance Workshop Notes*, 26-31.

Johnson, Gary C. "Small Estates," *1986 ICA Life Insurance Workshop Notes*, 10-17.

Summary and Affidavit Procedures For Settlement of Estates: Report of the Law Committee. International Claim Association, 1983.

Walker, Dennis. "Beneficiary Designation Problems," *1986 ICA Life Insurance Workshop Notes*, 64-69.

CHAPTER

10

Paying Life Insurance Benefits— Part II

Related to the question of who is to receive payment of the life insurance benefits is the question of how those benefits are to be paid. In the early days of life insurance, when benefit amounts were small and were designed just to pay funeral and last illness expenses, life insurance companies typically provided for only one benefit payment option—the lump sum payment option. However, as policyowners purchased larger amounts of life insurance benefits, insurance companies began to provide alternatives for managing and distributing the benefits payable. Thus, in addition to the lump sum payment option, insurance companies currently offer a variety of settlement options that allow the policyowner and/or the beneficiary to specify how the policy proceeds should be managed and distributed.

SETTLEMENT OPTIONS

The following settlement options have been traditionally offered by insurance companies:

- *The interest option*—The proceeds are temporarily left on deposit with the company and interest is paid on the proceeds. The

167

beneficiary may or may not have the right to withdraw all or part of the principal.

- *The fixed period option*—The company pays the proceeds and interest in a series of annual or more frequent installments for a preselected period.
- *The fixed amount option*—The company uses the proceeds and interest to pay a preselected sum in a series of annual, or more frequent, installments for as long as the proceeds last.
- *The life income option*—The company uses the proceeds and interest to pay a series of annual or more frequent installments over the entire lifetime of the person designated to receive the policy benefits.

In addition to these four traditional settlement options, some insurers have recently introduced a new method of paying life insurance claims that is a hybrid of the lump sum payment and the interest option. The **retained asset account (RAA)** is an interest-bearing money market checking account that is fully guaranteed and is managed by an insurer through a bank intermediary. Instead of being paid in a lump sum, the death benefit is automatically deposited into an RAA. The RAA provides the beneficiary with competitive interest rates, safety of principal, and the ability to defer major investment decisions until he or she has had time to recover from the emotional strain of the insured's death.

The companies that offer this option allow beneficiaries to choose the traditional lump sum payment if they wish, or another benefit payment option if they wish. Beneficiaries can even choose an alternate settlement option after the proceeds have been deposited into the RAA.

A primary advantage to the insurer of the RAA option is that the beneficiary remains in contact with the company. Thus, the insurer has gained a potential customer for other financial products and services offered by the company.

The Claim Examiner's Role in Administering Settlement Options

In the early days of life insurance, the claim examiner who approved the claim also generated the lump sum claim payment check and mailed the check to the beneficiary. By contrast, the claim examiner's role in paying life insurance proceeds today varies considerably depending upon the choice of settlement option and the company's size.

In both large and small insurance companies, the claim area usually oversees lump sum death benefit payments. However, claims that are to be paid under a settlement option may or may not be handled in the claim area. In the largest companies, once a claim examiner establishes that the claim is to be paid under a settlement option, the claim is transferred to another department or unit for administration. In the smaller life insurance companies, the responsibility for the administration of all claims, including those to be paid under a settlement option, may remain within the claim department. For simplicity's sake, we assume in the next section that the claim examiner oversees the administration of settlement options. However, the issues remain the same even if another organizational area maintains responsibility for administering settlement options.

The Administration of Settlement Options

When a lump sum payment is made to the beneficiary, the terms of the life insurance contract are fulfilled, and the contract terminates. When proceeds are to be paid under a settlement option, the insurance company establishes a contractual relationship with the person who is to receive the policy benefit. In recognition of this contractual relationship, the claim examiner sends to the payee information that outlines the amount of the proceeds and the method by which the proceeds will be held by the insurer and distributed to the payee.

For the interest option, the claim examiner usually sends to the payee a *certificate of indebtedness*, which specifies a guaranteed minimum interest rate and the frequency (typically annually) with which interest payments will be made. The certificate of indebtedness also notes whether the beneficiary will have the right to change from the interest option to any of the other settlement options and whether the beneficiary has the right to withdraw all or part of the proceeds.

For the other traditional settlement options, the claim examiner usually sends an *installment certificate*, which specifies the amount of each benefit payment and/or the period during which benefit payments will be made. The installment certificate will also specify whether the beneficiary is allowed to withdraw all or part of the funds during the payment period.

For a retained asset account, the beneficiary receives a checkbook along with a *confirmation certificate*, which outlines the amount of life insurance proceeds in the account, the account number, and the current interest rate. In addition, the beneficiary receives information explaining the company's policies with respect to minimum withdrawals, deposits, minimum balances, overdrafts, creditors, and inheritance issues.

Election of a Settlement Option by the Beneficiary

If a policyowner under an individual policy or an insured under a group policy did not elect a mode of settlement, the beneficiary may be able to do so after the insured's death. However, the claim examiner must examine the policy to determine if the payee is in a class that may make such an election. Some policies do not permit an assignee, a trustee, an executor, or an administrator to elect an optional mode of settlement. Instead, these policies require the lump sum payment of benefits to this class of payee. In addition, the claim examiner needs to ensure that a policyowner/insured did not irrevocably choose one of the optional modes of settlement. A beneficiary cannot later change an irrevocable settlement option.

Repayment of Policy Loan

Sometimes a policy loan is outstanding at the death of the insured. Occasionally a beneficiary wishes to repay such a loan to increase the amount of money used for settlement option purposes. Some companies are willing to accept such repayments of policy loans. Others, however, hold that policy provisions require that any outstanding loan be deducted from policy proceeds and that acceptance of a loan repayment after the death of the insured is really acceptance of a deposit, not part of a life insurance transaction.

Premiums Paid in Advance

Premiums paid in advance are those paid beyond the length of the specified premium-payment period. Many companies consider the refund of premiums paid in advance to be payable to the estate of the deceased insured. However, small amounts, such as up to $500, may be included in policy proceeds. Most companies will not permit a premium refund to be included in the proceeds held under a settlement option. However, some companies will include the refund in the sum held under an option if the interested parties agree to such a move.

Changes in Irrevocable Settlements

Some settlement option arrangements allow the beneficiary to alter the payment arrangement and receive all or part of the proceeds in a lump sum. Other types of settlement options are irrevocable and, thus, cannot be changed. An insurer in an irrevocable settlement option arrangement is committed to pay benefits in the mode specified by the policyowner. A major disadvantage of making an irrevocable settlement option is that as times change, circumstances may change. A settlement option providing for a fixed sum payment of $200 a month may have been generous when the policyowner chose it many years before, but the option may be inadequate at the time of disbursement.

Although an insurer has contracted with a policyowner to pay out the policy proceeds in a certain manner, the true intention of a policyowner was probably to provide an adequate income for the beneficiary. In some situations, the settlement mode chosen may impose a real hardship upon the beneficiary. Strict adherence to the settlement mode elected might violate the policyowner's true intention of providing for the beneficiary's well-being. Therefore, in certain circumstances, some companies might allow policy proceeds under an irrevocable settlement to be commuted, that is, paid in a single sum to the beneficiary.

In the United States, companies willing to change irrevocable settlements usually set several requirements. The most common requirements include the following:

- There must be a demonstrated need for the proceeds, such as economic hardship,
- The amount of the proceeds must be relatively small, and/or the settlement option must have been chosen at least several years before, and
- All of the parties (such as contingent beneficiaries) having an interest in the proceeds must agree in writing to the change of settlement.

In general, U.S. courts have been sympathetic to the commutation of settlement options under the aforementioned circumstances. In Canada, the Uniform Life Insurance Act provides that when proceeds are payable in installments and the beneficiary does not have the right to commute the installments, the insurer may not commute the installments without written direction from the insured. However, the Act also provides that the beneficiary may apply to a court for modification of this restriction.

Settlement Options Involving Minors

Claim questions can arise when optional settlements are to be paid to minors. If the payee is a minor, the payments may be made only to a guardian of the minor's property, unless there is a statutory exception. As discussed previously, some state statutes permit the payment of relatively small sums directly to a minor who is of a specified age, such as 16.

Another question involves whether a minor's guardian may elect an optional settlement for the minor. The risk to an insurer of a minor's disallowing a settlement option upon reaching the age of majority is minimal if the guardian elects the interest option for the minor. Nonetheless, many companies seek to avoid such risk by requiring the guardian to produce a court order authorizing the election of any optional mode of settlement. Some other companies require such a court order only if the guardian elects an option other than the interest option.

TAXES ON LIFE INSURANCE PROCEEDS

In certain situations, life insurance proceeds are subject to estate taxes and income taxes. In order to understand the problems of policyowners and beneficiaries and in order to comply with various government form requirements, the claim examiner must know basic tax features. Taxation, of course, is a highly specialized subject and one that changes frequently. The discussion that follows should, however, provide a basic understanding of taxation for claim purposes.

Estate Taxes

In the United States, the federal government and some states levy an estate tax on an individual's gross estate at the time of the individual's death. An **estate tax** is a tax on the transfer of property at death.

Life insurance proceeds that are payable to a policyowner/insured's estate must be included in that person's gross estate for estate tax purposes. In addition, even when a named beneficiary is to receive the proceeds of a policy, if the policyowner/insured had any incident of ownership in the policy, then the proceeds from that policy are included in the gross estate of the policyowner/insured. An **incident of ownership** is any policy right including the right to (1) change the beneficiary, (2) cancel or surrender the policy, (3) assign the policy, (4) obtain a policy loan, or (5) use the policy as collateral for a loan.

A policyowner/insured may be able to avoid estate taxes by yielding all incidents of ownership to someone else through an irrevocable absolute assignment of the policy. The absolute assignment must transfer all rights of ownership, and the assignee must not be legally obligated to use the proceeds for the benefit of the policyowner/insured's estate. In addition, if the policyowner/insured dies within three years of making the assignment, the proceeds are still included in the estate of the policyowner/insured for estate tax purposes. Under Internal Revenue Service (IRS) regulations, such an assignment is regarded as a gift in contemplation of death.

Proponents of group life insurance were concerned at first that an insured person covered by a group policy could never assign all incidents of ownership because he or she always would retain the right to leave the group. However, the IRS has ruled that if, as permitted by state law, the insured assigns both the right to convert the group insurance and all other policy rights, the insured is considered to have assigned all incidents of ownership.

Estate tax liability is determined by a series of computations, starting with the gross estate of the decedent. The gross estate is the total of all property in which the decedent had an interest at the time of his or her death. From the gross estate, deductions are permitted for funeral and administration expenses, taxes, debts, and casualty and theft losses. The resulting amount is the adjusted gross estate.

To arrive at the amount of the taxable estate, three deductions from the adjusted gross estate are permitted—a marital deduction, a charitable deduction, and an orphans' deduction. An unlimited marital deduction is allowed for the full value of property that passes to a surviving spouse who, in effect, has ownership of the property. The charitable deduction is allowed for any property that is transferred to a qualified charity. The orphans' deduction is allowed for certain transfers to orphaned children of the decedent when the decedent has no surviving spouse. The amount of the deduction varies according to the age of each orphan.

The federal government in Canada has not levied estate taxes since 1972. Nonetheless, some provinces still maintain an estate tax. However, life insurance proceeds are granted a special exemption that helps reduce the amount of the estate tax payable.

IRS Form 712

In the United States, the IRS requires that Form 712, the Life Insurance Statement, be filed by the executor or administrator of an estate along with a Federal Estate Tax Return. Form 712 is prepared by the insurer and is used by the IRS to determine the statutory gross estate of an insured. The form is not completed routinely by insurance companies but only upon request by a legal representative of the deceased's estate. Form 712 is shown in Figure 10–1. Most of the required entries are self-explanatory, but several deserve additional comment.

Item 3: The insurance company is not obligated to obtain the Social Security number if it is not known.

Item 13: An appropriate entry should be made to indicate the frequency of premium payment, such as "single" or "annual."

Item 22: If a termination dividend is payable, it should be included in the amount entered on this line.

Item 24: The net amount payable as of the date of death should be entered on this line. If premiums have been deducted from the proceeds, a parenthetical entry to show the net amount should be added on this line. Interest earned on the claim should not be considered, either here or elsewhere on the form. Such interest accrues subsequent to the date of death.

Items 31 & 32: These questions need be answered only if current information is available from the claim file. The claim examiner need not research other files.

Form **712** (Rev. Oct. 1981) Department of the Treasury Internal Revenue Service		**Life Insurance Statement**		

Part I   Decedent—Insured (File with Federal Estate Tax Return, Form 706)

1 Decedent's first name and middle initial	2 Decedent's last name	3 Decedent's social security number (if known)	4 Date of death

5 Name and address of insurance company

6 Kind of policy	7 Policy number

8 Owner's name. Please attach copy of application.	9 Date issued	10 Assignee's name. Please attach copy of assignment.	11 Date assigned

12 Value of policy at time of assignment	13 Amount of premium	14 Names of beneficiaries

15 Face amount of policy.. $

16 Indemnity benefits .... $

17 Additional insurance.. $

18 Other benefits .... $

19 Principal of any indebtedness to the company deductible in determining net proceeds .... $

20 Interest on indebtedness (item 19) accrued to date of death....................................... $

21 Amount of accumulated dividends .... $

22 Amount of post-mortem dividends .... $

23 Amount of returned premium.. $

24 Amount of proceeds if payable in one sum .... $

25 Value of proceeds as of date of death (if not payable in one sum) .... $

26 Policy provisions concerning deferred payments or installments.

    Note: *If other than lump-sum settlement is authorized for a surviving spouse, please attach a copy of the insurance policy.*

27 Amount of installments .... $

28 Date of birth, sex, and name of any person the duration of whose life may measure the number of payments.

29 Amount applied by the insurance company as a single premium representing the purchase of installment benefits............. $

30 Basis (Mortality table and rate of interest) used by insurer in valuing installment benefits.

31 Was the insured the annuitant or beneficiary of any annuity contract issued by the company?............................ ☐ Yes ☐ No

32 Names of companies with which decedent carried other policies and amount of such policies if this information is disclosed by your records.

    The undersigned officer of the above-named insurance company hereby certifies that this statement sets forth true and correct information.

Signature ▶   Title ▶   Date of Certification ▶

Instructions

Paperwork Reduction Act Notice.—The Paperwork Reduction Act of 1980 says we must tell you why we are collecting this information, how we will use it, and whether you have to give it to us. We ask for the information to carry out the Internal Revenue laws of the United States. We need it to ensure that you are complying with these laws and to allow us to figure and collect the right amount of tax. You are required to give us this information.

Statement of Insurer.—This statement must be made, on behalf of the insurance company which issued the policy, by an officer of the company having access to the records of the company. For purposes of this statement, a facsimile signature may be used in lieu of a manual signature and if used, shall be binding as a manual signature.

Separate Statements.—A separate statement must be filed for each policy.

Form **712** (Rev. 10-81)

Figure 10-1.   Internal Revenue Service Form 712.

Federal Income Tax

In both Canada and the United States, as a general rule, life insurance proceeds that are paid in one sum to a beneficiary upon the death of an insured are not considered to be taxable income to the beneficiary. Proceeds from accidental death policies are also excludable from income taxes. However, if the insurer holds the proceeds under the interest option or pays the proceeds in installments, the interest earned is part of the payee's gross income and is subject within certain exemptions to income taxation. In addition, the proceeds of policies that have been transferred for value (such as in consideration for property or promises received) and proceeds of policies paid to a divorced spouse by virtue of a property settlement agreement may be taxable as income to the beneficiary.

U.S. Federal Income Tax

Generally, in order for the proceeds of life insurance contracts issued after December 31, 1984, to be excludable from a beneficiary's gross income, the life insurance contract must be defined as such under applicable state law and also must satisfy the TEFRA Corridor requirement discussed in Chapter 2. If a contract does not qualify as a life insurance contract, then only the excess of the death benefit over the net surrender value will be excludable from the income of the beneficiary as a death benefit.

Information Returns.   Each year, insurance companies are required to file with the federal government an information return, Form 1099, for certain policyowners and beneficiaries. Form 1099 reports payments to policyowners and beneficiaries of taxable income in excess of certain minimum amounts. Income constructively received, as well as that actually received, must be reported. There are several varieties of Form 1099, including: Form 1099-INT for recipients of interest income of more than $10, and Form 1099R for recipients of total distributions from profit sharing, retirement plans, and individual retirement arrangements of more than $600. In computing the amount paid to each person, the company must total the amounts paid under all contracts. Thus, if a beneficiary receives $6 annual interest on each of two amounts held at interest, an information return must be prepared because the total interest exceeds the $10 minimum for reporting.

Federal law requires the company to show a payee's identifying number on the return. For individuals, a Social Security number is required. For other payees such as corporations, a taxpayer identification number is required. Although legally the payee is responsible for furnishing the insurer with the identifying number, many insurers have modified their claim forms to request this information at the time of a claim.

When the taxable amounts paid exceed the minimum amounts for reporting, the insurer is required to furnish the payee with an annual statement showing the amounts paid. A copy of the Form 1099 information return may be used for that purpose.

Nonresident Alien Reporting and Withholding.   United States federal tax regulations specify that certain income paid from sources within the United States to persons who are not citizens of the United States is subject to information reporting and taxation. In addition, for many of these taxable payments, the law requires the payor to withhold taxes. By failing to report or withhold the appropriate tax, the payor could become liable for the tax.

Tax regulations divide noncitizens, or aliens, into two classes: resident and nonresident aliens. An alien actually present in the United States (the fifty states and the District of Columbia) is considered a **resident alien** for purposes of federal income taxation if he or she is not a transient or a temporary visitor and has no definite intention as to his or her length of stay. If an alien has lived in the United States for as long as one year, a legal presumption exists that the individual is a resident alien, but the alien may rebut that presumption.

A person who comes to the United States for a definite purpose that may be promptly accomplished is a **nonresident alien**. An alien whose stay is limited to a definite period by the immigration laws is ordinarily considered to be a nonresident alien. However, if an extended stay is necessary to accomplish this purpose and, if the alien makes a home temporarily in the United States, the person becomes a resident alien even though he or she intends to return home when the purpose of the stay has been accomplished.

For income tax purposes, the difference between a resident alien and a nonresident alien is that resident aliens are generally taxed the same as citizens of the United States. Nonresident aliens are taxed only on income received from sources within the United States.

For claim purposes, several types of payments to nonresident aliens are subject to reporting and withholding requirements. Such payments include

- interest paid on death proceeds,
- interest paid on dividends left on deposit,
- interest paid on proceeds left on deposit,
- interest paid on prepaid insurance premiums,
- interest paid on overcharges of premiums,
- income derived from the maturity of an endowment, and
- capital gains on lump-sum payments under certain qualified employee retirement plans.

Currently, insurers are required to withhold 30 percent of the taxable income paid in such cases. However, residents of some two dozen countries may be entitled to reduced tax rates or complete exemption from taxation because of tax treaties with the United States. Nonetheless, government regulations require insurers to file Form 1042S for all payments, regardless of whether tax is withheld.

Tax Waivers, Consents, and Notices

Most states levy taxes on various types of insurance proceeds. In order to make certain that the taxes are paid by the beneficiaries, some of the jurisdictions have statutes which impose requirements on the insurers before the proceeds are paid. Those requirements include giving notice to the Department of Revenue, withholding a sufficient amount of the proceeds to pay the taxes on the proceeds, and either (1) obtaining consent from the Department of Revenue to pay the entire proceeds or (2) obtaining a waiver from the Department of Revenue of the withholding requirements.

In only one Canadian province, Quebec, insurers may be required by the Succession Duty Act to obtain the consent of the provincial government before paying insurance proceeds.

BENEFIT COUNSELING

Within the narrowest of legal terms, the payment of policy benefits to the proper beneficiary discharges the insurer's responsibility under the policy contract. But many insurance companies, recognizing their role as service companies, particularly financial services companies, provide financial counseling to beneficiaries at the time benefits become payable.

Such counseling offers advantages to both the beneficiary and the company. The beneficiary receives, at a minimum, information as to alternative settlements that are available or, on the other hand, an analysis of immediate and long-term financial needs. The insurer receives an opportunity to manage the proceeds that the beneficiary might otherwise withdraw and place elsewhere.

Benefit counseling requires specialized knowledge in a variety of areas: Social Security and other government benefits, company products, estate planning, alternative investments, estate taxes, and income taxes. Therefore, the role of the claim examiner is usually limited to recognizing the potential for benefit counseling. An agent, a financial consultant, or a professional benefit counselor will usually be the one to consult with the beneficiary.

References

Breston, Chris. "Companies, Beneficiaries Applaud New Way To Pay Claims: RAAs," *Resource Magazine*, (vol. XIII, no. 1) January/February 1988, 28-30.

Inheritance and Estate Taxes: Report of the Law Committee. International Claim Association, 1983.

Inheritance and Estate Tax Waivers, Consent and Notice Requirements: Report of the Law Committee. International Claim Association, 1979.

The Tax Companion, 1988. Indianapolis, IN: Longman Publishing Company, 1988.

Tax Facts on Life Insurance. Cincinnati, OH: Nulaw Services, 1987.

Medical Claim Administration

11

Examining
Medical Expense Claims

Because of the number of factors involved in determining the availability and the amount of medical expense benefits, medical expense claims are very complex to administer. The policies issued by an insurer contain hundreds of variations. For example, one policy may cover home health care services while another policy may not. Likewise, many different types of health care providers may be used by the insured; some of them may be qualified for payment under a medical expense policy's terms, whereas others may not. In addition, when an insured is eligible to receive medical expense benefits from a second insurance plan or government program, liability for benefits may be coordinated between the plans. Finally, an insured with medical expense coverage may submit multiple claims. One medical emergency, for example, can result in one or more prescriptions, one or more diagnostic tests, or perhaps even several admittances to a hospital. Thus, the sheer volume of medical expense claims makes the processing of this type of claim more difficult.

The process of examining medical expense claims is complicated for these and other reasons. Nonetheless, the basic claim process remains the same as for any other type of claim. In this chapter, we look at verification of (1) the insured's coverage, (2) the insured's loss, and (3) policy coverage of the loss, focusing on what benefits are typically provided under various medical expense coverages. In Chapter 12, we discuss payment of the benefits.

We cannot proceed with these topics, however, without first discussing a process that has revolutionized the payment of medical expense claims: automation of the medical expense claim system.

AUTOMATION OF THE CLAIM EXAMINATION PROCESS

Because of the large volume of medical expense claims, automation of the claim processing function has resulted in significant cost savings for many insurers. Companies vary in their degree of automation. Some insurers use computers to verify policy status and maintain an insured's claim history but still rely on human intervention for the calculation of benefits. Other companies maintain a fully automated system that can (1) verify a policy's in-force status, (2) verify a claimant's eligibility for benefits, (3) calculate benefit amounts, and (4) generate a letter containing an explanation of the benefits payable. With a fully automated system, human intervention is necessary only to authorize payment of the benefits and process problem claims.

An automated claim system contains master files on each policyholder's medical expense plan. Each master file contains information about the plan's benefit structure as well as information about each insured and his or her dependents. The master file is updated with each submitted claim to maintain the integrity and accuracy of the data base.

SUBMISSION OF THE CLAIM

As with life insurance claims, the processing of medical expense claims begins with the submission of the claim. Medical expense policies include a provision that specifies a period, typically 20 to 90 days after the occurrence or commencement of any loss covered by the policy, during which an insured must file a medical expense claim. The purpose of such a provision is to encourage prompt filing of claims.

The majority of medical expense policies require an insured, or sometimes an insured's employer under a group medical expense contract, to file medical expense claims directly with an insurer in a process called *direct claim submission*. The medical expense claim form contains information concerning the loss for which a claim is being made. This form must be signed by the insured and the insured's employer, if a claim is made for group employer-provided medical expense benefits. In addition, if the claim is for a dependent under an employer-provided group plan, the insured employee must also sign the claim form.

In the early 1980s, several insurers began experimenting with *electronic claim submission*, a system that allows the medical care provider to submit charges directly to the insurer via a computer terminal or magnetic tape, thus eliminating the need for the submission of a paper claim. In 1981, the National Electronic Information Corporation (NEIC) was formed by eleven major life and health insurance companies to provide for the electronic submission of claims from providers to insurers. The purpose of submitting claims electronically is to minimize the use of the labor-intensive and error-prone paper forms approach to claim data collection. Currently, the NEIC system is set up to accept claims only from enrolled hospitals. However, plans call for system enhancements that will allow physicians, dentists, and laboratories to eventually participate in the network. In addition, other electronic claim submission systems are in the development and introductory stages.

The key to the establishment of electronic claim submission has been the standardization of claim data. The Health Insurance Association of America, working in conjunction with the American Hospital Association, insurers, and providers of medical care, has developed uniform group health insurance claim forms. A sample form used for submitting physician expenses is shown in Figure 11–1.

In addition to allowing for the development of electronic claim submission, uniform claim forms have greatly simplified the traditional direct claim submission process. Since all uniform claim forms require standard insurance information, hospitals and other health care providers are able to complete claim forms more rapidly and with fewer mistakes.

VERIFICATION OF THE INSURED'S COVERAGE

After submission of the claim, the insured's eligibility for coverage is verified. In most instances, when an individual submits a claim for payment, the person is insured. Sometimes, however, an individual's coverage may have ceased. In such cases, the claim examiner must determine if the insured is still eligible to receive benefits. The individual may be entitled to benefits through a conversion of group coverage to individual coverage or, in the United States, through election of government-mandated continuation coverage. Conversion of group coverage to individual coverage was discussed in Chapter 3. In the next section, we discuss government-mandated continuation coverage.

Government-mandated Continuation Coverage

In the United States, the Consolidated Omnibus Budget Reconciliation Act

FORM APPROVED
OMB NO. 0938-0008

HEALTH INSURANCE CLAIM FORM

(CHECK APPLICABLE PROGRAM BLOCK BELOW)

☐ MEDICARE (MEDICARE NO.) ☐ MEDICAID (MEDICAID NO.) ☐ CHAMPUS (SPONSOR'S SSN) ☐ CHAMPVA (VA FILE NO.) ☐ FECA BLACK LUNG (SSN) ☐ OTHER (CERTIFICATE SSN)

PATIENT AND INSURED (SUBSCRIBER) INFORMATION

1 PATIENT'S NAME (LAST NAME, FIRST NAME, MIDDLE INITIAL) | 2 PATIENT'S DATE OF BIRTH | 3 INSURED'S NAME (LAST NAME, FIRST NAME, MIDDLE INITIAL)

4 PATIENT'S ADDRESS (STREET, CITY, STATE, ZIP CODE) | 5 PATIENT'S SEX MALE ☐ FEMALE ☐ | 6 INSURED'S I.D. NO. (FOR PROGRAM CHECKED ABOVE INCLUDE ALL LETTERS)

7 PATIENT'S RELATIONSHIP TO INSURED SELF ☐ SPOUSE ☐ CHILD ☐ OTHER ☐ | 8 INSURED'S GROUP NO. (OR GROUP NAME OR FECA CLAIM NO.) ☐ INSURED IS EMPLOYED AND COVERED BY EMPLOYER HEALTH PLAN

9 OTHER HEALTH INSURANCE COVERAGE (ENTER NAME OR POLICYHOLDER AND PLAN NAME AND ADDRESS AND POLICY OR MEDICAL ASSISTANCE NUMBER) | 10 WAS CONDITION RELATED TO A PATIENT'S EMPLOYMENT YES ☐ NO ☐ B ACCIDENT AUTO ☐ OTHER ☐ | 11 INSURED'S ADDRESS (STREET, CITY, STATE, ZIP CODE) TELEPHONE NO. 11 a CHAMPUS SPONSOR'S STATUS ☐ ACTIVE DUTY ☐ RETIRED ☐ DECEASED | BRANCH OF SERVICE

12 PATIENT'S OR AUTHORIZED PERSON'S SIGNATURE (READ BACK BEFORE SIGNING) I AUTHORIZE THE RELEASE OF ANY MEDICAL INFORMATION NECESSARY TO PROCESS THIS CLAIM I ALSO REQUEST PAYMENT OF GOVERNMENT BENEFITS EITHER TO MYSELF OR TO THE PARTY WHO ACCEPTS ASSIGNMENT BELOW SIGNED _____ DATE _____ | 13 I AUTHORIZE PAYMENT OF MEDICAL BENEFITS TO UNDERSIGNED PHYSICIAN OR SUPPLIER FOR SERVICE DESCRIBED BELOW SIGNED (INSURED OR AUTHORIZED PERSON)

PHYSICIAN OR SUPPLIER INFORMATION

14 DATE OF ◄ ILLNESS (FIRST SYMPTOM) OR INJURY (ACCIDENT) OR PREGNANCY (LMP) | 15 DATE FIRST CONSULTED YOU FOR THIS CONDITION | 16 IF PATIENT HAS HAD SAME OR SIMILAR ILLNESS OR INJURY GIVE DATES | 16 a IF EMERGENCY CHECK HERE ☐

17 DATE PATIENT ABLE TO RETURN TO WORK | 18 DATES OF TOTAL DISABILITY FROM _____ THROUGH _____ | DATES OF PARTIAL DISABILITY FROM _____ THROUGH _____

19 NAME OF REFERRING PHYSICIAN OR OTHER SOURCE (e.g. PUBLIC HEALTH AGENCY) | 20 FOR SERVICES RELATED TO HOSPITALIZATION GIVE HOSPITALIZATION DATES ADMITTED _____ DISCHARGED _____

21 NAME & ADDRESS OF FACILITY WHERE SERVICES RENDERED (IF OTHER THAN HOME OR OFFICE) | 22 WAS LABORATORY WORK PERFORMED OUTSIDE YOUR OFFICE? YES ☐ NO ☐ CHARGES _____

23 DIAGNOSIS OR NATURE OF ILLNESS OR INJURY RELATE DIAGNOSIS TO PROCEDURE IN COLUMN D BY REFERENCE NUMBERS 1 2 3 ETC OR DX CODE

1.
2.
3.
4.

EPSDT YES ☐ NO ☐
FAMILY PLANNING YES ☐ NO ☐
PRIOR AUTHORIZATION NO.

24 DATE OF SERVICE		B PLACE OF SERVICE	C FULLY DESCRIBE PROCEDURES, MEDICAL SERVICES OR SUPPLIES FURNISHED FOR EACH DATE GIVEN		D DIAGNOSIS CODE	E CHARGES	F DAYS OR UNITS	G TOS	H LEAVE BLANK
FROM	TO		PROCEDURE CODE IDENTIFY	(EXPLAIN UNUSUAL SERVICES OR CIRCUMSTANCES)					

25 SIGNATURE OF PHYSICIAN OR SUPPLIER (INCLUDING DEGREES OR CREDENTIALS) I CERTIFY THAT THE STATEMENTS ON THE REVERSE APPLY TO THIS BILL AND ARE MADE A PART THEREOF | 26 ACCEPT ASSIGNMENT (GOVERNMENT CLAIMS ONLY) (SEE BACK) YES ☐ NO ☐ 30 YOUR SOCIAL SECURITY NO. | 27 TOTAL CHARGE | 28 AMOUNT PAID | 29 BALANCE DUE 31 PHYSICIAN'S SUPPLIER'S AND/OR GROUP NAME, ADDRESS, ZIP CODE AND TELEPHONE NO.

32 YOUR PATIENT'S ACCOUNT NO. | 33 YOUR EMPLOYER I.D. NO. | ID NO.

*PLACE OF SERVICE AND TYPE OF SERVICE (T.O.S.) CODES ON BACK REMARKS | APPROVED BY AMA COUNCIL ON MEDICAL SERVICE 6/83 FORM HCFA-1500 (1-84) FORM OWCP-1500 FORM CHAMPUS-501 (1-84) FORM RRB-1500 FORM AMA OP-501

Figure 11-1. Health insurance claim form used for submitting bills from physicians and other health care providers.

of 1985 (COBRA) requires companies employing 20 or more employees to offer employees insured under a group medical expense contract the opportunity to continue their group medical expense coverage after leaving the insured group. Likewise, those employers must offer an insured's dependents the opportunity for continued group coverage after a loss of coverage. COBRA provides that qualified members of an insured group or their dependents who lose group medical expense coverage because of certain qualifying events can elect to continue their group coverage for a limited time (18 or 36 months) by paying the required premium amount for group coverage. Qualifying events and the maximum amount of continuation coverage provided are listed below:

- 18 months for an employee or dependent who loses coverage due to the employee's termination of employment or reduction in hours; and
- 36 months for a dependent who loses coverage due to:
  o the insured employee's eligibility for Medicare
  o the death of the insured employee
  o a divorce or legal separation from the insured employee
  o the loss of dependent child status.

For COBRA purposes, termination of employment is the severance of the employer-employee relationship for any reason, other than for the employee's gross misconduct. Thus, termination includes voluntary resignations, strikes, walkouts, or layoffs.

To illustrate, assume that Irwin Goldstein resigns from a teaching position at State University in order to research and write a book. During the time he will be writing the book, he will not be employed and will, thus, have no medical expense coverage. Because of the COBRA mandate, Irwin can elect to continue the group medical expense insurance coverage provided by State University for 18 months by paying the required premium amount.

A qualified individual has a period of 60 days after notification of his or her eligibility for continuation coverage in which to decide to accept or decline it. This 60-day period is called the **election period**. The first premium payment is due within 45 days of the date continuation coverage is elected. The continuation coverage takes effect as of the date of the first qualifying event. COBRA also provides that a person who elects continuation coverage must again be eligible to convert to an individual policy within the usual conversion period (31 days) after the maximum 18- or 36-month continuation of group coverage ceases.

When an employee elects continuation coverage, the employee must complete an election form. The election form is then submitted to the insurer's billing department. The billing department enters the information from the election form into the computerized master file. The master file will then indicate that an insured is covered under COBRA continuation coverage and will also specify the date on which the insured's coverage will terminate.

Continuation coverage will terminate at the end of the maximum allowable period or upon the date that the

- insured fails to pay the required premium amount,
- employer terminates all group health plans it maintains,
- insured becomes covered under another group health plan, or
- insured becomes eligible for Medicare.

VERIFYING THE LOSS

Verifying that an insured has incurred a covered loss is a complex process because of the diversity in health factors that may give rise to a loss and because of the wide range of medical care providers. In addition to the required claim form, a claim examiner must have adequate proof that a loss was incurred. An original itemized receipt from a medical care provider which lists (1) a diagnosis, (2) a description of the types of expenses incurred, (3) the date on which these expenses were incurred, and (4) the provider of the medical care services is the generally accepted proof of loss. Original itemized receipts are required because photocopies can more easily be tampered with than originals.

Fraud

The Federal Trade Commission estimates that medical insurance fraud totals $10 billion annually in the United States. There are two major types of medical insurance fraud: individual fraud and provider fraud. *Individual fraud* is perpetrated by individuals on their own medical expense claims for the purpose of obtaining insurance benefits in excess of their medical expenses. *Provider fraud* is initiated by providers on patients' claims in order to increase their own income. Provider fraud may affect a far greater number of insurance payments than may an isolated individual who alters personal claims.

Individual Fraud

A claim examiner who is aware of what to look for can eliminate honest errors in claim submissions and can more readily detect possible fraudulent situations. A claim examiner may detect potential individual fraud situations by identifying the following characteristics in the submitted claims:

- alterations of bills—dates, charges, diagnoses, descriptions of services rendered. Correct information may be altered by correction fluid, different color ink, etc.
- fabrication of bills—similar handwriting by claimant and provider, a mixture of typed and handwritten charges on a given claim
- misspelled medical terms
- unusual charges for a given service
- photocopied bills, particularly those where the typed portion is clearer than the letterhead or preprinted items
- handwritten hospital bills
- unassigned bills that are normally assigned, such as large hospital or surgery bills as well as large bills that are marked "paid" in handwriting similar to that of the insured
- provider not in the same geographical area as the claimant
- absence of the provider's medical degree on a form
- lack of any provider's signature on a claim form
- absence of duplicate insurance coverage information when both an insured and spouse are employed

A claim examiner who observes one or more of these characteristics should be alert to the possibility of individual fraud.

Provider Fraud

Provider fraud may be more difficult for the claim examiner to identify because (1) providers often have access to computers that can be used to generate bills, (2) providers have knowledge of medical techniques and terminology that might not be questioned by the claim person, and (3) claimants who suspect provider fraud may not bring their suspicions to the insurer's attention because they are reluctant to accuse their physician or other medical care provider of wrongdoing. Nonetheless, common characteristics that might indicate potential provider fraud are

- advertisements of forgiveness of coinsurance payments, which means that the patient will not be responsible for paying to the provider the portion of a medical charge that the insurance company does not pay
- provider's address on the claim form is the same as that of the insured
- provider uses post office box as return address

- alteration of fees on bills that have been submitted for payment by the provider
- photocopied claim forms with benefit assignments to the provider
- charges submitted for payment for which there is no supporting documentation available, such as x-rays, lab results, etc.
- services charged for but not rendered, or excessive amounts charged for services; such discrepancies are often brought to the claim examiner's attention by claimants after reviewing their explanation of benefit statements
- unqualified individuals posing as licensed providers; a provider's licensing status can be verified by checking with the appropriate licensing agency

Fraud Investigations

If a claim examiner finds discrepancies in an insured's claim, the claim should be investigated further either to resolve the discrepancy or to provide enough evidence for prosecution of the claimant and/or provider. The claim examiner may request additional information from the provider or the insured. Figure 11–2 is a sample letter requesting medical information from a physician. If the receipt of additional information does not resolve the problem or if the information is not forthcoming, then the examiner probably will turn the file over to an investigative unit of the company or to a private investigative firm. In addition, once a questionable claim is identified, insurance companies who have automated systems will monitor electronically any further claims from the insured or the provider. Upon receipt of a full investigative report, the claim either will be payable or will be turned over to the company's legal department or claim committee for a decision as to whether to prosecute.

VERIFYING POLICY COVERAGE OF THE LOSS

After a claim examiner has determined that a policy is in force, that the insured is covered, and that a legitimate medical expense has been incurred by the insured, then the next step is for the claim examiner to verify that the insured's policy actually provided benefits for the medical expense. As we mentioned earlier, some insurers are able to enter standard benefit and plan data into an automated system. However, automation of all plans is not possible because of the tremendous variety of customized policy provisions that result from customer demand and union bargaining. Most companies keep a copy of the master group contract on file in the claim department to be used as a reference.

Personal & Confidential   April 1, 1989
Dr. Sam Wienstock
200 Doctors' Building
Harbor Cove, ME 02020

Re: Group Account No. 001
Insured: Ralph Dryden
Claimant: Ralph Dryden
Control No: 1001

Dear Dr. Wienstock:

We have received a Major Medical claim for the above claimant with a diagnosis of heart disease. In order to properly evaluate this claim we will need some additional information from you.

Did you treat this patient and/or prescribe any drugs or medicine for this condition or any other condition before February 1, 1989? If so, please list the dates of treatment and/or prescriptions and the diagnosis made on the lines below.

_____

_____

Has the patient been hospitalized for this or any other condition in the last five years? If so, please list the dates of confinement and the name(s) of the hospital(s) below.

_____

Was the patient aware that he had this or any other condition prior to February 1, 1989? If so, please state the basis for which you believe that the patient was aware on the lines below.

_____

_____

Was the patient referred to you by another physician? If so, please provide us with the name and address of that physician.

_____

_____

Please sign your name on the lines provided below.

Signed: _____

Date: _____

Thank you for taking the time to give us this information.

Sincerely,

Group Claim Division

Figure 11-2. Sample claim letter requesting medical information from a physician.

Hospital Procedures for Verifying Policy Coverage

Hospitals in a number of states require a statement of the benefits for which the patient is covered at the time of admission to the hospital, or, if the admission is on an emergency basis, as soon after admission as possible. Group health claim forms may contain a section which provides information about what benefits would be payable to the hospital under the group policy. If the group policy has a deductible feature, that too is shown. A group health claim form may be obtained from an employer prior to the hospital admission, or the hospital personnel may obtain the information necessary by a phone call to the employer or the insurance company.

BENEFITS PROVIDED BY MEDICAL EXPENSE COVERAGE

In Chapter 3, we introduced the major categories of medical expense coverage. The remainder of this chapter discusses the typical benefits provided by each type of coverage. However, before we proceed, we should note that the information presented relates to group medical expense coverage, because the overwhelming majority of health insurance in force is group insurance. In addition, since Canadians are covered by government programs that pay benefits to cover most types of medical treatment, the discussion that follows pertains to medical expense coverage in the United States.

Basic Hospital-Surgical-Medical Expense Coverage

As the name implies, this type of coverage consists of three distinct types of benefits: hospital expense benefits, surgical expense benefits, and medical expense benefits. In addition, other types of benefits may be added to this basic coverage.

Hospital Expense Benefits

Hospital expense benefits cover charges incurred by an insured who is an inpatient or, in some circumstances, an outpatient of a hospital. Every policy defines the term *hospital*. While the actual wording may vary, the following definition is typical:

> The institution must be accredited as a hospital under the hospital accreditation program of the Joint Commission on Accreditation of Hospitals, or the institution must be engaged in providing

diagnostic or therapeutic facilities for the medical diagnosis, treatment and care of injured and ill persons on an inpatient basis by or under the supervision of staff physicians and with continuous 24-hour nursing service by Registered Nurses. It cannot be, other than incidentally, a place of rest, place for the aged, or a nursing home.

In addition, other facilities can qualify as hospitals if certain state licensing and accreditation requirements are met. These facilities include

- clinics and doctors' offices,
- psychiatric institutions,
- tuberculosis sanatoriums,
- freestanding ambulatory surgical facilities (surgicenters), and
- Christian Science sanatoriums.

The hospital directory of the American Hospital Association provides a detailed description of the services offered and the classification (such as general or psychiatric) of each accredited hospital in the United States and Canada.

Basic hospital expense plans generally provide benefits to cover two types of services: daily room and board in the hospital and other hospital expenses of a medical nature.

Room and Board.   Room and board benefits usually cover the cost of the hospital room, meals, and any other services normally provided to all inpatients, including routine nursing care. Policies usually specify a maximum dollar amount of room charges that will be reimbursed. Occasionally, this limit applies only to private room accommodations; semiprivate and ward accommodations are paid in full. The maximum period of hospitalization covered by insurance varies from one policy to another. Some contracts provide coverage for an unlimited number of days, but more frequently a maximum is set that may vary from 30 days to 1 year. When dependent coverage is included, the time limit applies separately to each person covered.

Miscellaneous Hospital Expenses.   Hospital expenses other than room and board are commonly referred to as miscellaneous hospital charges, ancillary charges, or other hospital charges. Miscellaneous hospital expenses are certain services and supplies ordered by a physician during an insured's hospital stay such as drugs, operating room charges, and laboratory services. Reimbursement is typically made for all miscellaneous medical charges up to a specified dollar limit. Nonmedical charges, such as for a telephone or television, are not covered. Also excluded from this benefit are hospital charges for professional services, such as for the services of physicians and nurses.

At one time, the maximum miscellaneous hospital benefit was stated as a multiple of the room and board benefits. A common plan provided miscellaneous hospital benefits of up to ten times the room and board benefit. Thus, if such a plan had a $75 daily room and board benefit, the maximum miscellaneous hospital benefit would be $750. Today, the maximum is generally stated as a dollar amount without reference to the room and board benefit; some plans are written with unlimited miscellaneous hospital benefits.

When the insured is placed in an intensive care unit of a hospital, the daily room and board charge is substantially increased because of the constant care provided. Usually the patient is on the critical list of the hospital and has no choice as to the accommodations. Companies differ in their approach toward such intensive care unit charges. Some insurers consider charges in excess of the usual rate as being payable under miscellaneous hospital benefits. Others believe that the charges do not qualify under the miscellaneous hospital benefit because they are due to the professional care rendered by physicians and nurses. Some policies provide a separate benefit for charges of intensive care units.

Many policies also provide benefits for outpatient treatment including (1) treatment rendered within 48 hours of an accidental injury, (2) treatment for outpatient surgery, and (3) preadmission testing. The amount payable may be limited to the maximum available for miscellaneous charges or may be a specified flat amount. The outpatient treatment will count toward the policy's maximum benefit limit if the patient later enters the hospital for additional treatment for the same accident or sickness. Outpatient hospital expenses are usually not covered if the insured is treated nonsurgically for a sickness.

Exclusions and Limitations. All types of medical expense coverages are subject to various policy limitations and exclusions. Before a claim examiner can determine the benefits payable under any claim, the examiner must apply the provisions of the policy under which the claim was filed.

All of the types of coverages described in this chapter usually exclude expenses that result from

- injury or sickness resulting from war or from any act of war,
- intentional self-inflicted injury,
- injury or sickness covered under Workers' Compensation or occupational disease laws,
- cosmetic surgery, unless required by injury or necessary to correct

congenital defects of newborn children who are covered by the policy, and
- pre-existing conditions, although only for a limited time.

Two other exclusions—one excluding maternity-related expenses and one excluding services furnished by or on behalf of government agencies—may be used in medical expense contracts. Prior to 1978, when an amendment to the Civil Rights Act was passed by the U.S. Congress, employers often excluded maternity-related expenses from medical expense contracts. Now, however, employers with 15 or more employees are required to treat pregnancy, childbirth, and related conditions the same as any other illness. Employers with fewer than 15 employees may, and many still do, exclude maternity-related expenses.

Medical expense plans commonly exclude payment for services rendered in a Veterans' Administration or military hospital. Until 1985, a veteran and his or her dependents were under no obligation to pay for such services. However, in 1985, with the passage of COBRA, responsibility for some of these expenses was shifted from the government to private medical expense plans. In addition to requiring employers to make available health continuation coverage, COBRA also requires employer-provided health care plans to provide coverage for retired veterans and their dependents who are treated in Veterans Administration (VA) hospitals for non-service-related conditions.

In addition to these general exclusions that are often found in all types of medical expense coverages, other exclusions apply to specific types of basic medical insurance. Hospital expense insurance may exclude expenses that result from

- voluntary confinement for physical health examinations not related to a disease or injury,
- nontreatment items, such as telephone, television, guest trays, and other personal items not necessary for treatment of the patient,
- take-home drugs,
- private duty nurses, or
- custodial care that normally can be performed by nonmedical persons without direct supervision by a physician or registered nurse.

Surgical Expense Benefits

Surgical expense benefits cover a surgeon's charges incurred during surgery. Insurance policies typically define surgery as cutting, suturing, electrocauterization, removal of a stone or other foreign body, and the treatment of fractures or dislocations. Traditionally, benefits were provided for surgery performed in conjunction with hospitalization. Today, however, to discourage unnecessary hospitalization, basic surgical benefits are often paid for outpatient surgery performed in an ambulatory surgical center or a physician's office.

Surgery benefits are usually paid according to either a surgical schedule or the reasonable and customary charges for the procedure performed.

A **surgical schedule** lists common surgical procedures and the maximum benefit amount the insurer will pay for each procedure. If the actual charge is greater than that listed in the surgical schedule, then the insured must pay the difference. If a surgical procedure is not included on the schedule, the amount that will be allowed for the unlisted procedure will be determined from publications which list the relative values for different surgical procedures, or through consultation with the insurance company's medical department or with medical consultants. These consultants will equate the unlisted procedure with one of similar difficulty that is listed on the schedule.

Although surgery benefits can be paid on the basis of a schedule, many policies provide for reimbursement on another basis. A **reasonable and customary charge** represents the charge most frequently made by surgeons of similar specialization and experience in a given geographical area for a specified surgical procedure. Reasonable and customary charges are usually determined from a database that identifies the cost of each procedure or service in various regions of the country. For example, if a statistical analysis indicates that 90 percent of all surgeons in the Northwest charge $1,000 or less for an appendectomy, then the maximum reasonable and customary charge for an appendectomy in the Northwest would be $1,000. Any amount charged over $1,000 would not be considered a covered expense under the medical expense plan. Schedules of maximum reasonable and customary charges are adjusted periodically to reflect changes in physicians' charges.

Exclusions and Limitations.   Surgical expense insurance may exclude charges that result from

- services performed by a resident physician or intern of a hospital;
- dental work or oral surgery except as specified in the policy;
- operating physician's charges for postoperative care or preoperative care;
- supplies furnished by an operating physician in connection with an actual surgical operation performed outside a hospital; and
- assistant surgeon's charges, unless the total charges from both the primary and assistant surgeons are within a scheduled benefit for the procedure.

Basic hospital and surgical policies usually include a **maximum benefits for related confinements provision**. This provision limits the maximum benefits for all hospital confinements and for all surgery performed during one period of sickness or for any single injury. For example, successive periods of hospital confinements are considered to occur during one period of sickness if there are two or more separate confinements within less than six full months for the same illness, or a related illness. Successive confinements for different illnesses are considered separate periods of sickness. All confinements and all surgical procedures resulting from the same accident are subject to one policy maximum for that accident. These rules are summarized in Figure 11–3. The following

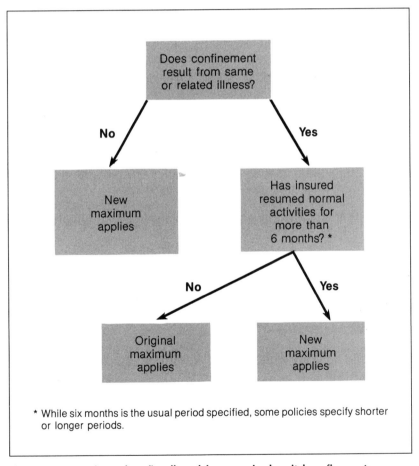

* While six months is the usual period specified, some policies specify shorter or longer periods.

Figure 11-3. **Maximum benefits allowed for succesive hospital confinements.**

example illustrates the application of this provision:

> Lucy Bennett is covered by a policy that allows $100 per day for room and board for up to 60 days, up to $1,000 for miscellaneous charges, and up to $2,000 for surgery. Lucy suffers a kidney disorder, enters a hospital, and undergoes a nephrectomy. Lucy is hospitalized for 40 days; the eligible miscellaneous charges exceed the $1,000 maximum; the surgical schedule allows $1,500 for a nephrectomy.

In this case, Lucy's policy will pay $4,000 in room and board charges ($100 x 40 days), $1,000 for miscellaneous charges, and $1,500 for the surgery. If Lucy reenters the hospital within 6 months of discharge for treatment of the same or a related condition, policy benefits will be limited to the remaining 20 days of room and board and benefits of up to $500 for surgery. No benefits will be available for miscellaneous charges. However, if the second confinement is for an unrelated condition, Lucy will be eligible for the policy's maximum benefits. Policy provisions vary greatly, of course. Some provide for longer or shorter periods between confinements and for the imposition of a new maximum.

Medical Expense Benefits

Medical expense benefits, also referred to as physicians' visits expense benefits, provide benefits for physicians' services and sometimes for diagnostic testing.

Physicians' Services.   Medical expense insurance provides benefits relating to the expenses of treatments performed by physicians other than surgeons. Benefits are generally payable in specified amounts for non-surgical treatment in a hospital, as well as for the expense of home or office visits. Policy benefits are usually based on a *reasonable and customary* charge rather than on scheduled amounts.

Diagnostic Tests.   Diagnostic testing, including x-rays, and laboratory services are often covered. Reimbursement is provided up to the limit of the contract when the testing and laboratory services are done as part of the diagnosis of disease or injury. Such tests and services are usually not covered when they are a part of routine physical examinations. However, symptoms of an illness or a suspected injury usually justify such testing, so the expense would be covered in such cases.

Exclusions and Limitations.   Medical expense insurance may exclude charges that result from

- treatment rendered by hospital employees;

- preventive treatment, such as inoculations and vaccinations;
- routine dental work or treatment, eye examinations, and fitting of glasses; and
- diagnostic x-rays.

Other Benefits

Many other benefits can be purchased to supplement the basic hospital-surgical-medical coverage including extended care benefits, home health care benefits, hospice benefits, prescription drug benefits, and vision care benefits. Dental benefits, which are one of the most popular supplemental benefits, are the subject of Chapter 13.

Extended Care Benefits. Often a hospitalized patient will not need the full level of medical care provided by a hospital but still will require a certain minimal level of medical care. Extended care facilities are designed to provide this minimal level of medical care at a lower cost than the hospital facility can provide. Extended care coverage pays for expenses incurred while the insured is an inpatient in an extended care facility (ECF). The usual policy wording defines an ECF as an institution or part thereof that

- provides room and board and skilled nursing care 24 hours a day, including a regular professional nurse and other nursing personnel needed to provide adequate medical care, under the full-time supervision of a licensed physician or registered nurse;
- has available the services of a licensed physician under an established agreement;
- complies with all applicable legal requirements and maintains adequate medical records;
- is not used principally for the treatment of alcoholism or drug addiction; and
- is not, except incidentally, a place for the aged or a hotel.

Extended care coverage typically pays room and board expenses up to a specified maximum. For example, one-half the daily room and board benefit of the policy might be paid for each day that a covered person is a resident inpatient in an ECF. Most policies set a maximum benefit period such as 60 days per calendar year for ECF benefits. Typically, an ECF stay must commence within 14 days after termination of a specified period of hospital confinement, and the ECF confinement must be for the same cause as that for which the insured was in the hospital.

Home Health Care. Home health care coverage provides that

home health care may be utilized in lieu of residency in an ECF. Home health care is usually defined as a formal program of care and treatment that is

- performed in the home of a covered person discharged from a hospital;
- prescribed by a physician as medically necessary and intended to result in a shortened hospital confinement;
- not available from members of the covered person's family; and
- organized and administered by, and under the direct supervision of, a hospital or Home Health Care Agency.

The home health care benefit usually covers the services of registered nurses or licensed practical nurses, as well as the medical services and supplies provided by a hospital at the insured's home. In addition, physical, occupational, and speech therapy are usually covered.

Benefits are usually limited either to a maximum number of visits or to a period of time such as 90 days. Several states have mandated policy coverage of home health care programs and treatment.

Hospice Benefits.   Although few plans currently cover hospice care, policyholders have shown widespread interest in such coverage. Hospice treatments can produce savings in the range of 20 to 30 percent over hospital-based treatments. **Hospice care** is designed to ease the physical and psychological pain associated with a terminal illness rather than to cure the illness. In addition to providing medical care for the dying patient, a hospice offers counseling to the patient and to family members. Most hospice care benefits pay for additional home care or hospice facility care, drugs, therapy, and family counseling.

Prescription Drug Plans.   The costs of prescription drugs prescribed for a patient while in a hospital are usually covered under the basic hospital/surgical coverage. However, other prescription drugs are not covered unless the insured has a separate prescription drug benefit. About 97 percent of full-time participants in basic medical expense plans at medium and large employers have prescription drug benefits for outpatient prescription drugs. A prescription drug benefit plan generally provides benefits only for drugs that are prescribed by a licensed physician for the treatment of illness or injury.

Vision Care Plans.   Basic hospital-surgical-medical coverages provide medical care for eye injury or disease. In addition, an insured may have a vision care benefit that will provide benefits for the costs of eyeglasses or contact lenses and sometimes for the cost of routine eye examinations. Vision care is most often covered on a scheduled basis that pays a fixed dollar amount for eye examinations, lenses, and eyeglass frames. The plan usually specifies the frequency of examinations and lens replacements.

Major Medical Insurance

Major medical insurance provides comprehensive protection for medical care expenditures. Major medical coverage can be provided through either (1) a superimposed major medical plan or (2) a comprehensive major medical plan. A *superimposed major medical plan* is coordinated with various basic medical expense coverages and provides benefits for expenses that exceed these coverages. Covered medical expenses not reimbursed under the basic plan are covered under the medical plan, subject to deductible and coinsurance requirements payable by the claimant. A *comprehensive major medical plan* covers virtually all types of medical expenses through a single major medical contract. A comprehensive plan applies one overall reimbursement formula to the total of covered expenses. Major medical plans, either of the superimposed or the comprehensive type, provide a wide range of benefits. The maximum benefit available is rarely less than $250,000 and often may be $1 million or even an unlimited maximum benefit. Major medical plans generally provide coverage for

- hospital expenses (with a limit on private-room expenses);
- fees of surgeons, physicians, and anesthetists;
- prescription drugs and medicines;
- radiology;
- physiotherapy;
- private-duty nursing care;
- laboratory fees;
- oxygen; and
- the rental of durable medical equipment such as wheelchairs.

Major medical insurance has not traditionally provided coverage for stays in extended care facilities, for hospice care, or for home health care. However, more major medical plans are now including such coverage.

Psychiatric Benefits

Major medical insurance generally provides coverage for psychiatric treatment given while a patient is either in or out of a hospital. Psychiatric treatment is generally defined as "treatment or care for a mental or emotional disease or disorder, or functional nervous disorder."

The benefit for psychiatric treatment given while the covered person is in a qualified hospital is typically 80 percent of covered psychiatric expenses in excess of the deductible up to a maximum number of days. Benefits for out-patient psychiatric treatment are typically 50 percent of covered expenses, subject to a maximum of $1,000 per calendar year. Other plans may specify a per visit psychiatric benefit or no benefit at all for out-patient services.

Exclusions and Limitations

Although major medical insurance provides broad coverage for necessary expenses, there are a few common exclusions for charges arising from

- transportation from one hospital to another solely for reasons of convenience;
- transportation in a public conveyance that does not have medical facilities;
- shoes purchased from a shoe store even though used as part of a leg brace;
- routine vision care and examinations, refractions performed in order to prescribe eyeglasses, and the cost of eyeglasses (these costs may be covered if required as the result of an accidental bodily injury);
- hearing aids; and
- experimental treatments, including drug treatments.

Medical Necessity

Most major medical expense plans include a **medical necessity provision** which states that medical services that are educational or experimental in nature are not covered. A claim examiner who suspects that a treatment is actually experimental or educational will submit the claim for benefits to the insurer's medical consultant who may seek information from an outside agency such as the Food and Drug Administration.

The medical necessity provision can be important in the payment of AIDS claims. At the present time, there is no known cure for AIDS. Thus, a claim for any treatment purporting to cure the disease would most likely be denied by a claim examiner as experimental in nature. Treatments that are not generally accepted by the medical community would probably be considered experimental. However, medical treatment designed to arrest the various medical conditions that are part of the AIDS syndrome, such as pneumonia or cancer, would generally be considered as medically necessary, and, as such, would routinely be paid by claim examiners.

References

"Automated Claims," *1982 ICA Group Insurance Workshop Notes*, 1–29.

"Automated Claim Systems," *1980 ICA Group Insurance Workshop Notes*, 1–10.

"Automation of Individual Medical Claim Payments," *1985 ICA Individual Health Insurance Workshop Notes*, 119–121.

"Fraud Identification," *ICA Claim Investigation Handbook*, 1987, 1/1–1/3.

"Fraud: Provider Abuse," *1987 ICA Group Insurance Workshop Notes*, 5–6.

Matter, Roxanna. "The Impact of COBRA and TRA'86 on Group Insurance," *Group Insurance Readings*, 1988, 1–16.

Nielson, Norma L. "Group Medical Expense Provisions and the AIDS Crisis," *Benefits Quarterly*, (Vol. IV, No. 1), 1988, 5.

Parks, Michael. "Medical Fraud on Uprise in Washington," *National Underwriter, P & C*, November 16, 1987, 26.

Vadakin, II, Charles and Lipton, Zelda. *The Health Insurance Answer Book*. Greenvale, NY: Panel Publishers, Inc., 1986, 56–57.

Young, John Hardin and Pannell, Susan J. "New Fangs on Cobra," *Best's Review Life/Health Insurance Edition*, August 1987.

12

Paying
Medical Expense Claims

Once the examination of a medical expense claim is complete, the claim
examiner is responsible for payment of the appropriate benefit amount
to the proper party. In this chapter, we describe the payment of the medical
expense benefit and the various methods companies use to calculate
benefits payable. We explain how benefits are coordinated between two
insurers or between an insurer and a government program. Finally, we
discuss programs such as utilization review and case management that are
designed to promote high quality medical care while ensuring greater control of medical costs.

METHODS USED TO CALCULATE THE
BENEFIT PAYMENT

Although medical expense benefits vary extensively according to the type
of coverage involved, insurers typically use one of three methods to determine the amount of medical expense benefits payable. One method involves the use of a schedule that lists various medical procedures or services and the maximum amount payable for each procedure. Another

method sets a maximum limit on the dollar amount of coverage or on the number of days of coverage. A third method sets benefit levels based on reasonable and customary charges for the medical treatment involved. All of these methods of payment were discussed in Chapter 11.

Such methods of paying benefits are known as **retrospective payment methods** because they provide benefits after costs are incurred by the insured. Retrospective payment methods encourage hospitals and physicians to provide the maximum level of care to a patient, but they provide no incentive for an insured or medical care provider to cut or control medical expenses.

Diagnostic Related Groups (DRGs)

In 1983, Medicare, a two-part federal insurance program that provides medical expense benefits for qualified persons over age 65 and for certain classes of disabled persons, stopped using a retrospective payment method and introduced a prospective payment system, called **diagnostic related groups (DRGs)**. Under this new system, the amount Medicare will pay to a hospital is based not on the number and kinds of medical services, but on the diagnosis of each patient. Proponents hope that the DRG system will encourage cost-effective care because if the care delivered by a hospital is less than the DRG-allowed sum, the hospital makes a profit. Conversely, if the care provided by the hospital exceeds the amount reimbursed, then the hospital will lose money.

DRGs classify all types of medical conditions into major diagnostic categories (MDCs). Figure 12–1 shows the 23 MDCs used in the Medicare system. Each MDC is broken down into its DRG components, of which the Medicare system uses 467. Each of the 467 components is split according to a specific operating procedure, the age of the patient, the sex of the patient, and the likely discharge date of the patient. DRGs are further refined to take into account **outliers**, patients whose illnesses are unique and whose conditions may not be classifiable under one of the DRGs. Payment of expenses incurred by outliers is handled on an individual basis.

DRG rates are based on a patient's probable usage of hospital resources. In other words, a patient is fitted into a DRG category which presupposes a consumption of a certain dollar amount of hospital services. Each DRG is weighted to reflect the probable cost of services incurred. For example, care of a newborn (DRG 391) is weighted .2218, which indicates low utilization of drugs and staff. In comparison, care of a premature newborn (DRG 386) is weighted 3.640, indicating a much higher utilization of hospital staff and services.

Effect of DRGs on Insurance Companies

The use of DRGs is not limited to the Medicare Program. New York, New

Major Diagnostic Categories

1. Diseases & Disorders of the Nervous System
2. Diseases & Disorders of the Eye
3. Diseases & Disorders of the Ear, Nose & Throat
4. Diseases & Disorders of the Respiratory System
5. Diseases & Disorders of the Circulatory System
6. Diseases & Disorders of the Digestive System
7. Diseases & Disorders of the Hepatobiliary System
8. Diseases of the Musculoskeletal System and Connective Tissue
9. Diseases of the Skin, Subcutaneous and Breast
10. Endocrine, Nutritional, and Metabolic Diseases
11. Diseases & Disorders of the Kidney and Urinary Tract
12. Diseases & Disorders of the Male Reproductive System
13. Diseases & Disorders of the Female Reproductive System
14. Pregnancy, Childbirth, and the Puerperium
15. Normal Newborns & Other Neonates with Conditions in the Perinatal Period
16. Diseases & Disorders of the Blood and Blood-forming Organs and Immunities
17. Myeloproliferative Disorders & Poorly Differentiated Malignancy & Other Neoplasm NEC
18. Infections and Parasitic Diseases
19. Mental Disorders
20. Substance Use Disorders and Substance Induced Organic Disorders
21. Injury, Poisoning, and Toxic Effects of Drugs
22. Burns
23. Selected Factors influencing Health Status & Contact with Health Services

Figure 12-1.   Medicare's 23 major Diagnostic Related Groups (DRGs).

Jersey, and Connecticut have passed legislation which specifies that certain acute care hospitals must use the DRG system to calculate hospital charges for all payers, not just Medicare participants. Other states such as Arizona, while not mandating DRG billing, will set rates and regulate hospitals that choose to bill on a DRG basis.

The long-term ramifications of DRGs on insurers' claim procedures are not yet known. At this time, insurers are aware of several potential problems. First, the medical coding of an insured's condition is to some degree discretionary. For example, assume that a patient is admitted to a hospital and is diagnosed with lung cancer. While hospitalized the patient receives a full treatment of chemotherapy and one dosage of radiation therapy. The hospital could code this case as DRG 082—respiratory neoplasms, DRG

409—admission for radiotherapy, or DRG 410—admission for chemotherapy. Average DRG payments for DRG 082 would be $8,408.80; for DRG 409, $6,050.80; and for DRG 410, $3,332.40. Obviously, the hospitals might tend to report the most remunerative diagnosis as the DRG diagnosis.

Insurers who wish to monitor DRG payments must develop a DRG validation program to look at unsubstantiated second diagnoses, or a designation of a principal diagnosis without a clear medical basis. If an insurer has a preadmission program, a preliminary DRG may be assigned by the insurer at the preadmission stage to be compared at a later date with the actual DRG assigned to the claim by the hospital. If a large discrepancy exists between the two, the claim warrants a more extensive DRG validation.

Another potential problem with the DRG system is that it could encourage doctors and hospitals to discharge patients too early in the recovery period. In a DRG system, a hospital's financial interest dictates that a patient leave as soon as is medically possible. Insurers need to monitor medical claims to ensure that an early discharge from a hospital does not later result in medical complications that require further treatment.

Finally, there is concern that hospitals are engaged in cost shifting the revenue they lose from Medicare DRGs to privately-insured individuals. Many insurers suggest the introduction of an all-payer system under which all providers of medical benefits are charged for medical services on a DRG basis.

ADJUSTMENTS TO THE AMOUNT PAYABLE

The amount of the benefit payment that results from the claim examiner's initial calculations is not necessarily the amount that will be paid to the insured. The amount of the benefit payment may be reduced if there is a deductible amount outstanding or if a coordination of benefits (COB) provision applies.

Deductibles

Basic coverages often reimburse an insured for the first dollar of incurred medical expenses. Thus, most basic coverages have no deductible. The type of deductible included in major medical coverages depends upon whether the coverage is comprehensive or superimposed. Comprehensive major medical plans typically use an initial deductible, which is the simplest type of deductible specified and is the type of deductible described thus far in this textbook. The *initial deductible*, also called the cash deductible, is a fixed amount that the insured must pay before any insurance benefits are payable for covered expenses.

Superimposed major medical plans typically use either a corridor or an integrated deductible. A **corridor deductible** is a fixed amount (e.g., $100) that an insured must pay after exhausting his or her basic medical expense benefits before major medical benefits are payable. For example, assume that Judy Jillian incurs $5,000 of covered medical expenses. Her basic insurance coverage provides first-dollar coverage and pays $2,500. Her major medical coverage includes a $100 corridor deductible and a 20 percent coinsurance requirement. Therefore, Judy must pay a $100 corridor deductible before her major medical plan will pay 80 percent of the remaining $2,400 in medical expenses.

An **integrated deductible** is a fixed amount (typically $500 or more) that an insured must pay for medical expenses before major medical coverage can begin. The amounts paid by the basic coverage can be used to satisfy the integrated deductible. Referring back to our earlier example, if Judy had had an integrated deductible of $500, then her deductible would have been satisfied by the amount paid in basic benefits.

Most deductibles are classified as **all-cause deductibles** because the deductible amount must be satisfied only once per benefit period regardless of the cause of the claims. However, a policy may include a **per-cause deductible**, which states that a separate deductible must be satisfied for each injury or illness per benefit period.

Most medical expense policies also include a **carry-over provision**, which provides that expenses incurred during the last three months of the benefit period, typically a calendar year, which are used to satisfy the current benefit period's deductible, may be used to satisfy any or all of the following benefit period's deductible. For example, assume that Jackson Millhouse, insured under a group medical expense plan with a calendar year benefit period, satisfied $75 of his $200 deductible requirement for 1987 in August of 1987. In December of 1987, Jackson submits eligible claims totalling $1,000 which were incurred in November of 1987. In such a case, $125 can be applied to satisfy the balance of the 1987 deductible, and an additional $125 can be applied to the 1988 deductible, leaving only $75 of the deductible to be satisfied in 1988.

In addition, most major medical coverages include a **common accident provision**, which states that if an insured and one or more of his or her covered dependents are injured in the same accident, only one individual deductible amount will be taken from the total expenses incurred as a result of the accident. This provision is applicable only to contracts that do not include a **waiver of deductible provision**, which waives the application of an initial deductible if a claimant incurs expenses resulting from accidental injury.

Coordination of Benefits Provision

Coordination of benefits (COB) provisions are designed to ensure that an

insured covered under more than one medical expense plan will not collect more in benefit payments than the medical expenses incurred. A COB
provision defines the primary provider of benefits in situations in which
the insured has duplicate medical expense coverage and specifies how
benefits are reduced for secondary providers of benefits.

Order of Benefit Determination

The primary provider of benefits is responsible for paying the full benefits
promised under the policy. The secondary provider of benefits will then
determine the amount payable under the terms of its coverage. The following rules are used to determine which insurer is primary and which is secondary for COB purposes:

- If one of the two plans under which an insured is covered does
  not have a COB provision, then that plan is the primary provider of benefits.
- If an insured is covered as an employee under one plan and as a
  dependent under another plan, the plan covering the insured as
  an employee is the primary provider of benefits.

There are two rules relating to dependent children covered under both
parents' group plans. One rule, in existence since the creation of COB provisions, states that an employer's plan insuring the male parent of dependent children is primary to a plan insuring the female parent. Large
employers of predominantly male employees object to this gender rule
because of the burden such a rule places on their group health insurance
plans. In 1985, the NAIC recommended that insurers change their COB
provisions from the gender rule to the birthday rule. The **birthday rule**
states that when a dependent child is covered under separate plans of each
parent, the plan covering the parent whose birthday (month and day) falls
earlier in the year is primary to the plan of the parent whose birthday falls
later in that year. When both parents have the same birthday, the plan which
has covered a parent longer is primary to the other plan. In the majority
of states, insurers are required by law to use the birthday rule.

However, if the parents are separated or divorced, then special coordination of benefits rules apply. If a court decree sets responsibility for the
child's health care, then the plan that covers the child as a dependent of
the parent with such responsibility will be required to pay its benefits before
any other plan that covers the dependent child. For example, both Debbie
Knapp and her former spouse, Charles Knapp, have group medical expense
insurance. Debbie has custody of their son, Tom. Both parents have elected
to purchase dependent group medical expense coverage for their son, and
Charles is under a court order to provide major medical health insurance

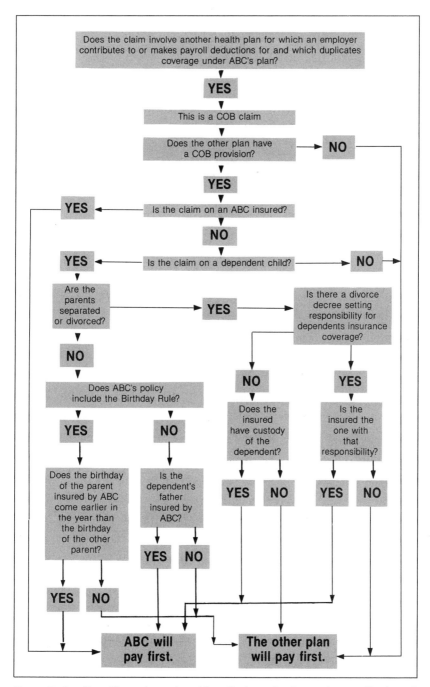

Figure 12-2.   Chart illustrating order of benefit determination under coordination of benefits.

for Tom. For COB purposes, Charles' insurance is the primary carrier, and Debbie's is the secondary carrier. In situations similar to this one, the claim examiner should request a copy of the divorce decree to resolve any discrepancies.

If the divorce decree does not specify which parent is responsible for maintaining health care, and if the parent with custody of the child has not remarried, then the plan of the parent with custody will pay its benefits before the plan of the parent without custody. Assume in our previous example that the Knapp's divorce decree did not provide for Tom's medical care; since Debbie has not remarried, her insurance carrier is the primary provider of benefits.

However, if the parent with custody has remarried, then the order of benefit determination is as follows:

1. Parent with custody
2. Step-parent with custody
3. Parent without custody

Computation of Benefits under COB

Historically, COB provisions have limited the combined payments of two insurers to "not more than 100 percent reimbursement of actual covered charges incurred." To illustrate, assume the following information:

> Shelton Bains is insured under his employer-sponsored group insurance plan and is also insured as a dependent under his wife's employer-sponsored group plan. Shelton's employer-sponsored plan specifies an 80 percent coinsurance percentage and a $100 deductible. His wife's plan provides for a 75 percent coinsurance percentage and a $100 deductible. Both plans have COB provisions.

Shelton incurs $500 of covered medical expenses. His plan, which is the primary plan, pays $320 [($500−$100) x .80]. If there were no COB provision, his wife's plan would pay $300 [($500−$100) x .75] and Shelton would receive $120 over the cost of his actual medical expenses [($320+$300) −$500]. However, because of the COB provision, his wife's plan, the secondary provider of benefits, pays only $180, which is the total amount of his incurred medical expenses ($500) less the amount paid by the primary carrier ($320).

Although COB provisions ensure that an insured does not profit from an accident or illness, these provisions still reimburse an insured for 100 percent of incurred medical expenses. Because of this 100 percent reimbursement level, COB provisions are frequently criticized for eliminating the cost containment advantages of coinsurance percentages and deductible amounts. In 1984, the NAIC recommended that states allow insurers to reduce benefits to a level below 100 percent of allowable expenses. As a result of the NAIC recommendation, several states now allow insurers to use one of the following two methods for coordinating benefit payments. Both of these methods result in less than 100 percent of all allowable expenses being reimbursed.

The first method allows the secondary plan to pay the difference between some percentage (typically 80 percent) of total allowable expenses actually incurred and the amount that was paid by the primary provider. In the preceding example, the total allowable expenses incurred were $500. Eighty percent of $500 is $400. Since the primary carrier paid $320, the secondary carrier is liable for $80 ($400–$320).

The second method, often called the nonduplication of benefits provision, allows the secondary carrier to pay the difference, if any, between the amount paid by the primary plan and the amount that would have been payable by the secondary plan had that plan been the primary plan. If, in the previous example, the secondary plan included a nonduplication of benefits provision, then no secondary benefit would have been payable because the amount paid by the primary plan ($320) exceeded the amount that would have been payable by the secondary plan ($300), had the secondary plan been the primary provider of coverage.

In order to use one of these two methods, the plan must comply with the following NAIC rules:

- Plan participants must be given notice of the COB change before it is implemented so that they can discontinue duplicate coverage under one of the plans.
- The plan must allow a person who is eligible for coverage under the plan but who is not enrolled because the person has coverage under another group plan, to enroll if that person's coverage under the other group plan terminates for any reason.

In addition, a plan using a nonduplication of benefits provision *cannot* (1) cover less than 50 percent of the expenses associated with mental or nervous disorders or alcohol and drug abuse treatments, (2) reduce benefits to less than 50 percent for a person who fails to obtain or follow cost containment provisions such as obtaining second surgical opinions, and (3) cover less than 75 percent of all other covered expenses, except for dental care, vision care, hearing care, or prescription care.

Coordination of Benefits with Alternate Providers

In addition to the medical expense benefits provided by traditional insurance plans, medical expense benefits may be provided by health maintenance organizations or a variety of government-sponsored benefit programs. When an insured is covered under an insurer-provided benefit plan and also under an alternate benefit plan, the insurer will coordinate benefits with the other plan.

Health Maintenance Organizations

A *Health Maintenance Organization (HMO)* is an organization that provides health care on a prepaid basis to subscribing members. HMOs are an approach to health care that has gained popularity in recent years. Subscribers of the HMO must obtain their medical care from providers who either are salaried employees of the HMO or have contracted with the HMO to treat HMO subscribers. When a subscriber is treated by an HMO provider, the subscriber is not charged for the cost of the service but may be responsible for paying a small, two- to five-dollar co-payment.

HMOs are unique in that they are both providers of benefits and insurers of benefits. This unique characteristic complicates the COB process. If an individual, covered under an HMO and also as a dependent under a family member's group medical expense policy, submits the co-payment charge to the insurer as a claim, coordination of benefits is seldom involved. The insurer would consider the co-payment charge from the HMO to be the medical care provider's charge for the service. Such a claim would be subject to applicable coinsurance and/or deductible provisions.

However, assume that the individual in our previous example is referred to a non-HMO facility (usually a specialist), or that an emergency necessitates that the individual go to a non-HMO facility. In such a case, the HMO will act as an insurer and pay a portion of the medical expense charges incurred by the individual. If the insured submits a claim to the insurer for the medical expenses not paid by the HMO, then the insurer must determine how to coordinate benefits with the HMO. For example, assume that a non-HMO physician charges an insured $75 for emergency services. The HMO pays $50 of the insured's expenses. The insurance company receives a claim for medical expenses totalling $25 ($75 minus the HMO payment of $50).

In order to coordinate benefits between the insurer and the HMO, the claim examiner must first determine if the $50 HMO payment qualifies as a basic benefit under the insurance company's group major medical policy. If the insured's employer funds any part of the insured's membership in the HMO, or if the employer makes payroll deductions for the insured's premium payment, then the $50 HMO payment may well qualify as a basic benefit. In such cases, the insurer's major medical would provide coverage for all benefits not covered by the basic benefits and would thus pay the remaining $25 charge.

If the HMO's $50 payment does not qualify as a basic benefit, then the claim examiner must determine who is the primary provider of benefits. If the HMO has no coordination of benefits provision, then the insurance company will assume a secondary position and will pay accordingly. If the HMO does have a coordination of benefits provision, then the claim examiner must apply the appropriate order of benefit determination rule discussed previously to determine who is the primary and who is the secondary provider of benefits.

Medicare

Medicare was created in 1965 by amendment to the Social Security Act. One part of the program (Part A) provides basic hospital insurance for persons entitled to Social Security or Railroad retirement benefits. In addition, state and federal government workers who have worked a specified length of time and certain classes of disabled workers are eligible for benefits. Insured individuals support the Medicare program through compulsory payroll taxes.

Until 1983, most medical expense policies terminated an insured's group coverage when the insured became eligible for Medicare coverage. An amendment to the Age Discrimination in Employment Act, passed in 1983, made it discriminatory for an employer with 20 or more employees to discontinue employee benefits for workers age 65 or older. Thus, employers with 20 or more employees must now provide medical expense coverage for their active employees age 65 or older and for such employees' spouses who are eligible for Medicare.

Employees who are eligible for Medicare can choose to participate only in their employer's plan, only in the Medicare plan, or in both plans. If they choose to participate only in the Medicare plan, then the employer-provided coverage may be cancelled as of the day Medicare coverage is elected. If they choose to participate in both plans, benefits are coordinated between the private group medical expense plan and the Medicare plan to avoid duplicate coverage. In situations in which an employee works for an employer with 20 or more employees and participates in both Medicare and the company's medical expense plan, the employer's group medical expense plan is the primary provider of benefits and the Medicare plan is the secondary provider of benefits. If an employee works for an employer with fewer than 20 employees, then Medicare is the primary provider of benefits and the private insurance is secondary.

Sometimes employers may wish to continue medical expense coverage on retired employees who are age 65 or older. These retired employees are not protected by the provisions of the Age Discrimination in Employment Act. In such situations, either a Medicare carve-out or a Medicare supplement is used to avoid duplicate coverage.

Medicare carve-out coverage reduces medical expense benefits payable by the group plan to the extent that those benefits are payable under Medicare. For example, assume that Margaret Miller, a retired employee of ABCO, Inc., incurs $750 of covered expenses. ABCO's group plan would pay $520 in the absence of any Medicare coverage. However, Medicare reimburses $450 of Margaret's expenses. Therefore, her ABCO group coverage will pay only $70, which is the difference between the benefit that would have been payable by the group coverage and the Medicare benefit.

Medicare supplement coverage provides benefits for certain expenses not covered under Medicare. In addition, a Medicare supplement usually pays a portion of any deductibles or coinsurance payments required by Medicare.

Civilian Health and Medical Program of the Uniformed Services

The Civilian Health and Medical Program of the Uniformed Services (CHAMPUS) is a medical benefits program provided by the United States federal government. CHAMPUS provides broad medical expense coverage for the following individuals:

- spouses and dependent children of active-duty military personnel;
- spouses and dependent children of persons who died while on active duty;
- spouses and dependent children of retired military personnel;
- surviving spouses and dependent children of deceased retired military personnel;
- retired military personnel; and
- spouses and dependent children of persons having a service-connected 100 percent disability, as certified by the Veterans Administration.

CHAMPUS provides benefits for both inpatient and outpatient hospital services and for medical services rendered by physicians. Benefit amounts are based on reasonable and customary fees for such services. CHAMPUS also provides benefits for care of mentally retarded children and any seriously physically handicapped spouse or children of active-duty military personnel.

Legislation effective in 1982 provides that no CHAMPUS funds "shall be available for the payment for any service or supply for persons enrolled in other insurance, medical service, or health plan to the extent that the service or supply is a benefit under the other plan . . . ." In other words, CHAMPUS is a secondary payer to all other insurance plans.

Workers' Compensation Programs

Laws mandating Workers' Compensation insurance have been enacted in all states in the United States. Workers' Compensation insurance provides benefits for work-related injuries or illnesses. Benefits are statutorily established by each state legislature and are periodically reviewed for adequacy. For work-related injuries or illnesses, Workers' Compensation provides 100 percent reimbursement for medical treatment, physical therapy, prescriptions, and orthopedic appliances. In addition, temporary or permanent disability benefits are provided if necessary and will be discussed in Chapter 14.

Most group medical expense contracts exclude coverage for work-related injuries or illnesses that are covered by Workers' Compensation. Sometimes, however, claim examiners are not notified that a claim has been filed with Workers' Compensation, or an insured worker may not be aware that a claim is eligible for coverage under Workers' Compensation. Thus, claim examiners typically investigate all claims that are obviously work-related, as well as any claims for accidents, cancer, heart disease, respiratory problems, and anxiety, which may be work-related. To avoid charges of bad faith during an investigation, insurers may proceed with the payment of any benefits due under the group insurance contract. Later, if the facts show that the insured is eligible for coverage under the Workers' Compensation system or is receiving duplicate payments from the Workers' Compensation system, the insurer can attempt to collect the benefit amounts from the Workers' Compensation system or the insured.

Detection of Duplicate Coverage

Insurance industry experts estimate that 30 percent of the medical coverage written today is duplicate coverage. Of this 30 percent, only 10 percent is detected by insurance companies and thus subject to coordination of benefits provisions. The other 20 percent of the duplicate coverage goes undetected and costs the industry billions of dollars annually in unnecessary benefit payments.

Automated detection systems present a great opportunity for insurers to discover duplicate coverage. Under such a system, insurers sharing a common data base can identify duplicate claims through the computer network. However, automated systems are still in the introductory stages of development. Currently, the majority of duplicate coverage information must be obtained through either correspondence or communication with the group policyholder, the insured, the provider of medical care, or another insurance company.

In most instances, duplicate coverage is identified from the information provided by the insured on the claim form. If an insured's spouse is employed, the odds are good that the spouse has coverage provided by his or her employer. Most claim forms include a question regarding other coverages that an insured might have in force. If an insured with an employed spouse answers "No" to the question regarding other coverage or leaves the question regarding other coverage blank, then the claim examiner may wish to contact the employer of the insured's spouse to discover if the insured is also covered under that plan. If the insured repeatedly denies other coverage and if the claim examiner obtains information that the insured filed claims with another carrier, the insured's intent to defraud may be established.

For example, assume that Pierre Joshi submits a medical expense claim and indicates on the form that he has no other insurance in force. Pierre's wife, Sonya, is employed as a financial analyst with a large investment banking firm. The claim examiner calls the investment banking firm and discovers the name of their insurance company. A phone call to the other insurer reveals that Sonya does indeed have coverage under the banking firm's group plan, and that Pierre is also covered. In such cases, the claim examiner should complete a thorough investigation of the nature and circumstances surrounding the duplicate coverage issue. At a minimum, the claim examiner will consult with the other involved insurer to coordinate payment of the benefits. Then, if the case warrants further action, it should be turned over to the legal department for possible prosecution.

PAYMENT OF THE MEDICAL EXPENSE BENEFIT

Medical expense policies provide for payments to be made to the insured unless the insured voluntarily elects to have payments made to a provider of service.

Assignment of Benefits

Through an *assignment of benefits*, the insured may authorize the insurer to make payment directly to the provider of benefits. Some assignments may be valid only for the particular claim being submitted at the time, while others may be valid for the duration of the condition being treated.

An assignment-of-benefits form must be signed and dated by the insured. If the insured is a dependent spouse rather than the primary insured, then the claim examiner must ascertain that the primary insured and the dependent spouse are not separated or divorced. If there is any indication of a separation or divorce, then the claim examiner should obtain written verification from the insured that benefits should be assigned before paying the claim.

The completion of an assignment is routine procedure on the part of most hospitals at the time an insured is admitted to a hospital. However, the advent of computer-produced hospital bills has eliminated separate assignment forms. Instead, an assignment will be indicated on the hospital's billing form. A claim examiner will honor such an assignment unless he or she has a reason not to do so.

Death of the Insured

Sometimes an insured will die before medical expense benefits are paid. In such situations, the claim examiner must ensure that the proper individual receives payment and that the laws of the jurisdiction in which payment will be made are observed.

If an assignment of benefits form was signed by the insured prior to his or her death, then that assignment may be honored. In some instances, payment of the benefits may be made under a facility of payment clause. A *facility of payment clause* allows the insurer to pay the whole amount or any part of a medical expense benefit to (1) any institution or person to whom payment is owed for charges upon which the benefit is based, or (2) a legal relative such as spouse, child, mother, or father.

In many cases, the benefit will be paid to the estate of the deceased insured. Many states require that insurance companies notify the state tax department of benefit amounts transferred to an estate of a deceased insured. Refer to Chapter 10 for a discussion of tax notice and waiver and consent laws.

CLAIM COST MANAGEMENT PROGRAMS

In Chapter 3, we mentioned many ways in which insurers and policyholders attempt to control medical expense claim costs through plan design. For example, deductibles, coinsurance percentages, exclusions, preadmission testing requirements, second surgical opinion requirements, and coordination of benefits provisions are all plan design features aimed at reducing medical expense claim costs. Recently, insurers have implemented a variety of other programs such as case management, utilization review, and hospital claim audits that are designed to contain the rising costs of health care.

Case Management

Case management, also called large claim management, medical case management, or catastrophic claim management, is designed to identify alternate, less costly methods of treatment for seriously ill patients without sacrificing the quality of care the patients receive. The rapid rise in the popularity of case management can be attributed to the savings that can be realized from a relatively small number of claims. The statistics shown in Figure 12–3 represent the payments and savings of one insurance company during the first full year of its case management program.

A case management program is usually a voluntary program that brings together all of the parties involved in a patient's care—the providers of care, the patient's family, and the insurance company—to evaluate the patient's needs and to arrange quality, cost-efficient medical care for the patient. A case management program consists of four basic elements: (1) identification of a catastrophic claim, (2) evaluation or assessment of the insured patient's needs, (3) coordination of services, and (4) ongoing evaluations, recommendations, and monitoring.

Number of claims in case management program	874
Estimated claim savings	$ 5,108,115
Cost of program	$ 647,017
Net savings	$ 4,461,098

Source: "Large Claim Management," *1987 ICA Group Insurance Workshop Notes*, 72.

Figure 12–3. **Annual payments and savings from one insurer's case management program.**

Identification

Early identification of the catastrophic claim is important to the success of a case management program. Claim professionals agree that a patient is most likely to accept a case management program before medical treatment has begun. At the time an insured is admitted to a hospital, the claim examiner should receive (1) the admitting diagnosis, (2) the reason for hospitalization, (3) the condition of the patient upon admittance, and (4) if the insured was admitted in an emergency, information as to the need for immediate surgery.

Although any medical condition can develop to the catastrophic level, claim examiners should recognize the following diagnoses that are most likely to result in catastrophic claims:

• acquired immune deficiency syndrome (AIDS)
• accidents involving multiple fractures, major burns, amputations

- Alzheimer's disease
- anorexia nervosa
- cancer
- cardiovascular conditions
- cerebral palsy
- cerebral vascular accident (stroke)
- chemical dependency
- head injury
- congenital anomaly
- cystic fibrosis
- multiple sclerosis
- muscular dystrophy
- neurological disorders (Guillian Barre syndrome, quadriplegia, paraplegia)
- organ transplants
- premature birth
- pregnancy complication
- psychiatric conditions
- renal failure
- respiratory conditions (emphysema, chronic asthma, or bronchitis)

Other indicators of potentially catastrophic claims include (1) repeat hospital admissions, (2) transfers from one hospital to another, and (3) hospital admissions for a relatively insignificant diagnosis.

Evaluation

An insurance company's initial evaluation of the catastrophic claim is normally conducted by a nurse coordinator—a nurse who has extensive claim experience and who is employed by the insurance company either directly or on a contract basis. Some insurers that maintain long-term disability rehabilitation programs or preadmission certification programs find that maintaining an in-house staff of nurses is cost-effective. Other insurers find it more economical to obtain such expertise from a third-party administrator (TPA), an organization that administers insurance benefits but accepts no responsibility for providing the funds to pay claims. If a TPA is used, claim personnel must closely supervise the nurse coordinator's activities to ensure adherence to company policy and claim guidelines.

After the nurse coordinator evaluates the patient's condition and consults with all interested parties—the patient, the patient's family, and the patient's physician—the coordinator will make recommendations for future health care. The patient can accept or reject any recommendation without sacrificing the normally covered expenses. However, insurers can encourage a patient to accept an alternate method of health care by providing liberalized benefits under the alternate program.

Coordination of Services

Once the attending physician, the family, and the coordinator have agreed upon the course of treatment, the coordinator will assist in making any necessary arrangements, appointments, or transfers. Claim examiners administering the case management program should have the authority to make extra-contractual decisions such as approval of home health care beyond policy limits in lieu of hospitalization, or approval of a wheelchair purchase in lieu of rental.

Ongoing Evaluation and Monitoring

Once the patient's treatment is established, the coordinator will continue to check and report on a periodic basis to determine if the treatment remains appropriate and the patient's condition remains stable. Such reports contain recommendations for future treatment. If the current treatment does not seem appropriate or if the treatment does not appear to be cost effective, the company, with the patient's consent, may elect a secondary method of treatment.

Utilization Review

Somewhat related to a case management program is a utilization review program that evaluates the appropriateness, necessity, and quality of health care provided at various stages in its delivery. These services usually focus on hospital review, but some utilization review programs provide review of outpatient surgery, treatment of mental illness, and long-term care. A utilization review program usually consists of three components:

1. *Preadmission review* requires an insured person, or that person's physician, to obtain prior authorization from an insurer before any nonemergency hospitalization. An insured who is admitted to a hospital in an emergency usually must obtain certification from the insurance company within 24 to 48 hours of admission.
2. A *concurrent review* monitors an insured's care while the insured is hospitalized. Concurrent review encourages the dismissal of an insured from the hospital as soon as the insured's medical condition no longer warrants continued in-patient hospital care.
3. *Retrospective review* provides the insurer with periodic reports on physicians' practice patterns and hospitals' average lengths-of-stay.

Although a large insurance company may operate its own utilization review program, it is more common for an insurer to obtain such services from a TPA or from a professional review organization (PRO).

A TPA is completely independent of the local medical society and has no legal or administrative ties to the providers of medical service. In fact, TPAs typically conduct their reviews over the telephone or through written inquiries. A PRO is a physician-sponsored organization that reviews the appropriateness of the duration of either a hospital stay or medical treatment. PROs were chartered by the provisions of the Tax Equity and Fiscal Responsibility Act (TEFRA) to review the appropriateness and necessity of the care provided under Medicare and Medicaid. However, many insurance companies have since contracted with PROs on a fee-per-patient basis to review the appropriateness and necessity of the care given their privately insured patients.

Hospital Audits

The administration of hospital claims is one of the most difficult aspects of claim administration. The financial amounts are large, and the amount and quality of information provided on hospital bills varies widely from one facility to another. Many insurers routinely audit hospital bills, particularly those that exceed some amount such as $5,000 or $10,000. Other insurers selectively screen hospital claims to determine which claims should be audited. In hospital audits, insurers check for errors in length of stay, services performed, and billed charges. Some insurers report that a hospital audit program can result in a *sentinel effect*, whereby hospitals prepare hospital bills more carefully because they know the bills will be reviewed in detail by insurers.

References

"Case Management of the Catastrophic Claim," *1986 ICA Individual Health Insurance Workshop Notes*, 47–53.
"COB Industry Task Force/New Concepts," *1984 ICA Group Insurance Workshop Notes*, 86–88.
Claim Investigation Manual, 1987, International Claim Association, 1/9.
"Diagnostic Related Groups," *1987 ICA Group Insurance Workshop Notes*, 79–86.
Garrigan, Lisa. "DRG Dangers," *Business Insurance*, July 25, 1988, 21.
"Hospital Employment Under Revised Medicare Payment Schedules," *Monthly Labor Review*, August 1986, 40.
McGregor, Miriam. "IDP Automates Coordinations of Benefits Services," *National Underwriter*, Life/Health Edition, February 22, 1986, 36.
"Medical Utilization Management," *1984 ICA Group Insurance Workshop Notes*, 53–55.
"Large Claim Management," *1987 ICA Group Insurance Workshop Notes*, 72–78.

"Large Medical Claim Management," *1986 ICA Group Insurance Workshop Notes*, 36–39.

Rejda, George E. *Social Insurance and Economic Security*, 2nd Edition. Englewood Cliffs: Prentice-Hall, Inc., 1984.

"Update on Coordination of Benefits," *1985 ICA Group Insurance Workshop Notes*, 23–24.

Vanner, Bruce S. "Cut Beneath the Abuse of Workers' Compensation," *Personnel Journal*, April 1988, 30.

13

Dental Expense Claims

Dental expense insurance is designed to help pay for both routine dental care and dental damage caused by accidents. Insurance companies are currently the largest providers of dental expense protection, covering 62 million of the 133 million people with dental coverage in the United States and 6 million of the almost 9 million with coverage in Canada. The remaining dental coverage is provided by Blue Cross/Blue Shield Plans, dental service corporations, and self-insured employer-provided plans.

Dental expense benefits are one of the fastest growing employee benefits. From 1975 to 1985, the number of persons in the United States with dental insurance grew from 19 million to 62 million. There are several reasons for this growth. First, there is a basic need for such protection; dental disease is one of the most prevalent of all diseases. Second, this need has not yet been widely met; the number of persons in the United States protected by dental insurance is only about one-half the number covered by hospital or medical insurance. Third, dental insurance is a logical area of benefit expansion for unions, now that relatively complete levels of benefits are provided under many group hospital, surgical, and medical programs. These factors point to a continued strong growth of sales of dental expense insurance over the next decade. Accompanying that growth will be a need for increased knowledge about claim processing for such policies.

CHARACTERISTICS OF DENTAL EXPENSE INSURANCE

Although dental expense insurance is a form of medical coverage, its characteristics differ from those of hospital, surgical, and medical expense insurance.

Dental Problems are a Predictable Risk

Insurance risk usually involves relatively infrequent claims and a comparatively high degree of loss severity. A classic insurance risk situation is unpredictable for the individual as to either the frequency or the time of occurrence, but it is predictable for the group as a whole. With some exceptions, such as for small group and association business, antiselection is not a major concern.

In contrast, many persons can forecast their need for dental care with a fair degree of certainty. Although some dental expenses are unanticipated, the need for dental care can be predicted more accurately than, for example, the need for major surgery. Thus, individuals can select against a dental care program much more effectively than is possible with other forms of health insurance. Evidence of this potential for antiselection can be found in the claim volume of a new dental plan. In the first three to six months of a new dental plan, claim volume generally runs between 20 and 30 percent higher than the expected long-term annualized volume, as new insureds take advantage of their coverage to receive long-postponed treatment.

One means by which group insurers attempt to reduce this antiselection is to require a high level of participation. In general, insurers require higher participation in group dental plans than in other group plans; 85 percent participation is a popular level, although for larger groups the traditional 75 percent level has been accepted. One method for increasing participation is to require employers to contribute toward the cost of the premiums.

Dental Coverage Encourages Preventive Care

Major dental problems and their costs can be avoided through early treatment. For example, a person with periodontal disease can receive early care, such as scaling and curettage, at a cost of perhaps $100; postponing the treatment could lead to later surgery at a cost of $800 or more. Thus, unlike traditional health care coverage, dental plans encourage early and regular treatment. Such care is typically encouraged by providing full coverage for the cost of preventive treatments, whereas other treatments may have coinsurance or deductible limitations. Some policies provide an inducement for regular dental care through use of *incentive coinsurance*

provisions, whereby the percentage paid by the insurer is higher if the insured person receives regular dental examinations.

Large Claim Volume and Low Claim Amounts

Unlike medical expense claims, dental claims are characterized by relatively large claim volumes and small benefit amounts. Although claim volume varies depending upon plan design and whether the plan has a deductible feature, annualized claim volume typically averages three times the number of insureds. For example, a plan that covers 10,000 employees probably incurs as many as 30,000 claims per year.

The majority of dental procedures are low in cost. Even in comprehensive plans, most reimbursements are for relatively inexpensive items. In 1984, the average amount of dental benefits paid per insured in the United States was $48.09, whereas the average for regular medical benefits was $224.97. Therefore, an insurer's system for processing dental claims must be able to handle a large volume of claims in a cost-efficient manner while still maintaining a high level of accuracy. Both large and small insurance companies have automated their dental claim processing to achieve such processing economies.

A Wide Range of Acceptable Treatments

Dental insurance plans also differ from medical insurance plans in that while there is usually only one acceptable treatment for a medical problem, there are usually many acceptable alternative treatments for a dental problem. For example, silver amalgam, a gold inlay, or a gold crown are all acceptable treatments for a cavity. A missing tooth or teeth may be replaced by a unilateral partial denture, a bilateral partial denture, or a fixed bridge, with inlay, onlay, or crown abutments. The choice of service depends on a variety of factors. In addition to the condition of the patient's mouth and teeth, the cosmetic effects of the service and the price often guide the dentist and the patient in choice of treatment. For the most part, dental plans are intended to cover adequate methods of treatment. Therefore, the dental claim system must provide for a review of treatment performed in order to identify situations in which the choice of treatment may have been more costly than was necessary.

DENTAL EXPENSE COVERAGE

Insurance coverage is available for practically all types of dental services. Dental services are typically classified according to eight treatment categories:

- *Diagnostic*—Oral examinations, x-rays, and laboratory tests to

evaluate the condition of the mouth and to determine the existence of dental disease.

- *Preventive*—Prophylaxis, fluoride treatment, and other procedures
  designed to prevent dental decay and tissue disease and to maintain dental health.
- *Restorative*—Fillings, crowns, and inlays used to restore the functional use of the patient's natural teeth.
- *Endodontics*—Diagnosis and treatment of diseases of the dental
  pulp within existing teeth, such as root canal therapy.
- *Periodontics*—Treatment of diseases of the bone and soft tissues
  of the mouth.
- *Oral Surgery*—Surgical extraction of teeth and other operative
  treatment relating to the teeth and jaw.
- *Prosthodontics*—Replacement of missing teeth by artificial
  devices, such as dentures and bridgework.
- *Orthodontics*—Straightening of teeth and correction of other ir-
  regularities through the use of such devices as appliances and
  retainers.

As we mentioned previously, insurers structure their dental plans to
encourage preventive maintenance. Thus, preventive and diagnostic services are often covered at 100 percent. Coverage for other service varies
depending upon the nature of the service. **Basic services**, which typically
consist of fillings, endodontics, periodontics, and oral surgery, are often
covered at 80 percent of their reasonable and customary charges. **Major
services**, which typically consist of inlays, crowns, prosthodontics, and orthodontics, are often covered at 50 percent of their reasonable and
customary charges.

VERIFYING THE LOSS

In order to verify that an insured has incurred a covered dental expense,
a claim examiner usually needs only the completed and signed claim form.
However, in some cases, the insured or the insured's dentist must also submit proof-of-loss materials or submit a proposed treatment plan for a
predetermination of benefits.

Claim Form

The completed claim form contains information about the insured, the patient, the policyholder, the carrier, and the dentist. In addition, the claim
form includes the dental treatment plan, which lists each dental procedure
performed and the dental code for each procedure. In both Canada and

the United States, dental associations working in conjunction with insure
have developed uniform claim forms for reporting dental treatments. Figur
13–1 shows the uniform claim form used in the United States. Uniform
coding systems permit the practitioner to specifically identify the procedure
involved in treating a patient. A claim examiner is thus better able to cross-
reference procedure codes to the various dental plans offered by the insurance company.

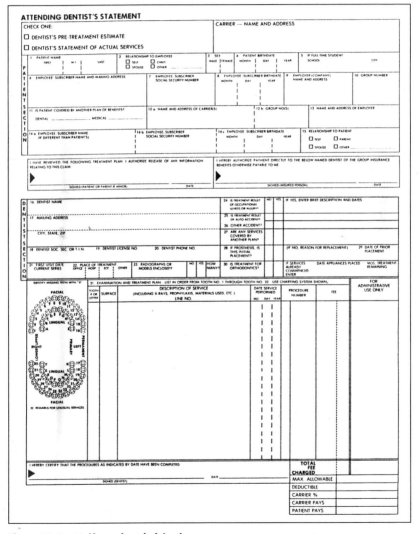

Figure 13-1.   Uniform dental claim form.

Proof-of-Loss Materials

Because of the high volume of dental claims, claim examiners do not require proof-of-loss materials for every dental claim. Instead, they require such materials only when necessary to determine benefits. X-rays are probably the most commonly required proof of loss. Other items sometimes requested include photographs, narrative descriptions, accident reports, and diagnostic casts.

Predetermination of Benefits

The *predetermination of benefits provision*, also called preauthorization of benefits, precertification of benefits, or pretreatment review, typically specifies that when dental treatments are expected to exceed a stated level, such as $100, $150, or $200, the dentist should submit to the insurer the proposed treatment plan for the patient. The purpose of predetermination is to enable the insurer to specify the amount of benefits it will pay for the proposed treatment before the cost is incurred. Predetermination is not intended to limit the patient's choice of an attending dentist, nor to advise either party of what treatment should be performed. Failure to submit the proposed treatment plan does not result in any forfeiture of benefits because benefits are always payable in accordance with the terms of the contract.

Properly accomplished, predetermination of benefits has several advantages:

- The patient's eligibility for coverage is certified in advance of any treatment.
- The patient gains a better understanding of planned treatment, charges, and benefits.
- The dentist has an opportunity to discuss with the patient the financial aspects of treatment before costs are incurred.
- The insurer has an opportunity to evaluate treatment plans and to discuss questionable items prior to actual treatment.
- A peer review committee, which consists of a panel of licensed dentists, can be used, if necessary, to resolve disputes between the insurer and the dentist.

The Predetermination Process

The predetermination process typically consists of the following steps: (1) a dentist makes a diagnosis and outlines on a claim form a proposed treatment plan and the fees for the insured; (2) the dentist submits the claim form to the insurer before treatment is initiated; (3) the claim examiner reviews the claim form, determines the amount of benefits payable, and identifies any ineligible services; and (4) the claim form is then returned to either the dentist or the insured. In most cases, the claim form is returned to the dentist so that he or she can discuss alternative treatment plans and costs with the patient.

Sometimes the dentist is required to submit x-rays with the proposed treatment plan. Some dentists feel that such requirements are an infringement on their professional judgment and an intrusion into the relationship between dentist and patient. This opposition can be considerably lessened through the use of certain guidelines by claim personnel in requesting and using x-rays, including the following:

- X-rays should not be required indiscriminately, but only in those cases in which they are essential to determine the extent of liability under the program and to clarify the benefits to which the insured is entitled under terms of the contract.
- The x-rays taken by the dentist are a part of the dentist's records; they are not the property of the patient, the insurer, or any other third party. X-rays should not be furnished to anyone else, including peer review committees, without the written consent of the dentist.
- X-rays should be examined only by dentists.
- X-rays should be returned to the dentist promptly, such as within ten days. As an alternative, the insurer can pay the additional expense of using dual packs, or duplicate x-rays, so that x-rays need not be returned and will be less vulnerable to being lost in transit.
- The insurer should not require post-treatment x-rays unless they are a part of proper dental treatment or unless they are required for peer review purposes.

VERIFYING POLICY COVERAGE OF THE LOSS

After a claim examiner verifies that a dental expense has been incurred, the examiner must determine if the insured's policy provides coverage for the expense. Dental plans include numerous exclusions and limitations designed to control claim costs and to eliminate unnecessary dental care.

Policy Exclusions

Policy exclusions identify services that are not covered under the plan. Some exclusions are standard in all types of health insurance policies; others are unique to dental insurance.

Standard Health Insurance Exclusions

The following charges are generally excluded from all health insurance coverages:

- treatment of injury or disease caused by an act of war whether declared or undeclared or incurred while engaged in the armed forces,
- charges arising out of or in the course of employment (for pay or profit) which is covered under Workers' Compensation or occupational disease law,
- services for which no charge would be made in the absence of insurance,
- charges for services and supplies that are either experimental or obsolete, and
- charges for any services to the extent that they are provided for by other plans (coordination of benefits).

Special Dental Exclusions

The following charges are typically excluded from most dental insurance plans:

- charges for the replacement of lost or stolen prosthetic devices,
- expenses for plaque control or dental hygiene programs that are educational,
- expenses for services received prior to the effective date of coverage, and
- charges for services and supplies that are essentially cosmetic in nature.

Of these special dental exclusions, those pertaining to the effective date of coverage and to cosmetic treatment are described more fully in the next section.

Incurred Date of Treatment.   For the most part, medical services have a fairly well-defined date of occurrence. In dentistry, however, the question of when an expense is incurred becomes more complex. Treatments such as root canal therapy or full mouth reconstruction may well extend over a lengthy period of time. Thus, a portion of the charges may be incurred before or after the period of eligibility under policy coverage.

Determining whether a treatment qualifies for coverage requires that the claim examiner understand specific policy provisions. These provisions vary from company to company; however, the following general observations can be made:

- For most ordinary services, the charge is incurred on the date the service is performed. When an expense represents more than one date of service, the expense should be broken down by dates to determine the portion covered under the policy. Claim payment is not made until the procedure or service is actually performed.
- Oral examinations, dental prophylaxis, and dental x-rays are not generally considered the start of a procedure or series of treatments. Hence, the discovery of a diseased tooth and the development of a treatment plan do not represent the incurred date of expense for the treatment of that tooth.
- For dentures and fixed bridgework, most companies regard the expense as incurred on the date impressions are taken to prepare the denture or bridge.
- For crowns, some companies regard the charge as incurred when impressions are taken or when the teeth are prepared.
- For root canal therapy, expense is incurred upon the initial surgical work of opening the canal.
- For orthodontics, charges are usually deemed to be incurred on the date the appliance is first installed.

Cosmetic Dentistry.   The purpose of dental insurance is to provide for sound dental care and healthy mouths, not to provide perfect teeth. Therefore, the cost of dental coverage is based on providing care that has been variously described as "regular and customary," "reasonably necessary," or "essential or necessary for care." As already pointed out, many dental problems lend themselves to a variety of procedures with a wide range of costs. In many cases, a more costly procedure is chosen for sound medical reasons. In some cases, however, the choice is made primarily for cosmetic reasons.

Dental cosmetics may be interpreted as being those services performed primarily to enhance the appearance of the mouth by changes in shape, color, or position of teeth. Examples include

- crowns placed on otherwise sound teeth that overlapped or were not in normal alignment,
- crowns placed on teeth that are discolored but not diseased,
- crowns placed on adjacent anterior teeth to close a space for cosmetic purposes, and
- use of veneer crowns on posterior (rear) teeth.

In many cases, the improvement of appearance is the sole purpose of cosmetic treatment. In other cases, some treatment is required, but the procedure chosen may be more complex and expensive than the insurer believes necessary. When a procedure is performed solely for cosmetic purposes, the policy exclusion would normally mean that the treatment is not covered, and hence no benefits would be payable. When the insurer believes that an unnecessarily expensive procedure has been used, the benefit payable is an amount equal to that which would have been payable for a less expensive but adequate treatment.

A reduction in the amount of benefits or a denial of benefits should be made only after the claim examiner has carefully reviewed the case. In many cases, the claim examiner will require the assistance of a **dentist-consultant**, a licensed dentist who understands the underwriting intent of dental plan language as well as the accepted standards of dental practice, to determine the benefits payable. Nevertheless, a dentist-consultant's opinion should remain advisory in nature, with final benefit determination being made by the insurer after taking all known factors into consideration.

Policy Limitations

Policy limitations are provisions that limit the frequency of service covered and/or the amount of benefits payable. Like exclusions, limitations vary considerably from plan to plan in terms of both their inclusion and the degree of limitation imposed.

Deductibles

Dental plans usually include one or more deductibles for various types of dental services. Because dental plans are designed to encourage preventive care, most dental plans require no deductible or a very low deductible amount for preventive and diagnostic services. Deductibles typically are required for basic and major services. For example, a dental plan may specify a $50 annual deductible for basic services and a $50 deductible for each major service. Under this plan, the insured must pay the first $50 of dental expenses before any benefits for basic services will be payable by the insurance company. If the insured requires a major service, such as oral surgery, then the insured would have to pay an additional $50 before benefits would be payable.

Coinsurance

As do medical insurance policies, dental insurance policies usually contain a coinsurance provision, which requires the insured to pay a stated percentage of the covered expenses. As we mentioned previously, the percentage usually varies according to the type of service. For example, preventive and diagnostic services are often covered in full. Other types of services are covered at 80 percent or 50 percent of their reasonable and customary charge.

In addition, some dental plans include incentive coinsurance provisions which specify that the insurer will pay a higher percentage of the dental charges if the insured person receives regular dental examinations. For example, a dental plan might have a coinsurance factor of 70 percent during the first year of coverage. If the insured has a dental examination during that year, the coinsurance factor increases to 80 percent for the second year. If the insured has dental examination during the second year, the coinsurance factor rises to 90 percent, and so on until it reaches 100 percent. If the insured does not meet the conditions of the incentive provision, however, the coinsurance factor decreases, but not lower than a specified percentage.

The purpose of such incentive coinsurance is to encourage regular visits to the dentist, thus avoiding mouth deterioration which may result in higher long-term dental expenses. However, there are two drawbacks: greater confusion on the part of the insured as to what benefits are payable, and increased administrative processing for the insurer.

Maximums

A maximum is the amount of benefit dollars to which the insured is entitled for covered dental services during some stated period or for a certain type of service. Maximum amounts may be stated in various ways. Calendar-year maximums are common and typically vary from $500 to $1,500. Lifetime maximums are also common and may be included in a plan along with calendar-year maximums. Lifetime maximums typically vary from $5,000 to $10,000 for each insured. In addition, maximum amounts may be placed on certain services. For example, some plans limit periodontal benefits to a lifetime maximum of $1,000, in order to encourage insureds to practice good dental hygiene.

Placing maximum limits on benefits can substantially affect the cost of dental insurance without affecting most persons covered by the plan. In a typical plan, most of the insureds account for only a comparatively small percentage of the aggregate costs of the plan; conversely, a comparatively small percentage of insureds account for a large portion of total costs.

Waiting Periods

Some dental plans include a waiting period, which is a period of time that must pass after an insured becomes eligible for dental coverage before benefits are payable. A few dental plans include a waiting period for all types of dental services. However, in most plans, waiting periods apply only to certain services, such as prosthetic and orthodontic work.

A waiting period for all services is most commonly found in situations in which the employer-policyholder has a high rate of personnel turnover. The waiting period acts as protection against a situation in which a person joins the employer primarily for the dental benefits, intending to leave as soon as the treatment is completed.

Other Limitations

Most dental plans specify the frequency with which some dental benefits will be paid. For example, routine oral examinations are usually limited to two times per year, and fluoride treatments are often limited to one time per year. The replacement of dentures may also be limited to one time in some specified period, such as five years.

DETERMINING THE AMOUNT OF BENEFITS PAYABLE

The methods insurers use to determine the amount of dental benefits payable are the same three types of methods used to determine the amount of surgical and medical expense benefits payable. These methods include

- *Scheduled benefits*—The plan lists benefit amounts for specific procedures in a policy schedule, with individual consideration given to unlisted items.
- *Reasonable and customary charges*—The plan provides a percentage reimbursement of the reasonable and customary charges.
- *Combination benefits*—The plan includes a percentage reimbursement of reasonable and customary charges for diagnostic and preventive services, with a scheduled benefit for all other covered services.

Coordination of benefits provisions are included in dental contracts, as they are in medical expense insurance contracts, so that when an insured is covered under two separate policies, the insured does not receive benefits in excess of the expenses that he or she incurred. Chapter 12 includes a detailed description of coordination of benefits provisions.

TERMINATION OF BENEFITS

The majority of dental plans provide a limited period of extended benefits, payable after termination of coverage. To be eligible for such extended benefits, a patient must have been insured prior to incurring a dental expense. Extended benefits apply for only a limited period of time, such as 30 to 90 days following termination of coverage. In addition, dental coverage is subject to the continuation rules of COBRA that were discussed in Chapter 11.

PREPAID DENTAL PLANS

Some insurance companies have developed dental plans that provide dental care on a prepaid basis to subscribing members. Like a health maintenance organization, the prepaid dental plan allows insureds to obtain their dental services from a panel of approved dentists. The contract between the participating dentists and the insurance company includes a set fee schedule for dental services. Generally, the fees are lower than the fees dentists receive under regular dental expense coverages. However, the dentist is usually guaranteed a specified number of patients. The insured member pays no deductible but is responsible for a low copayment (between $2 and $5) per visit. In addition, the panel dentist is responsible for completing all dental forms.

References

Garwood, Richard L. *Dentistry and Dental Insurance Claims*, Los Gatos, CA: International Claim Association, 1985.
Kozlowski, Joseph G. *The Health Insurance Answer Book*, 1988 Update, Greenvale, NY: Institute for Management, 1988.

Disability Claim Administration

14

Examining
Disability Claims

Disability insurance, a relatively new product with origins in the late 19th century, is still evolving. New disability benefits, variations in policy provisions, legal rulings, the potential long-term nature of a disability claim, and many other factors combine to make the administration of disability claims one of the greatest challenges for a claim examiner.

In this chapter, we present the examination process for disability claims. Because the administration of disability claims varies extensively depending upon the type of benefit involved, we first describe the major types of disability benefits. Then, we review the claim administration process, noting similarities and differences in the ways the various types of disability claims are handled. In Chapter 15, we look at the payment of disability benefits.

DISABILITY BENEFITS

Disability benefits take two basic forms: a waiver-of-premium benefit and a cash benefit. A **waiver-of-premium benefit** provides that if an insured becomes totally disabled, and if the total disability continues for a specified length of time, the policyowner will be allowed to forego the payment of all premiums falling due under the policy for as long as the total disability continues. This disability benefit is usually offered in conjunction with any life insurance contract and with any disability insurance contract that is guaranteed renewable.

Cash benefits for disability are provided through (1) disability income coverages that provide a series of cash benefit payments to the insured in the event of his or her disability, and (2) business insurance coverages that are designed to provide financial protection for business owners in the event of their disability.

Disability Income Coverages

Insurers offer many different types of disability income coverages. All disability income policies include a basic benefit that is payable when an insured is totally disabled according to the policy's definition of total disability. In addition, most policies provide a benefit that is payable in situations in which the insured is not totally disabled but is suffering from a partial disability or an income loss that is a direct result of a disability.

In this book, we describe four major categories of disability income benefits: (1) a basic disability income benefit, (2) a partial disability benefit, (3) a residual benefit for partial disability, and (4) a recovery benefit or an income replacement disability benefit. Some insurers offer all of these types of benefits. Others may offer only the basic disability income benefit or disability income with a partial disability benefit. These types of benefits may be sold on both an individual and a group basis as well as through riders to individual life insurance policies.

Basic Disability Income Benefits

A basic disability income benefit will replace a portion of an insured's income should the insured become *totally disabled* according to the definition of disability included in the policy. (Total disability is defined later in this chapter.) The benefit provided is designed to be somewhat lower than an individual's pre-disability earnings in order to motivate the individual to return to work. Benefits are payable after the completion of an **elimination period**, or a **waiting period**, which is a specified number of days, typically 30 to 180 days, that must pass after the onset of total disability before any disability benefits are payable.

The benefit provided is either a fixed amount or a percentage of the insured's pre-disability earnings. If the policy provides a fixed amount benefit, then the benefit amount is determined at the time the policy is purchased and is specified in the policy. This fixed amount is usually paid to the insured regardless of the amount of any other income benefits payable during the disability. Most disability income policies issued to individuals specify a fixed amount benefit.

If the policy provides a benefit that is a percentage of the insured's pre-disability income, then the formula for determining the benefit amount is specified when the policy is purchased. The benefit percentage may vary according to the length of the disability. For example, the benefit amount might equal 100 percent of the insured's pre-disability earnings for 4 weeks of a disability and then 75 percent of the insured's pre-disability earnings for the remainder of the benefit period. In addition, when a percentage formula method is used, the benefit amount is often subject to an overall maximum. For example, the policy may specify that the income benefit is the lesser of (1) 75 percent of the insured's monthly pre-disability income or (2) $1,500 per month. A percentage formula is often included in group contracts.

Basic disability income benefits can be classified either as short-term disability benefits or long-term disability benefits depending upon the duration of the benefit period. Short-term disability benefits are payable for a relatively short period of time, between 13 to 26 weeks. Long-term disability benefits are payable for a lengthy duration such as 5 years, 10 years, to age 65, or the lifetime of the insured.

Partial Disability Benefits

Along with the benefit for total disability, some disability insurers offer a benefit for partial disability that is one-half of the benefit for total disability. A *partial disability* exists when an insured is unable to work full-time or complete one or more important job duties because of a disability. In order to receive a partial disability benefit, an insured must be partially disabled according to the policy's definition and must satisfy an elimination period. The partial disability benefit is paid regardless of the amount of income that the insured receives. The policy usually states that the partial benefit is payable for only a short time, such as three to six months.

Residual Benefits for Partial Disability

Most disability insurers currently offer a **residual benefit for partial disability**, that varies according to the percentage of the insured's earnings that is lost during a period of partial disability. The amount of each benefit payment depends upon how much the insured earns following a return to work, compared to pre-disability earnings. As an insured's post-disability earnings increase, the amount of the residual disability benefit decreases.

In order for a residual disability benefit to be paid, the insured must be partially disabled. Furthermore, the insured must demonstrate that the disability resulted in a loss of at least a specified percentage, such as 20 or 25 percent, of pre-disability earnings. (We will describe the process for determining whether a claimant has suffered an insurable earnings loss later in this chapter.) In order for a residual disability benefit to be paid, the insured must also satisfy an elimination period, which is sometimes called a qualification period in these types of policies. In residual disability policies, the elimination period or qualification period may be satisfied by a period of total disability, a period of partial disability, or any combination of the two types of disabilities. In other words, the insured does not have to suffer a period of total disability in order to satisfy the elimination or qualification period in such policies.

Recovery Benefits or Income Replacement Benefits

Like the residual benefit for partial disability, a recovery benefit or income replacement benefit varies according to the insured's pre-disability and post-disability earnings. The *recovery benefit* or *income replacement benefit* is payable after an insured (1) satisfies an elimination or qualification period, (2) returns to work, and (3) then suffers a loss of earnings, usually a minimum of 20 or 25 percent, which is a direct result of a preceding total or partial disability.

However, unlike the residual benefit for partial disability, the recovery benefit or income replacement benefit is payable even if the insured has fully recovered from the disability and has resumed *all* occupational duties on a full-time basis. The following example illustrates the difference between the residual benefit for partial disability and the recovery or income replacement benefit:

> Gladys Goldsmith is a self-employed accountant. After a year of total disability, she returns to work on a full-time basis and is able to perform all of her usual duties. However, she experiences a 60 percent loss in monthly earnings because while she was disabled and unable to serve her clients, she lost several large accounts.

If Gladys has a disability income policy with a residual benefit for partial disability, she will not be eligible for a disability benefit after returning to work because she is not partially disabled. However, if Gladys has a disability income policy with a recovery or income replacement benefit, most insurers would consider her 60 percent loss of earnings to be a direct result of the preceding disability. Therefore, Gladys would be qualified to receive a payment of the recovery benefit.

Business Insurance Coverages

In the late 1960s, insurers began offering disability insurance benefits designed to meet the needs of business owners. Overhead expense insurance and disability buy-out insurance are the two major types of such coverages.

Overhead Expense Coverage

Overhead expense coverage provides cash benefits to pay the ongoing expenses of a business while the business owner is disabled. Overhead expense contracts will usually reimburse the disabled business owner for the following expenses:

- utilities,
- rent,
- property taxes and mortgage interest,
- compensation of employees,
- interest on loans/equipment,
- depreciation of assets, and
- any other normal fixed business expenses.

Overhead expense contracts may have a 30 to 180 day elimination period and a benefit period of one year or two years. Benefit amounts depend upon the expenses incurred up to a maximum benefit amount. For example, assume that Johnny Rodriguez has an overhead expense policy that provides a maximum $5,000 benefit per month in the event of his disability. However, Johnny's business incurs only $4,500 in expenses during one month of his disability. For that month, Johnny would receive a $4,500 benefit rather than the maximum $5,000 benefit. Overhead expense policies are issued in large amounts, frequently in the $5,000 per month range. Most disability insurers will insure amounts up to $20,000 or more per month on an overhead expense policy.

Disability Buy-out Insurance

Disability buy-out insurance provides cash funds to a business or professional partnership so that the business interests of a totally disabled partner or shareholder may be purchased. Since the need for a business buy-out exists only when the disability is long-term or permanent, the elimination period in such contracts is normally at least one year and sometimes longer. After the elimination period is satisfied, the benefits are payable. The benefits are frequently paid in a lump sum but may be paid monthly in a settlement arrangement over a period of one to five years.

The method for determining the benefit payment is established at the time the policy is purchased. The benefit may be a flat amount such as $300,000, or a benefit formula may be stated that is based on the value of the business at the time of the buy-out.

THE CLAIM EXAMINATION PROCESS

The process for examining disability claims is different in many ways from the process of examining either life or medical expense claims. First, the examination of disability claims is more subjective than the examination of either life or medical claims. Disability is not as easily verifiable as death or illness. To be sure, some disability claims are for manifest disabilities—for example, multiple dismemberment or quadriplegia. However, in many other cases there may be a genuine question as to whether the insured is truly disabled.

Second, the examination of disability claims involves more personal interaction between claim examiners and claimants than does the examination of medical or life claims. Direct personal contact is necessary to satisfy two basic needs: (1) the claimant's need for information about policy benefits and procedures for initiating and continuing disability benefit payments, and (2) the insurer's need for information about the insured's medical condition and its prognosis, as well as the insured's occupation, sources of income, and future plans. Most companies find that direct contact with their claimants—through telephone calls, correspondence, or personal visits— is an effective method of promoting good will and of satisfying these two needs.

Despite these differences, the examination of disability claims is similar to medical expense claim examination in some ways. In both areas, automation has radically changed the way claims are handled. Further, over-insurance and fraud are major concerns of claim examiners in both areas.

In the remainder of this chapter, we describe the process for examining disability claims, noting differences and similarities between claim examination for disability insurance and life or medical expense insurance.

Verifying the Loss

The nature of the loss in a life insurance claim is a singular occurrence that usually can be easily verified. With a medical expense claim, the loss is usually verifiable from the provider of the service. However, with a disability claim, two different medical specialists may disagree on whether an insured person is disabled within the applicable policy's definition. In addition, the individual and the individual's personal circumstances may affect the degree of disability. Different persons have different thresholds of pain and endurance, both physical and mental. Some individuals are able to continue to work with a physical impairment; others with the same impairment will be considered disabled. Studies suggest that an insured's weight, occupation, age, education, and motivation may affect his or her disability. Consider the examples below:

- *Weight*—An obese person is likely to be disabled longer from a low back strain than is an individual of normal weight.

- *Occupation*—A fractured finger could be totally disabling to a professional baseball pitcher, but not to a teacher.
- *Age*—Older persons recover more slowly from fractures than younger persons.
- *Motivation*—People who are motivated to return to work have shorter periods of disability.

What all this means to the claim examiner is that it is difficult to cite definite rules for evaluating disability claims. Nonetheless, the disability claim examiner's job is to determine whether an individual is disabled according to a disability contract's terms. The claim process begins when the examiner receives notice of the claim.

Notice of Claim

As with all claims, the examination of a disability claim begins with notice of the claim. Disability policies specify a period—usually 30 days or less after the onset of disability—within which the insured must notify the insurer of the claim. Such a time limit is included in disability contracts so that the claim examiner can make a timely investigation of the claim. Proof of an insured's disability can be more easily established at the onset of disability rather than later.

Insurers generally do not adhere strictly to the time period required for notification of a claim but often accept claim notices beyond the period specified in the policy, particularly if the nature of the disabling incident (injury or sickness) prevented the insured from filing a claim within the time limit. Still, an insured should notify an insurer promptly because some disability policies specify that benefits will not be paid for any period prior to the receipt of written notice of a claim. Other policies may allow retroactive benefits, but for not more than one year prior to the receipt of notice of a claim.

Proofs of Loss

After receiving notice of a disability claim, the claim department sends the insured a claim form that must be completed and returned to the insurer with supporting documentation in order for the claim examiner to establish proof of the insured's loss. The claim form, according to most policy provisions, must be sent to the claimant within 15 days of the receipt of the notice of the claim.

General Information

The proof of loss requirements will vary according to the type of disability benefit involved. However, all disability claim forms require identifying information about the insured—the name, address, date of birth, telephone number, and occupation of the insured—in order to set up the insured's claim file. In addition, the following information is usually required: (1) the name and address of the insured's employer; (2) the cause of the disability; (3) the dates of disability; and (4) an Attending Physician's Statement that states the diagnosis and the proposed treatment of the insured.

Name and Address of the Employer. Information from the insured's employer is valuable for several reasons. The most obvious reason is to verify the insured's work record. For example, if an insured states that he was disabled and unable to work from August 1 through November 15, then the employer can affirm the fact that he did not work. Beyond this, an insurer may learn such facts as

- the employment status of the insured immediately prior to the disability: full-time or part-time, temporarily laid-off, or on strike;
- the occupational title and the specific duties of the insured immediately prior to the disability;
- whether the injury or illness is covered by Workers' Compensation;
- the amount of the insured's pre-disability income;
- any income, such as a salary or wage continuation or union benefits, that the insured may be receiving during the period of disability; and
- whether the insured will be rehired when the disability ceases.

Cause of Disability. Information describing the cause of the insured's disability is critical to the processing of disability claims for several reasons, including the following:

- *To determine whether the disability was caused by accident or sickness.*

  Some disability policies provide different elimination periods depending upon whether the disability results from an accident or sickness. Some policies specify a short elimination period (such as seven days) for disabilities resulting from accidents, and a longer elimination period (such as six months) for disabilities resulting from sickness.

  All disability policies specify a ***maximum benefit period***, which is the maximum period during which disability income benefits will be paid. The maximum benefit period may be as short as a few weeks or as long as the insured's lifetime. The maximum benefit period may differ depending upon whether the disability was caused by an accident or sickness. For example, an individual who has coverage with a lifetime maximum benefit period for accidents may have only a five-year maximum benefit period for sickness.

It is important to note, however, that the distinction between accident and sickness is not as critical as it once was because many policies now provide identical benefits—in terms of the elimination period and the maximum benefit period—for sickness and injury.

- *To determine if the cause of disability is a risk that is excluded from policy coverage.*

Disability policies usually exclude disability caused by (1) attempted suicide or an intentionally self-inflicted injury, (2) war, or any act or hazard of war, and (3) injury sustained or sickness contracted during military service. In addition, employer-provided group disability insurance policies usually exclude occupationally-related disabilities or sicknesses for which the insured is entitled to receive benefits under a government program, such as Workers' Compensation.

Some disability policies specify that disability resulting from pregnancy or childbirth will not be paid. However, this exclusion is subject to the same legal restrictions in the United States as is the pregnancy exclusion in medical expense coverage. Therefore, this exclusion is rarely used in group disability income policies.

Further, a few disability policies may exclude disability resulting from mental or nervous disorders. Others may provide coverage only for psychotic conditions and exclude neurotic conditions. Some policies covering mental or nervous disorders require the insured to be institutionalized to receive disability benefits. Currently the most common approach is to provide coverage for a specified period, such as 12 or 24 months, after which coverage continues only if the insured is institutionalized for the mental or nervous condition.

Dates of Disability.   A claim examiner must know the dates of an insured's disability in order to determine if the policy's elimination or qualification period has been satisfied. In addition, the claim examiner must ensure that the maximum benefit period is not exceeded.

An Attending Physician's Statement.   An Attending Physician's Statement (APS), shown in Figure 14-1, is one of the most important sources of information for the disability claim examiner. The attending physician usually provides the claim examiner with an insured's medical diagnosis, medical test results, record of medication, and dates of treatment. However, the attending physician may not be willing to make a determination as to whether the individual is or has been disabled. The physician may state

Attending Physician's Statement of Disability
Group Insurance

The patient is responsible for the completion of this form without expense to

You may mail this form directly to:

Please print

Name of patient _____ Date of birth | Month | Day | Year

Patient's address _____ No. ____ Street ____ City ____ State or Province ____ Zip Code

Employer's name _____ Control number

I hereby authorize release of information requested on this form, by the below named physician for the purpose of claim processing.

Signed (Patient) ►

Date _____

1. History

(a) When did symptoms first appear or accident happen? .... Mo. _____ Day _____ 19 _____

(b) Date patient ceased work because of disability . ... Mo. _____ Day _____ 19 _____

(c) Has patient ever had same or similar condition? .... ☐ Yes ☐ No If "Yes" state when and describe.

(d) Is condition due to injury or sickness arising out of patient's employment? ☐ Yes ☐ No ☐ Unknown

(e) If condition due to automobile accident, indicate state in which it occurred _____

(f) Names and addresses of other treating physicians

2. Diagnosis (including any complications)

(a) Date of last examination .... Mo. _____ Day _____ 19 _____

(b) Diagnosis (including any complications)

(c) If disability is due to pregnancy what is expected/was delivery date . . . . . Mo. _____ Day _____ 19 _____

(d) Please describe any complications that would extend this disability longer than for a normal pregnancy.

(e) Subjective symptoms

(f) Objective findings (including current X-rays, EKG's, Laboratory Data and any clinical findings)

3. Dates of Treatment

(a) Date of first visit .... Mo. _____ Day _____ 19 _____

(b) Date of last visit .... Mo. _____ Day _____ 19 _____

(c) Frequency .... ☐ Weekly ☐ Monthly ☐ Other (specify)

4. Nature of Treatment (including surgery and medications prescribed, if any)

5. Progress

(a) Has patient .... ☐ Recovered? ☐ Improved? ☐ Unchanged? ☐ Retrogressed?

(b) Is patient .... ☐ Ambulatory? ☐ House confined? ☐ Bed confined? ☐ Hospital confined?

(c) Has patient been hospital confined? .... ☐ Yes ☐ No If "Yes", give name and address of hospital

Confined from _____ through _____

6. Cardiac (if applicable)

(a) Functional capacity · · · · · · · · · · · · · ·☐ Class 1 (No limitation) ☐ Class 2 (Slight limitation)

(American Heart Association) ☐ Class 3 (Marked limitation) ☐ Class 4 (Complete limitation)

(b) Blood pressure (last visit) .... Systolic _____ / Diastolic _____

Figure 14-1. Attending Physician's Statement of Disability.

that he or she does not know the details of the insured's occupational duties, nor the provisions of the insured's policy.

The best way to overcome such objections is to supply the physician with an explanation of the pertinent policy provisions and a copy of the patient's job description as furnished by the employer. With such information, the physician can determine if the insured should be restricted from performing any or all of his or her occupational duties. However, even with the necessary information, a physician may still be hesitant to offer a professional determination on the question of disability. In such cases, some companies have reported good results from telephone contacts with the physician. In many cases, the attending physician is willing to discuss informally the condition of the insured.

If the information from the attending physician does not verify the extent of the claimant's disability to the claim examiner's satisfaction, then the claim examiner may request an independent medical examination of the claimant by someone other than the insured's attending physician. Most disability income policies sold today include a provision authorizing the insurer to conduct an independent medical examination of the claimant. The principal reason for requesting such an examination is to verify the nature and extent of the claimant's disability. However, the examination may also be used to establish a possible plan for the claimant's rehabilitation.

The manner in which an independent medical examiner is selected varies from company to company. Some companies seek the advice of their medical department in the selection. Others use the services of an inspection company. Still others prefer to select an examining physician on a random basis from a directory of medical specialists. The reason for making a random selection is that such a process precludes any accusations that the company has used a medical practitioner who always finds in the company's favor.

Financial Information

In addition to the general information necessary to process all types of disability claims, the insurer requires financial information about the insured or the insured's business if the claim is a disability claim with residual or recovery benefits, or a business expense benefit claim.

Residual or Recovery Benefits.

The key factor in determining whether a compensable residual disability claim exists is whether the insured has suffered an earnings loss. Policies with residual or recovery benefits specify that the company has the right to require financial information that will document this earnings loss.

Most insurers define *earnings* as income received for personal services rendered. Earnings can consist of salary, wages, profits, commissions, bonuses, and other remuneration, depending upon the type of business for which the insured works. In this context, earnings do not include income from rent, royalties, annuities, investments, or any other income not derived from job activities. In order to verify an insured's earnings, the claim examiner must first identify the type of business entity for which the insured works. After making such a determination, the claim examiner will then know what type of financial information to request from the claimant.

For residual claim handling purposes, the five basic types of business entities are

- *Individual/employee*—Most disability claims are submitted by individuals who are employees with, but have no ownership interest in, a particular business. Individual employees are compensated in the form of a salary or wage. In the United States, a federal income tax "W-2" form documents this type of income. In some cases, a claim examiner may request that the individual submit a copy of his or her federal income tax return with all of the accompanying schedules.
- *Owner/sole proprietor*—A sole proprietor is the sole owner of a business. A sole proprietor's earned income is generally considered to be the net profit of the business and is documented in the United States by the sole proprietor's federal income tax return or an Income Statement, or Profit and Loss Statement.
- *Partnership*—A partnership is a legal business entity owned by two or more people. The earned income of a partner is typically represented by a proportionate share of the partnership's net income or profit. The profits would be documented in the United States by the use of the partnership's income tax return Form 1065, Schedule E of the partner's personal tax return Form 1040, or an Income Statement (Profit or Loss Statement) of the partnership.
- *Regular corporation*—A regular corporation is a legal business entity that is separate and distinct from its owners. The owners of the corporation, called **shareholders**, receive **dividends**, or periodic income payments from the corporation. For a regular type of corporation, these profits would be documented in the shareholder's federal income tax forms, 1099 Form, Form 1040, Form 1120, Schedule E (1120), or Annual Business Statements.
- *"S" corporation*—A Sub-S or "S" corporation has the same legal purpose as a regular corporation. The primary difference between the two types of corporations is that the profits of an "S" corporation are distributed to the shareholders, in a manner similar to that of a partnership. In order to adequately document the sources of earnings for a shareholder in an "S" corporation, the claim examiner must have Form 1120, 1120S, or a business financial statement as well as the shareholder's individual income tax return.

Overhead Expense Benefits. An overhead expense policy provides for reimbursement of business expenses in the event of the business owner's disability. Thus, a disabled insured must submit itemized expenses from the insured's business, as well as supporting documents such as bills, cancelled checks, or cash disbursement journals, as verification that the expenses were incurred. A claim examiner should be cautious about accepting photocopies of actual bills or receipts, since photocopies can be altered by the insured.

Continuation of Claim Proofs

How frequently an insurance company requires further claim filings during a continuing disability depends on the company's practices. During the first 6 to 12 months after disability payments commence, the usual practice is for the claimant to submit a claim form at monthly intervals. Beyond this initial period, the frequency and extent of claim filings depend to a large extent on the anticipated duration of the disability involved.

A number of companies provide their claim examiners with reference material on the expected length of various disabilities based on the diagnosis. Some of these companies have developed their own data for this use; others use generally available references, including *The Medical Handbook for Claims Executives*, by Paul V. Reinartz; *The Human Body— Its Function in Health and Disease*, by Walter S. Clough; *The Merck Manual*, published by Merck, Sharp and Dohme Research Laboratories; and *Current Diagnosis and Treatment*, published by Lang Medical Publications. Figure 14–2 contains a portion of the Duration of Disability list found in *The Human Body—Its Function in Health and Disease*. This list assumes that the insured individual's job entails only light physical activity.

These sources serve as useful guides to the claim examiner at two points during the claim examination process: first, when the claim is initially evaluated, in determining whether the anticipated length of disability is compatible with the diagnosis; and second, at the time such a disability might be expected to end, as an indication of the possible need for an investigation of the claim. For example, if a disability is expected to last 12 months, but at the end of 12 months the insured is still claiming continued disability, the claim examiner may need to investigate more thoroughly the circumstances surrounding the insured's disability.

Almost all companies relax their requirements for claim proofs when an insured is permanently and totally disabled. A **permanent and total disability** exists when the insured is, and is expected to remain, unable to return to any gainful employment. In such situations, most companies will require a medical report on a semi-annual or an annual basis. In addition, a statement may be required from the claimant, possibly on a semi-annual basis. Some companies will establish regular contact with the insured through either a personal visit or a telephone call. The personal visit or telephone call can be a substitute for written claim forms if a company's

Operation/condition	Duration of disability
Caldwall-Luc operation	3–4 weeks
Carotid endarterectomy	6 weeks
Carpal tunnel surgery	4–6 weeks
Cataract extraction	3–6 weeks
Cholecystectomy	8–10 weeks
Colostomy	8–10 weeks
Colporrhaphy, anterior and posterior	6 weeks
Commissurotomy, mitral valve	3 months
Cone biopsy of cervix	2 weeks
Coronary artery bypass	3 months
Cystocele repair	6 weeks
Cystoscopy	0–2 weeks
Cystotomy	6 weeks
Dilation and curettage	1–2 weeks
Gastroenterostomy	8 weeks
Gastrectomy	8–10 weeks
Hallux valgus surgery	6 weeks
Heart valve replacement	3 months
Hemorrhoidectomy, external	2–3 weeks
internal and external	3–4 weeks
Herniorrhaphy	4–8 weeks
Hip replacement	4–6 months
Hysterectomy, abdominal	8–10 weeks
radical abdominal	3–4 months
vaginal	6–8 weeks
Ileostomy	8–10 weeks
Iridectomy	3–5 weeks
Knee cartilage, excision of	6 weeks
Laminectomy	6–12 weeks
Laparoscopy	0–3 days
Laryngectomy, partial	6–8 weeks
total	3–4 months
Laser therapy for retinal detachment	0–2 weeks
Lobectomy, pulmonary	8–10 weeks
Lumbar disc surgery	2–3 months
Mastectomy, simple	6–8 weeks
radical	2–3 months
Nephrectomy	8–10 weeks

Figure 14–2. Sample duration of disability list.

primary intention is to determine the whereabouts and the physical status of the insured.

Verifying Policy Coverage of the Loss

After the disability claim examiner has received adequate proof of loss, then the examiner must ensure that the policy actually covers the loss. Some disability income policies pay benefits only if the insured is totally disabled. However, other types of policies specify that benefits are payable if the insured is only partially disabled, or if the insured has suffered a loss of earnings because of a disability.

Determining Total Disability

A key factor in the determination of whether an insured is totally disabled is the definition of disability contained in the policy. At the beginning of this chapter, we mentioned that disability insurance is still evolving. Much of the current evolutionary process is a result of the continuing attempts of insurance companies, insureds, and courts to define total disability.

Definition of Total Disability: "Any Occupation" Clauses.
Early definitions of total disability were quite stringent. They typically defined total disability as the inability of the insured to perform the duties of any occupation for remuneration or profit. Under this type of definition, a neurosurgeon unable to act as a surgeon but able to park cars would be barred from recovery of disability benefits.

Because such a strict interpretation of disability would prevent most people from qualifying for disability benefits, most insurers have stopped using this definition. However, if this definition is used, courts usually interpret it to mean any occupation for which the insured is suited by virtue of education, training, or experience. According to usual court interpretation and the practices of most companies, the neurosurgeon in our previous example would be able to receive disability income benefits.

Definition of Total Disability: "Own Occupation" Clauses.
Insurers liberalized the definition of total disability by introducing disability policies that defined it as the inability of the insured to perform the duties of his or her own occupation. Under this type of definition, a lawyer who is unable to practice law but who can still teach law classes would probably qualify as totally disabled.

Definition of Total Disability: Combination Clauses.   Combination clauses used in disability income contracts merge the "any occupation" and "own occupation" provisions. A combination clause specifies

a point at which the definition of total disability changes from that of "own occupation" to that of the general "any occupation." That point is often set at two or five years after the start of disability. According to typical combination clauses, insureds are considered totally disabled if their disability prevents them from working at 'their own occupation" for a specified period, usually two or five years. After the specified period, insureds are considered totally disabled only if their disabilities prevent them from working at "any occupation" for which they are reasonably suited by education, training, or experience.

It is generally easier for the claim examiner to determine disability based on the "own occupation" definition than on the "any occupation" definition. Disability under the "any occupation" clause requires consideration of the insured's personal and occupational background as well as the insured's potential for rehabilitation. In many cases, the change in the controlling definition makes no difference—the insured remains unable to assume any occupation. But in other cases, the change may be significant. For this reason, evaluations of the insured's condition after the specified period must be particularly careful, because if the insured does not satisfy the "any occupation" test of disability, then disability payments will be discontinued. Applying the combination clause with a two-year specified period to our previous example of the lawyer would result in payment of benefits for two years. After two years, benefits would be denied because teaching law is an occupation for which the lawyer is reasonably suited.

Definition of Total Disability: Presumptive Disability.   Most disability policies and the statutes of some jurisdictions classify certain disabilities as presumptive disabilities. A *presumptive disability* exists when an individual has an irrecoverable loss of sight in both eyes, the severance of both entire hands or both entire feet, or the severance of one entire foot and one entire hand. An insured who suffers from a presumptive disability is considered totally disabled even if the insured is able to engage in his or her occupation on a full-time basis.

Determining Partial Disability

A partial disability exists when an insured is unable to work full-time or complete one or more important job duties. Policies usually specify that the insured must be under the care of a physician and that the insured must satisfy loss-of-time or loss-of-duty requirements. Claim problems usually arise in determining what constitutes full-time work for the insured, the degree of an insured's disability, and whether some factor other than the insured's disability, such as a business slump, is keeping the insured from working full-time.

Partial disability claims, more so than total disability claims, require close supervision by claim personnel. The claim must be carefully evaluated initially to ensure that an insurable loss exists, and the insured's work activities must be verified. If the insured is not self-employed, then the insured's employer may be able to verify the insured's work activities to the claim examiner's satisfaction. Many insurers find that verification of a self-employed worker's activities can be accomplished only through a visit to the insured's workplace.

It is important that a claim examiner continue to scrutinize a partial disability claim throughout the claim's duration. Continuing investigation should include a verification of the insured's day-to-day activities as well as any changes that may have occurred in his or her medical treatment since the initial claim.

Determining an Income Loss

As we mentioned earlier, a recovery or residual benefit becomes payable when the insured can substantiate that a disability resulted in a loss of at least a specified percentage of earnings, such as 20 or 25 percent. The documentation necessary for this substantiation was described in an earlier section of this chapter.

The first step in determining the insured's percentage of earnings loss is to establish the insured's monthly earnings prior to and after a disability. Prior earnings are calculated as the greater of (1) the insured's average monthly earnings for the six months immediately prior to disability; or (2) the insured's average monthly earnings for any two successive calendar years during the five-year period just prior to the start of disability. Post-disability earnings are the average monthly earnings after the insured returns to work. Most insurers do not use gross earnings figures to determine an earnings loss. Instead, they deduct normal and customary business expenses from an insured's gross earnings to determine the insured's net earnings. The purpose of allowing these deductions is to avoid unfairly penalizing an insured whose business expenses remain relatively constant before disability and after a return to work. To illustrate, consider the following example:

A physician, Barry Williams, has a disability income policy that specifies that he must suffer a 25 percent earnings loss in order to qualify for a maximum monthly residual benefit of $3,000. Barry earned $20,000 in monthly gross earnings before his disability. Upon his return to work following his disability, he earned only $16,000 in monthly gross earnings. His office expenses before and after disability remained constant at $12,000 per month. The formula for determining an earnings loss is as follows:

$$\frac{\text{Previous Monthly Earnings} - \text{Current Monthly Earnings}}{\text{Previous Monthly Earnings}} = \text{Earnings Loss}$$

If Barry's earnings loss is calculated using his gross earnings, his earnings will only be reduced by 20 percent, and no benefits will be payable.

$$\frac{\$20,000 - \$16,000}{\$20,000} = \frac{\$4,000}{\$20,000} = 20\% \text{ Earnings Loss}$$

By contrast, if net earnings are used, his earnings will be reduced by 50 percent, and benefits will be payable.

$$\frac{\$8,000 - \$4,000}{\$8,000} = \frac{\$4,000}{\$8,000} = 50\% \text{ Earnings Loss}$$

Once a claim examiner has determined that an insured's earnings loss qualifies the insured for benefits, then the earnings loss percentage is multiplied by the maximum monthly benefit amount in order to determine the amount of the monthly benefit payable. Continuing with our example, the maximum monthly benefit Barry would receive in the month outlined would be $1,500 (.50×$3,000=$1,500). To collect benefits for the next month, Barry must submit financial data that verifies an income loss in that month greater than 25 percent of net earnings before disability.

References

"Administering the Residual Disability Claim," *1987 ICA Health Insurance Workshop Notes*, 103–116.
"Are you Insuring Occupation or Income?" *1983 ICA Health Insurance Workshop Notes*, 24–30.
"Business Overhead Expense Claims," *1984 ICA Health Insurance Workshop Notes*, 22–27.
"Claim Proofs, How Often and How Much?" *1982 ICA Health Insurance Workshop Notes*, 77–79.
"Residual Disability Claims—Using a CPA to Understand Tax Returns," *1985 ICA Health Insurance Workshop Notes*, 44–50.
"Residual Disability ... More on Its Concept and How It Works," *1986 ICA Health Insurance Workshop Notes*, 14–19.
"Residual Disability—The Concept, and How It Works," *1985 ICA Health Insurance Workshop Notes*, 32–42.
Soule, Charles E. *Disability Income Insurance—The Unique Risk*, Homewood, IL: Dow Jones-Irwin, 1984.
"Use of In-house Experts to Process Residual Claims," *1987 ICA Health Insurance Workshop Notes*, 82–83.

15

Paying
Disability Benefits

As we discussed in Chapter 14, disability claims differ greatly from life and medical expense claims. Perhaps the greatest difference between disability claims and other types of claims lies in the payment area.

A life insurance policy usually will result in only one claim for death benefits. Once the life insurance claim is paid, the insurer's obligation under the life insurance contract ceases. A medical expense policy, by contrast, may result in numerous claims, but each claim is independently evaluated and paid according to the contract's terms. Although the company retains an obligation to pay for any valid medical expense claims that are incurred in the future, future claims are not usually a continuation of a previous claim.

A disability policy may, however, require an insurer to pay benefits for many years under the same claim. An insured's disability may cause an insured to be unable to work for one month or for one year before recovering, or the insured may never be able to work again. As long as the insured satisfies the requirements of the disability policy, disability benefits will continue to be paid under the same claim until the policy's maximum benefit period is reached. The claim examiner must continue to verify that the insured satisfies the policy's requirements and to authorize payment of the disability benefit. Thus, the evaluation and payment of a disability claim can be an ongoing process for a disability claim examiner.

In this chapter, we first describe the process of paying valid disability claims. This payment process involves many claim considerations including (1) what type of disability benefit is involved, (2) whether benefits are to be coordinated with other income replacement plans, and (3) whether the insured is a candidate for rehabilitation. In the last portion of this chapter, we describe the termination of disability benefits and the settlement of disability claims.

TYPES OF DISABILITY BENEFITS

The method used to pay disability benefits depends to a large extent on the type of benefit involved. Some disability benefits, such as the waiver-of-premium benefit, are simple to calculate. In such cases, the amount of the benefit is the premium being waived. For other disability coverages, the benefit amount is established at the time the policy or rider is purchased. For example, a basic disability income policy may specify that the insurer will pay $2,000 a month for total disability. However, most disability benefit policies, particularly residual disability income policies, specify a formula that the claim examiner must use to determine the claimant's benefit amount. Figure 15–1 lists major categories of benefits and reviews the type of benefit payable under each type.

THE COORDINATION OF DISABILITY INCOME BENEFITS

If the benefit payable is for disability income benefits, then the claim examiner must be alert to the possibility of overinsurance. As in medical expense insurance, an overinsured claimant may profit from a disability if he or she is eligible for benefits under two or more separate plans. If the claimant receives the maximum benefit payment from each plan, he or she will probably receive more income while disabled than while working and thus will have little motivation to return to work. Disability insurers seek to protect themselves from such situations by designing their individual and group policies to avoid overinsurance.

Group Disability Income Policies

The disability benefits provided through group disability income plans are usually coordinated with other income replacement plans so that benefit amounts are reduced to reflect any amounts that the insured received from other sources, including

- salary continuation plans,

Type of Disability Benefit	Benefit Payable
Waiver of Premium Benefit	Benefit is the amount of the insurance premium being waived.
Disability Income—Basic	Benefit may be a fixed amount or a percentage of insured's pre-disability income, up to a maximum amount.
Disability Income—Partial	Benefit is one-half of the basic disability income benefit.
Disability Income—Residual or Recovery Benefit	Benefit varies according to a percentage formula that compares an insured's pre-disability income with post-disability income.
Overhead Expense Insurance	Benefit payment is the amount of itemized expenses submitted by the claimant, up to a maximum benefit amount.
Disability Buy-out Insurance	Benefit amount either is fixed at the time of policy application or is based on the value of the business at the time of claim.

Figure 15-1. Major types of disability benefits.

- Workers' Compensation programs,
- government-sponsored disability programs, and
- other insurer-provided disability plan benefits.

Salary Continuation Plans

Many employers provide self-insured salary continuation plans that are designed to continue an employee's salary during short periods of disability. Typical employer salary continuation programs may be for periods as short as four weeks or as long as one year and are frequently tied to the employee's length of service.

Because of the short duration of coverage, salary continuation plans do not present a significant overinsurance threat. Most group disability income policies are designed so that the elimination period of the group policy is at least as long as the employer's self-insured salary continuation plan. However, if there is an overlap of a week or so when benefits are payable under both the employer's salary continuation plan and the insurer's disability plan, then the salary continuation benefits should be applied to offset the long-term disability benefit.

Workers' Compensation Programs

Workers' Compensation programs were the first broad-based government disability programs enacted in the United States and in all provinces of Canada. As we described in Chapter 12, Workers' Compensation programs provide a variety of benefits including a disability income benefit for injuries or illnesses that arise in the course of employment. Most Workers' Compensation programs exclude self-inflicted injuries or accidents resulting from the worker's willful disregard of safety rules.

Most Workers' Compensation programs require an insured worker to satisfy a waiting period before benefits are payable. A seven-day waiting period is quite common. The disability income benefit is usually a percentage of the disabled employee's average weekly wage over some period of time, commonly the 13 weeks immediately preceding the disability, up to a maximum benefit amount. All state plans provide for the rehabilitation of disabled workers.

Because of the administrative difficulties of coordinating insurer-provided benefits with the benefits that are payable under various Workers' Compensation programs, most group disability contracts provide only nonoccupational benefits. In other words, benefits for occupationally related disabilities are excluded from coverage. In cases in which an insurer-provided plan and Workers' Compensation covers the same occupational injury or illness, the benefits paid by Workers' Compensation are deducted from the normal benefits payable under the disability insurance contract. If the insured's disability continues, the claim examiner should periodically contact the administrator in charge of the Workers' Compensation program to determine the status of the insured's benefits—to see if the insured's benefits have increased or decreased.

Social Security Disability Income

In the United States, the federal government provides disability benefits primarily through the Old-Age, Survivors, Disability and Health Insurance (OASDHI) Program, better known as Social Security. However, disability benefits are also available through

- a Supplemental Security Income Program,
- the Veterans Administration,

- the Civil Service Disability Program, and
- the Railroad Retirement Act.

Social Security disability income (SSDI) coverage began in 1956. It is funded through contributions paid by employers, employees, and self-employed individuals.

Eligibility. In order to be eligible for SSDI benefits, a person generally must have contributed to the SSDI Program for a certain number of years. The number of years of work required depends upon the age at which the person becomes disabled. For example,

- *If disabled before age 24:* Credit is needed for 1½ years of work in the three-year period ending when disability begins.
- *If disabled from ages 24 through 30:* Credit is needed for having worked half the time between age 21 and the time disability begins.
- *If disabled at age 31 or older:* Except for the blind, credit is needed for at least 5 years of work during the 10 years immediately preceding the date disability begins. (Years need not be continuous nor in units of full years.) A person disabled by blindness needs 1½ years of credit, on the basis of ¼ year of credit for each year worked since 1950 or since the year of reaching age 21 if that is later.

If a worker has accumulated sufficient work credits, disability benefits may be payable to

- *disabled workers under age 65 and their families.* Those older than 65 are eligible under regular Social Security retirement benefits.
- *persons disabled before age 22.* These benefits are payable as early as age 18 when a parent (or sometimes a grandparent) receives Social Security or disability benefits, or after an insured parent dies.
- *disabled widows and widowers and, under certain conditions, disabled surviving divorced wives of workers who were insured at their death.* These benefits are payable as early as age 50.

Determination of Disability. A strict definition of disability is used for SSDI benefits. The worker must have a medically determinable physical or mental condition that (1) prevents him or her from engaging in any substantial gainful work and (2) is expected to last (or has lasted) at least 12 months or is expected to result in death. Therefore, a person who is not able to perform his or her regular work but who can do other substantial gainful work is not considered disabled under SSDI. The determination is based upon medical evidence, age, education, training, and work experience.

Waiting Period. If the worker is eligible for disability benefits and satisfies the definition of disability, then he or she still must complete a five-month waiting period. Benefits are payable for the sixth full month following disability, payable at the beginning of the seventh month. For example, Dale Hutchinson was disabled according to the SSDI definition of disability on January 1. He completed a five month waiting period on May 31st and his first benefit check covering June was payable July 1. A new waiting period is not required if the worker recovers and returns to work but becomes disabled again within five years.

Disability Benefits. SSDI provides a monthly benefit equal to the monthly benefit that would normally have become payable when the worker retired. The monthly benefits are paid until the disabled worker reaches the normal retirement age—at which time regular Social Security benefits become payable—recovers from the disability, or dies. If the medical condition improves so that the person can perform substantial gainful work, the payments are continued for a three-month adjustment period that includes the month in which the disability ceased.

Special Claim Considerations. As we mentioned earlier, group disability plans frequently specify that the benefit which the insurer will pay is reduced or offset by any SSDI benefit payable. However, many disabled people will be content to accept the benefits of the insurer-provided plan and will not make the necessary effort to qualify for SSDI benefits. The claim examiner may be able to encourage qualified claimants to file for SSDI benefits by explaining the following advantages of SSDI:

- Regardless of age, the claimant will qualify for Medicare after having been entitled to monthly SSDI benefits for 24 months.
- The claimant will be considered for possible vocational rehabilitation services by the State Rehabilitation Agency.
- If the claimant recovers, SSDI payments continue through an adjustment period of three months.
- A claimant may continue receiving full disability benefits for up to nine months while testing his or her ability to work.
- If the claimant qualifies for SSDI benefits, monthly benefits may also be payable to other family members. For example, the dependent of a disabled individual may qualify for a benefit payment. Some long-term disability plans offset only the benefits

received by the disabled insured; thus the benefits received for dependents will increase the household income and will enhance the financial situation for the family.
- SSDI benefits include cost-of-living increases that may not be included in the insurer-provided plan.

However, assuming that the claimant can be encouraged to file, qualification for benefits is far from automatic. In fact, fewer than 50 percent of the people who apply for SSDI benefits are accepted on their initial application. Unless claimants understand the process involved, they are likely to accept the initial rejection as final. If a claim examiner has reason to believe that a claimant meets the requirements for SSDI benefits, then the claimant should be encouraged to apply for a reconsideration within 60 days of the initial denial. If the second application is denied, then the claimant may request a hearing with an Administrative Law Judge. If the Administrative Law Judge's decision is to deny benefits, then the claimant may request a review by the Appeals Council. If the Appeals Council declines to review the Administrative Law Judge's decision, then the claimant may bring suit in a Federal District Court.

During this process, which may take as long as a year, the claim examiner should stay in close contact with the claimant. Very often, the insurer will have information that can be useful in helping the claimant establish a right to SSDI benefits. In addition, some insurers aid the claimant in obtaining legal assistance by either agreeing to pay a portion of the attorney's fee or agreeing to offset the amount of the attorney's fee from any retroactive benefits.

Canada Pension Plan/Quebec Pension Plan (CPP/QPP)

In Canada, the federal government provides disability benefits primarily through the Canada Pension Plan/Quebec Pension Plan. However, government-provided benefits are also available through the Unemployment Insurance Program.

The CPP/QPP automatically covers almost all employees and self-employed persons in Canada who earn more than $2,000 annually and who are between the ages of 18 and 65.

Eligibility for Benefits.   In order to qualify for disability benefits under the CPP/QPP, a person must have contributed for a specified period— typically, at least five calendar years. In addition, the person must be suffering from a severe and prolonged mental or physical disability such that he or she is unable to engage in any substantially gainful occupation. The impairment must be expected to last well into the foreseeable future, much beyond the 12-month requirement for the Social Security program in the United States.

Benefits.   The disability benefit is payable monthly, beginning with the fourth month following the month in which the person became disabled. The disability benefit is paid for as long as disability continues, up to age 65. At age 65, it is replaced by the CPP/QPP retirement pension.

The benefits payable before age 65 are a fixed monthly sum, plus a percentage (currently 75 percent) of the individual's monthly retirement pension benefit amount, plus benefits for any minor children. If a disabled person is receiving benefits for a child who attains age 18 and who is still going to school, the benefit is then payable to the child, not to the disabled individual.

State Government Disability Plans

The statutes of five states—California, Hawaii, New Jersey, New York, and Rhode Island—provide state residents with a disability income benefit for nonoccupational disabilities. Benefits from these plans often start after one week of disability and continue for 26 to 39 weeks.

If a claimant is a resident in one of these states, the claim examiner should ask for a copy of the state's disability award. The disability award will specify the amount of benefits that are being paid to the claimant and the starting and ending dates of those benefits. The claim examiner can then reduce the insurer-provided benefits by the amount of state-provided disability benefits.

Other Disability Benefits

Sometimes an employer-provided pension plan or an employer-provided group life insurance plan will include a monthly benefit payment for total and permanent disabilities. If a claimant's disability appears to be permanent, the claim examiner should secure the relevant plan documents from the claimant's employer. Normally, if an employer offers employees long-term disability coverage, the employer's pension plan or group life plan will not provide a disability benefit. However, if a disability benefit is provided under an employer-provided pension or life insurance plan, those payments will be used to offset the long-term disability benefit.

Individual Disability Income Policies

Individual disability benefits are not generally coordinated with other sources of disability income. Instead, at the time an individual disability income policy is purchased, the insurer considers all sources of a proposed insured's income and limits the amount of disability income coverage the individual may purchase to a percentage, usually 75 or 80 percent of the proposed insured's monthly net earnings, up to a maximum amount. For example, the amount that can be purchased may be limited to 75 percent of the proposed insured's usual monthly net earnings up to a maximum of $2,000 per month.

If a claim examiner discovers during a policy's contestable period that an insured's income was misrepresented on the policy application, the claim examiner will refer the information to the underwriting department. An underwriter will determine whether the policy would have been issued as applied for, had the correct financial information been known to them at the time of application. If a different underwriting action would have been taken, then the claim department may take action to either reform or rescind the policy.

In addition, some guaranteed renewable or noncancellable individual policies include a *relation of earnings to insurance clause*, also known as a participation limit, that limits the amount of benefits in which the insurer will participate when the total amount of benefits from all insurers exceeds the insured's usual monthly net earnings. This clause takes effect *only* if the insurer was not notified of the other coverage at the time of application. An insurer utilizing such a clause must return the premiums for the excess coverage.

To illustrate how this clause would operate, assume that John James received monthly net earnings before disability of $1,000 per month. He applied for and was issued a disability income policy from *Insurer A* that paid $600 per month and one from *Insurer B* that paid $800 per month. Neither *Insurer A* nor *Insurer B* was notified of the other insurance coverage at the time of policy issue. If John's policy had a relation of earnings to insurance clause, and if he became disabled, he could collect $429 from *Insurer A* and $571 from *Insurer B*, or a total of $1,000. The amounts payable may be calculated as follows:

$$\frac{\text{Monthly Net Earnings before Disability}}{\text{Total Amount Payable from All Insurers}} = A$$

$$A \times \text{Benefit Amount Specified in the Policy} = \text{Benefit Payable by Insurer}$$

$$\frac{\$1,000}{\$1,400} \times \$600 = \$429 \text{ Payable by } \textit{Insurer A}$$

$$\frac{\$1,000}{\$1,400} \times \$800 = \$571 \text{ Payable by } \textit{Insurer B}$$

$$\$429 + \$571 = \$1,000 \text{ Total Benefit to Insured}$$

REHABILITATION

After the appropriate disability income benefit payment has been determined, the claim examiner authorizes payment of the benefit to the claimant. At this time, or perhaps even earlier in the claim process, the claim examiner will determine whether the claimant is a candidate for rehabilitation. *Rehabilitation*, as defined by the National Council on Rehabilitation, is "the restoration of the handicapped to the maximum physical, mental, social, vocational, and economic usefulness for which they are capable." Insurance companies are primarily interested in returning the disabled person to an occupation of economic usefulness.

Successful rehabilitation of a disabled person benefits all of the parties involved. The disabled person returns to being a self-supporting member of society. The insurance company, in addition to saving money, enhances its image with the disabled individual and, as a result, with friends, family, and business associates of the claimant. Other policyowners benefit from the lower premiums made possible by the insurer's reduced claim costs.

The most critical element of a rehabilitation program is flexibility. There is no one way to rehabilitate all disabled persons. Nonetheless, all rehabilitation programs usually include

- payments to the insured for medical treatment and counseling,
- continuation of disability income during a trial work period,
- provision of rehabilitation services and vocational training, and
- job placement services.

Identifying Likely Candidates

For any type of rehabilitation program to be successful, the program must concentrate on the early identification of likely candidates for rehabilitation. The passage of time brings acceptance of disability on the part of not only the disabled individual but also the disabled individual's family, friends, and employer. Therefore, the best time to screen disability claims for rehabilitation potential is at the time the claim is first approved. Early identification enables the candidates to be referred immediately to the rehabilitation specialists, who can determine rehabilitation possibilities and institute a rehabilitation program at the earliest possible stages of disability.

Not all disabled persons are candidates for vocational rehabilitation. In fact, the vast majority usually are not. Studies by several health insurance companies indicate that only from one to four percent of long-term disability cases are candidates for rehabilitation. Companies differ in their approach to identifying possible rehabilitation candidates; however, the criteria for selection usually includes the following considerations:

1. *Age*—The age of the insured is a critical factor. A younger person is generally more responsive to rehabilitation and more motivated to return to employment than is an older person.

2. *Cause of disability*—In general, injury lends itself more to rehabilitation than does sickness.
3. *Education and training*—The more highly educated the insured, the better the prospects for rehabilitation following any required retraining.
4. *Occupation*—Professionals are often easier to place in appropriate positions than are nonprofessionals. For example, a college professor may welcome the challenge of writing textbooks on a home computer.
5. *Marital status*—In many cases, persons who are married are better prospects for rehabilitation than are single disabled persons who feel comfortable living and being alone. The encouragement of a spouse is often a key factor in successful rehabilitation.
6. *Income*—Persons who are financially self-sufficient may not feel a need to undergo rehabilitation.
7. *Geographical location*—Proximity to needed rehabilitation facilities can be important. Also, compared to a rural location, an urban location may offer more job openings.
8. *Amount of liability*—The amount of potential benefits payable on a case is important in determining the feasibility of incurring the costs of rehabilitation. For this reason, most rehabilitation efforts are aimed at persons suffering from long-term, rather than temporary, disability.
9. *Motivation*—Motivation is generally accepted as being the most crucial factor. The insured must be willing to try rehabilitation and to continue trying during what may be a long and difficult process. In the absence of such motivation, success is very unlikely.

Sources of Rehabilitation

The rehabilitation process involves many professional disciplines. Vocational counselors, nurses, therapists, social workers, psychologists, and physicians with various specialties all play a part in the rehabilitation process. Although the claim examiner has an important role in first identifying potential candidates for rehabilitation, the administration of a rehabilitation program is usually outside the claim administration area for several reasons:

- Few claim personnel have the skills necessary for the responsibility.
- Rehabilitation involves continual contacts with the medical community. A professional with medical credentials usually has better direct access to medical personnel than does a lay person.

- A claimant might be suspicious of the motives of a claim examiner in advocating and managing his or her rehabilitation program.

Insurers may use one or a combination of three different sources for rehabilitation services: sources within the company itself, private rehabilitation services, and public rehabilitation services.

Rehabilitation Units Within the Company

Some companies have established separate rehabilitation units that work closely with the claim department. The rehabilitation units evaluate claimants with potentially long-term disabilities and determine whether they can be rehabilitated. If it appears that they can be, then members of the rehabilitation unit oversee the disabled individuals' rehabilitative therapy. Rarely do the rehabilitation units actually provide rehabilitative therapy themselves; instead they schedule therapy for a disabled person at rehabilitation centers located near the claimant.

Internal rehabilitation units have both advantages and disadvantages. With an internal rehabilitation unit, the insurance company can establish the greatest degree of control over the quality of the professionals involved and over the management of the rehabilitation process. However, an insurer often has difficulty in locating medical professionals who can manage the case and who live in the same area as the insured. Further, this approach requires that the insurer incur the costs of establishing a separate unit within its organization.

Private Rehabilitation Agencies

An alternative is for the insurer to use the services of a private rehabilitation agency. Some of these agencies provide initial screening of cases at no charge. In any event, charges are made only on a per-case basis; the company does not have the continuing overhead expense it has with an internal unit. As a purchaser of rehabilitation services, the insurer has some direct say in managing the process. However, services rendered by these private agencies are generally more expensive on a per-hour basis than are those of an internal rehabilitation area.

Public Rehabilitation Agencies

A third alternative is public rehabilitation agencies. Every state has a department of vocational rehabilitation to assist disabled persons in obtaining the highest level of recovery and placement in suitable employment. Most of these agencies provide listings of facilities and workshops located within their jurisdictions, along with summaries of the types of services available and the admission procedures of the facilities. Included among such facilities are specialized rehabilitation centers, rehabilitation departments of hospitals, workshops that offer employment for disabled persons, vocational training schools, and special institutions and schools for people with particular disabilities, such as the blind or the deaf.

Health insurers utilizing these public agencies report mixed results, which is probably not surprising considering the number of separate agencies involved. When using these public agencies, the insurer has no control over either the persons involved in the rehabilitation process or the medical management of the case. The obvious offsetting factor is that the services of such agencies are paid for by governmental funds, not by the insurer. In choosing whether to use private or public rehabilitation agencies, the insurer must balance the costs of utilizing a private agency against its lack of control over the public agency.

Methods of Rehabilitation

The methods of rehabilitation for any case depend on the circumstances of that case: the nature of the disablement, the type of medical correction used, and the demands of the job for which the insured is being prepared. Ideally, rehabilitation should return the disabled to their former jobs on a full-time basis. If it is apparent that this is not feasible, the insurer can consider making arrangements to modify the work area for the disabled person, to retrain the disabled person in a new field, or to find a self-employment opportunity for the disabled person.

Modifying the Work Area

In some cases, a disabled person will be able to resume his or her regular occupation after being fitted with artificial limbs or a wheelchair, and no modifications to the work area or job will be necessary. However, it is more likely that the disabled person will be prevented by some characteristic of the work area from returning to the original occupation. For example, a factory may not have entrance facilities suitable for use by wheelchair workers. An insurer might remedy such a situation by working with an employer to provide a ramp entrance to the building. Other ways the insurer might seek to modify the work area include making parking spaces available close to the building, lowering desks, raising chairs or work benches, modifying file drawer arrangements, and rearranging office furniture.

In some cases, the United States federal government may reward employers for making such modifications. Firms doing over $2,500 of business with the federal government are required by the Rehabilitation Act of 1973 to accommodate the needs of handicapped persons. Businesses may receive credit toward fulfilling this requirement for their efforts to reemploy disabled workers.

Training in a New Field

In many cases, work area modifications will not enable a disabled person to resume his or her former occupation. Training in a completely new field is required to allow the individual an opportunity to return to gainful employment. Training is more costly than work area modification; it also entails more risk, both to the insurer and to the disabled individual. Before underwriting the costs of training, the company will want to satisfy itself that the insured stands a reasonable chance of success in the new occupation. The insured, on the other hand, risks the loss of disability benefits during employment that may not work out satisfactorily. The insurer may reduce that risk by offering a subsidy for a specified period of time after the worker begins work in the new occupation.

In the United States, severely handicapped persons may qualify for special, noncompetitive appointments under civil service. These persons include, among others, the blind, deaf, cerebral palsied, paraplegic, and quadriplegic.

Self-Employment

The last method of rehabilitation is self-employment. Sometimes a disabled individual is truly not employable in a competitive market, but has business skills or hobbies that can be used for self-employment. Even home-bound persons may be successfully rehabilitated under this method. The cost to the insurer is the investment needed to set the person up in business, plus a subsidy during the early stages of the business operation.

TERMINATION OF DISABILITY BENEFITS

As we have already mentioned, a claim examiner's responsibility under a disability claim does not end with the initial authorization of payment. The claim examiner continues to monitor the circumstances surrounding the claim in order to verify that the claimant remains qualified to receive benefits.

A disability claimant typically relies heavily on the benefits of a disability contract in order to provide for basic living expenses. The loss of those benefits can place the claimant and his or her family in a very difficult situation. Therefore, a claim examiner must carefully consider all facts of the case before deciding that benefits are no longer payable.

Of course, disability benefits will automatically terminate when the policy's maximum benefit period is reached. In addition, the termination of disability benefits is likely to be triggered by one of the following events: (1) the controlling definition of disability changes from "own occupation" to "any occupation," (2) the insured is no longer disabled, or (3) the insured's income has increased so that it no longer satisfies policy requirements.

Change in Controlling Definition of Disability

In many disability policies, the definition of disability changes after a stated period of time from "own occupation" to "any occupation." At that time a review of the case may show that the insured is capable of employment for which he or she is reasonably fitted by training, education, or experience. In such cases, the insured may no longer be considered disabled and hence is entitled to no further benefits.

Change in Insured's Condition

The second situation leading to termination of benefits can arise at any time during the benefit period when the claim examiner verifies that the insured's physical condition or activities preclude a finding of disability. For example, the insured may have undergone surgery that corrected the disability, or the insured may have successfully completed a rehabilitation program that allows him or her to be gainfully employed.

In some cases, the insured may have recovered from the disability without notifying the insurer. Some cases may involve fraudulent activities on the part of the claimant. For example, the claimant may forge a physician's signature on an Attending Physician's Statement, which is required to verify continuing disabilities. If the claim examiner suspects that the insured is no longer disabled, the claim examiner will initiate an investigation into the claimant's activities in order to prove that the insured is no longer disabled.

Change in Insured's Income Level

Recovery or residual disability income benefits are payable when an insured suffers a loss of income because of a disability. Thus, if the insured's income exceeds a specified limit, then disability income benefits cease. Claim examiners monitor the insured's income flow through financial statements and income tax records.

SETTLEMENTS

Life and medical expense claims typically are either payable or not payable.

Claims for valid contractual liabilities are paid; those for which there is no liability are not paid. However, in the disability area, in addition to paying or denying claims, insurance companies may utilize another course of action—a settlement. According to the terms of a typical **settlement**, the insurer agrees to pay the claimant a lump sum of money in exchange for a termination of the insurer's obligation under the policy. There are basically two types of settlements: disputed claim settlements and financial settlements.

Disputed Claim Settlements

In situations involving disputed claims, the claim itself, or the policy, is the focus of the settlement. In such cases, the insurer and the claimant legitimately disagree over one or more aspects of the claim—for example, whether the disability was caused by accident or by sickness, whether the disabled person is totally or partially disabled, or whether the condition is excluded by a policy provision. When both parties are able to present evidence supporting their case, the insurer frequently will offer the claimant a settlement amount in order to avoid costly litigation, to alleviate lengthy and costly investigations, and to avoid charges of bad faith.

Financial Settlements

Some settlements, called **financial settlements**, **commutations**, or **buyouts**, are designed to aid an insured's rehabilitation or simply to terminate the insurer's obligation when the insured does not need or desire the monthly benefit payment. For example, the claimant may agree to a settlement in order to purchase a business so that he or she can be gainfully employed. Alternatively, the claimant, who is insured under an "own occupation" type of policy, may agree to a settlement after beginning another occupation. Financial settlements do not typically involve an adversarial relationship, and there is usually no question as to the company's liability for the claim.

Financial settlements can be advantageous to both the insurer and the claimant. From the insurer's perspective, the primary advantage of a settlement is cost savings. The insurer saves the costs of administering the long-term claim, including staff time, materials, and computer time. In addition, the amount of the reserve that must be set aside to fund the claim is often considerably more than the settlement amount. In such cases, the insurer will realize a net savings for that claim in the year in which the settlement is negotiated.

From the claimant's perspective, a settlement is an opportunity to acquire a lump sum of capital. A claimant may want to use the capital to produce an income that is not fixed or limited, as is the disability benefit.

The capital can also be used to pay off extraordinary expenses, to buy a house, or to enter any of a number of other ventures that require a large amount of capital. However, settlements do involve some risks to the claimant since the insurer's obligation under the policy usually ceases with the settlement.

References

Coward, Laurence E. *Mercer Handbook of Canadian Pension and Welfare Plans.* Toronto, Canada: CCH Canadian Limited, 1984.

"Disability Income Offsets," *1985 ICA Group Insurance Workshop Notes*, 12–13.

Harnett, Bertram and Lesnick, Irving L. *The Law of Life and Health Insurance*. Volumes 2 and 3, 1988.

"The Negotiation and Settlement of Questionable Claims," *1983 ICA Individual Health Insurance Workshop Notes*, 16–17.

"Rehabilitation Can Work For You," *1986 ICA Individual Health Insurance Workshop Notes*, 1–6.

"Rehabilitation/Case Management," *1985 ICA Group Insurance Workshop Notes*, 6–8.

"Rehabilitation—Is It Cost Effective?," *1983 ICA Individual Health Insurance Workshop Notes*, 1–9.

Rejda, George E. *Social Insurance and Economic Security*, Second Edition. Englewood Cliffs, NJ: Prentice-Hall, Inc., 1984.

Ross, Kenneth S. "Overinsurance-Problems and Cures," *1981 ICA Individual Health Insurance Workshop Notes*, 68.

Ross, Kenneth S. "Pros and Cons for Settlement Actions," *1982 ICA Individual Health Insurance Workshop Notes*, 91–97.

"Settlements and Settlement Negotiations—A Fundamental Analysis," *1987 ICA Individual Health Insurance Workshop Notes*, 66–76.

"Social Security Intervention," *1986 ICA Group Insurance Workshop Notes*, 11–15.

"Social Security Update," *1983 ICA Group Insurance Workshop Notes*, 38–40.

"What's Social Security Disability Doing Now?," *1986 ICA Individual Health Insurance Workshop Notes*, 150–155.

Other Types of Claims

16

Credit Insurance Claims

Consumers routinely borrow money to purchase cars, major appliances, or other items. The money they borrow is repaid either over a period of time or in one lump sum. Repayment of the debt is often dependent on the borrower's continuing ability to earn money. Should a borrower die or become disabled, the loan might not be repaid. Credit life insurance is designed to protect creditors against financial loss if the insured borrower should die. Credit disability insurance is designed to protect against financial loss if the insured borrower should become disabled.

If a borrower with credit life insurance dies, a term life insurance benefit pays the outstanding balance of the loan. When a borrower with credit disability insurance becomes disabled, the insurance benefit will either pay the loan installments as they come due or pay the outstanding balance of the loan. Credit insurance relieves the family of a deceased or disabled borrower from the financial strain of repaying the debt incurred by the insured.

The examination of a death claim or a disability claim under a credit insurance policy involves many of the same questions and principles described in earlier chapters. However, credit insurance does differ significantly in some respects from ordinary insurance. This chapter describes the characteristics of credit insurance and how credit insurance claims differ from other types of claims.

CHARACTERISTICS OF CREDIT INSURANCE

Insurance companies that provide credit insurance market it through banks, finance companies, credit card companies, loan companies, and other institutions that are eligible lenders according to applicable laws. Credit insurance is normally associated with short-term loans of a maximum of five or ten years' duration. However, a growing amount of credit insurance is being written on long-term loans, primarily home mortgages, of 20 to 30 years' duration. In this chapter, long-term credit insurance designed to insure home mortgages is called *mortgage protection insurance*. Since the handling of claims for mortgage protection insurance differs significantly from the handling of claims for credit insurance, mortgage protection insurance claims are described separately later in this chapter.

Credit insurance is not generally underwritten in the same manner as life or health insurance. The only underwriting qualification is that the insured must be below a maximum age limit—typically age 65. The same premium rate is charged to every consumer, regardless of age or sex. Generally, even if two or more persons cosign a note for a loan, only one person is covered by credit insurance. Sometimes, however, *joint credit life insurance* is provided that pays the full benefit to the lender upon the death of any of the loan cosigners. Once a benefit has been paid, no further benefit is payable even if another cosigner dies, because the death of any debtor terminates the certificate of insurance. As a rule, corporations, partnerships, and associations are not eligible debtors under credit insurance.

GROUP CREDIT INSURANCE

Credit insurance can be obtained through either group or individual insurance policies. However, the vast majority of credit insurance is issued through group insurance policies. Very little, if any, difference exists in the administration of group and individual credit insurance claims. In this chapter, we focus primarily on group credit insurance.

Group credit insurance policies are similar in many ways to other types of group policies. Under both types of policies, the contractual relationship is between the insurer and the group policyholder. Under credit insurance, the lender is the group policyholder and the borrowers of a particular lender are considered to be the insured group. The group credit insurance master contract is issued to the lender/policyholder, and the lender/policyholder is responsible for issuing certificates of insurance to eligible debtors. The certificates of insurance describe the essential features of the coverage and specify the benefits of the policy.

The major difference between group credit insurance and other types of group insurance is that under group credit insurance, the policy benefit must be used for the specific purpose of repaying the amount of the debt. Thus, the group credit master policyholder is also the beneficiary of the insurance.

A group credit insurance program may be either contributory or non-contributory. If the plan is contributory, the debtor may be required either to pay a single premium at the time the loan is established or to pay premiums through an insurance charge that is included in the loan payment installments. If the plan is noncontributory, the lender/policyholder absorbs the entire cost of the credit insurance as an operating expense, insuring all debtors automatically. Under either type of plan, the lender/policyholder remits the premium to the insurer.

GROUP CREDIT LIFE INSURANCE

Group credit life insurance is designed to insure a variety of debt obligations, including installment loans, single-payment loans, balloon loans, and open-ended loans. The type of debt obligation being insured determines the type of credit insurance coverage issued, as discussed below.

Types of Loans that are Insured

Installment loans account for the majority of loans insured by credit life insurance. **Installment loans** are typically fixed-amount, fixed-term loans that are repayable in equal monthly payments. Thus, the debt decreases through periodic payments made by the borrower. Decreasing term life insurance is commonly used to insure such loans. The initial amount of coverage is usually determined on a *gross basis*, that is, the initial amount of coverage is the total amount of money borrowed, which is known as the **principal**, plus interest, plus the premium cost of the credit insurance.

Single-payment loans are short-term loans that are repaid in a single sum at the loan's maturity date. In such cases, level term life insurance is used for credit protection. Generally, the purchaser of the coverage pays a single premium at the time the coverage is bought. However, the purchaser has the option of including the premium payment in the amount of the loan. Short-term loans are often renewed at the loan's maturity date. If a loan is renewed, new credit life coverage is issued, and the previous coverage is cancelled.

A **balloon loan** requires monthly installment payments, plus a lump-sum (balloon) payment at the loan's maturity date. Decreasing term and level term insurance are combined for credit life insurance covering this type of loan agreement. The level term insurance portion covers the amount of the final payment, and the decreasing term insurance portion covers the periodic payments.

For some types of debt, such as credit card debt, the amount of the loan is unspecified. Such loans are called *open-ended loans* because the amount of debt can vary throughout the period of the loan—decreasing, increasing, or remaining the same. The amount of credit life insurance on this type of debt fluctuates monthly according to the amount of the outstanding balance but can never exceed the amount of the outstanding balance. The premium, calculated monthly, is based on the amount of the balance for that month.

Policy Provisions

Although group credit life insurance is similar in many ways to conventional group life insurance, the group credit life insurance contract has been modified to adapt to the creditor-debtor relationship.

Policy Provisions Not Required in Group Credit Life

Provisions for beneficiary designation, facility of payment, settlement options, and policy conversion are not included in group credit policies because all benefits are payable to the lenders.

The usual misstatement of age provision is not needed because the premium rate does not depend upon the age of the individual debtor; the premium rate is the same for all ages acceptable for coverage. The group credit policy usually does give the insurer the right to refund a premium if the insurer discovers that the age of the insured debtor was above the highest age allowed by the insurer at the time of policy issue.

The incontestable clause is often omitted from group credit life policies because evidence of insurability is normally not required from an individual debtor. However, an insurer usually reserves the right to include an incontestability clause in a group credit life policy if a debtor is required to furnish evidence of insurability.

Modification of the Suicide Exclusion Provision

The typical suicide exclusion provision in group credit life insurance specifies that no benefit is payable if the insured commits suicide within a specified time after policy issue. The suicide exclusion period varies by company and by policy type; it may be as short as six months or as long as two years. For insurance on loans that are renewed periodically, such as 12-month lines of credit, the suicide exclusion is generally applicable only during the initial loan agreement period and does not begin again with each loan renewal. If benefits are not payable because of the suicide exclusion provision, the insurer will return any premiums paid. Premiums are refunded to the lender/policyholder. The lender will then credit the payment to the account of the debtor or, if the coverage was contributory, refund the premium amount to the next of kin, or to the insured's estate.

Inclusion of a Good Health Provision

Some group credit policies contain a *good health provision*, which states that a policy is void if the insured was not in good health either when the application was signed or when the policy was delivered, whichever was specified in the policy. Usually, all the applicant must do to satisfy this provision is to sign a statement saying that he or she is in good health, to the best of his or her knowledge. Since such statements are merely opinions, good health provisions are difficult for an insurer to use to support a rescission of coverage unless the insurer can present information (e.g., evidence of symptoms, treatments, disability) showing that the insured was in poor health on the effective date of policy coverage.

Even if a credit insurer presents information proving that the applicant was in poor health on the date of application, agent negligence may prevent the insurer from using the good health provision as a basis for rescission. For example, the proposed insured may charge that the insurer's agent (the sales representative) accepted the application knowing the actual health of the proposed insured.

Examination of Claims

The proofs of loss required under a credit life insurance claim usually include a certified copy of the death certificate and a claimant's statement completed by the creditor. The claimant's statement typically contains the

- name of the insured-debtor,
- number of the certificate of insurance,
- original amount of the loan,
- repayment schedule,
- total amount repaid to the date of death,
- amount due the creditor, and
- amount, if any, due the insured's estate.

The information on the claimant's statement and on the death certificate is matched with that in the insurer's records. The claim examiner verifies that the deceased is the insured, that the insured's age was not misstated, and that, if underwriting questions were asked and if the policy is still contestable, there is no evidence to indicate misrepresentation. If the claim examiner cannot verify any one of these items, then an investigation may be necessary. A claim examiner investigating a credit life insurance claim should pay particular attention to the eligibility of the debtor for insurance and to any errors that the lender/policyholder may have made.

Ineligible Debtors

Group credit life insurance policies typically exclude persons who are not considered to be eligible debtors. To be an eligible debtor, the borrower must incur indebtedness that is a binding obligation at and from the date the life insurance becomes effective. According to an NAIC model law, persons eligible for credit insurance are all the debtors of an eligible lender who meet any or all of the following three conditions:

- Their indebtedness is repayable in installments, or
- Their indebtedness is repayable in one sum at the end of a specified period that is no longer than 18 months from the date of the loan, or
- They belong to a class "determined by conditions pertaining to the indebtedness or to the purchase giving rise to the indebtedness."

Debt is an important element of a credit life insurance contract because the debt creates the beneficiary's insurable interest in the life of the insured. In reviewing a credit life insurance claim, the examiner should verify that the debtor was a debtor at the time of the insurance claim. In some cases, the debt may not exist because it has been paid. In other cases, as the following example illustrates, the debt may not have come into existence at the time of the claim.

> Doug Daniels signs an automobile purchase agreement. As a part of that agreement, Doug agrees to purchase credit life insurance on a contributory basis. Two days later, prior to signing the loan papers and prior to the delivery of the automobile, Doug dies. A claim is presented for the amount of the credit insurance.

The creditor in this case evidently believes that the credit life insurance was in force on the date of the purchase agreement. However, an indebtedness does not occur until the time of disbursement of funds or delivery of merchandise to the debtor. In this case, the signing of the purchase agreement did not cause a loan. On that basis, no insurance was in effect because there was no debt at the time of Doug's death.

Errors Made by the Lender/Policyholder

The lender/policyholder is authorized to issue certificates of insurance, to calculate and remit premiums, and to process cancellations. Mistakes by the policyholder are not uncommon and often are not discovered until a claim is presented. For example, at the time of a claim, a claim examiner might find that a certificate of insurance was never issued to the debtor. Faced with this situation, the claim examiner should request documents that could indicate whether the deceased debtor intended to purchase the insurance. If it is found that the deceased was an eligible debtor who signed a document agreeing to the purchase of the insurance, a certificate of insurance should be issued, retroactive to the original effective date. The claim then should be evaluated on that basis.

Lender/policyholders are authorized to issue certificates of insurance only within certain specified limits. For example, credit life policies usually specify a maximum age limit for the debtor and maximum loan amounts and loan durations. But sometimes the lender/policyholder, unintentionally or intentionally, exceeds one of these limits. With no knowledge of the provisions of the master contract, the debtor assumes that the stated coverage is in effect. When considering such a claim, some companies pay the benefits as described in the certificate. Other companies, however, stand by the limits specified in the master policy, declare the insurance contract null and void, and refund the amount of the premium paid.

Some claims involve the legal issue of whether the lender, acting in a capacity both as the writer of the certificate and as the beneficiary, is acting as agent of the insurer or as agent of the debtor. Court rulings have varied on this issue. The majority view has been that the lending institution is not acting as the agent of the insurer, but as the agent of the debtor. Acceptance of this viewpoint means that the insurance company is not liable for erroneous acts on the part of the lender. Thus, if a lender/policyholder issues a certificate of insurance by mistake and the insurer makes a benefit payment under this certificate, the insurance company may take legal action against the lending institution to recover the benefit payments. But, of course, taking such legal action would have a highly adverse effect on the relationship between the insurer and the lender and probably would be taken only in extreme situations.

Payment of Benefits

Group credit life insurance benefit checks are normally sent to the lender/beneficiary. Occasionally during the claim payment process, the insurer will discover that the outstanding loan amount is less than the amount of insurance in force. In such a case, the insurer can issue either one check for the gross amount of insurance to the lender, or two checks, one payable to the lender and the other to the estate of the insured. If only one check is issued, the lender is responsible for distributing the proceeds in excess of the outstanding debt to the estate of the insured. However, at least one state—Kansas—requires the insurer to pay the lender only the amount needed to satisfy the debt; any unearned premiums and unearned interest amounts must be refunded to the estate of the insured.

Conversely, the amount of the loan outstanding at the date of death is sometimes more than the amount of insurance in force. Such a situation can occur if a loan payment is delinquent and the amount of insurance decreases automatically on the scheduled basis. In such cases, many insurance companies, to promote goodwill, would increase the insurance benefit to allow for one, two, or three months of delinquent scheduled monthly payments.

Even though credit insurance benefits are payable to a lender, they fall within the scope of state inheritance or estate tax laws which require that states be notified as to the disposition of proceeds. Many states also require the insurer to pay interest on the policy proceeds from the date of death to the date of disposition of the funds.

Termination of Coverage

An individual debtor's group credit life coverage may terminate under any of several occurrences, including the following:

- The indebtedness is repaid.
- The debtor fails to make a scheduled repayment when due.
- The indebtedness is assigned to another creditor (although coverage may continue if the assigning creditor continues to service the debt and retains sufficient equity in the loan to justify continuance as beneficiary of the insurance).
- The group master policy is terminated by either the lender or the insurer, for reasons such as nonpayment of premiums or failure to meet underwriting requirements, such as maintaining a minimum volume of insurance or a minimum number of debtors in the group.

GROUP CREDIT DISABILITY INSURANCE

Group credit disability insurance provides a monthly benefit equal to the required monthly loan payment, while the insured remains disabled or until the scheduled maturity date of the loan, whichever occurs first. Generally, if a benefit is payable for part of a month, the insurance pays a pro rata portion of the disability benefit for those covered days. Benefit checks are paid directly to the lender with notification of payment to the insured-debtor.

Group credit disability insurance is generally offered only in conjunction with group credit life insurance. Unlike group credit life insurance, group credit disability insurance is generally not provided on a joint basis that insures both or all cosigners of a loan. Normally, only the primary debtor is eligible for disability coverage. In some cases, the joint debtors may elect which debtor will be eligible for disability coverage.

Definition of Disability

The definition of disability is an important consideration in the examination of all types of disability claims, including credit disability claims. Credit disability policies usually insure disabilities that result in the insured's inability to perform "any occupation." However, some states require that the "own occupation" definition be used during the first 12 or 18 months of disability. Thereafter, the "any occupation" definition must be satisfied in order for benefits to continue.

Elimination Period

As do all disability policies, credit disability policies specify an elimination period, or a waiting period, which is a specified number of days that the insured must remain disabled after the onset of disability before any disability benefits are payable. The typical elimination period under group credit disability policies is 14 or 30 days. However, some states permit the use of a seven-day elimination period.

Once the insured has satisfied the elimination period, benefits are paid on either a retroactive or a nonretroactive basis. **Retroactive benefits** are paid from the first day of disability, once the elimination period is satisfied. **Nonretroactive benefits** are payable for the period of disability after the elimination period. For example, assume that Margaret Lupo is insured under a credit disability policy with a 14-day elimination period and a nonretroactive benefit. Margaret becomes disabled and remains disabled for 50 days. She will receive 36 days of benefit payments. However, if her policy had had a retroactive benefit, then she would have received benefit payments covering the entire 50 days of disability.

Policy Exclusions and Limitations

Credit disability policies typically contain the same exclusions as do other disability policies. Policy provisions typically exclude from coverage disability resulting from

- attempted suicide or intentionally self-inflicted injury,
- war or any act or hazard of war,

- pregnancy or childbirth, and
- non-prescription drug use.

In addition, many credit disability policies have pre-existing conditions exclusions and actively-at-work requirements.

Pre-existing Conditions Exclusion

Credit insurance is not underwritten; that is, insurance is generally offered to all borrowers regardless of existing medical problems. Credit disability insurers have the option of placing a provision in their policies, called a *pre-existing conditions exclusion*, that excludes coverage of disabilities resulting from medical impairments for which the insured has been treated within a specified period, typically six months, prior to the effective date of coverage. Some states allow the specified period to be extended to 12 months if the term of the indebtedness is more than 36 months.

The pre-existing conditions exclusion most often used by credit disability insurers is called a *six and six* exclusion. According to the terms of a **six and six exclusion**, an insured's disability is not covered if the insured was treated for a condition within six months prior to the effective date of coverage and becomes disabled from that same condition within six months after the effective date of coverage.

To illustrate, assume that the effective date of credit disability coverage on Kim Wong was July 25, 1988. His credit disability policy had a six and six exclusion. The term of the insurance coverage was 36 months. On January 5, 1989, Kim became disabled from a herniated disk. A subsequent investigation disclosed that Kim had suffered a related injury on April 3, 1988, and had received continuing medical treatment, culminating in hospitalization on January 5, 1989. In this case, the insurer probably would not pay the disability benefits because (1) Kim received treatment for the injury during the six months prior to coverage and (2) disability commenced within the six months following the effective date of coverage.

Sometimes credit disability policies include a more liberal version of the pre-existing conditions exclusion than the six and six exclusion. Some insurers specify the following provision that excludes from coverage disability caused by

> Any pre-existing illness, disease or physical condition, which totally disabled the debtor at any time during the six-month period immediately preceding the effective date of coverage, and which causes loss within the six-month period following the date of insurance.

If Kim Wong's policy had included this type of pre-existing conditions exclusion, his disability would have been covered because the pre-existing condition did not result in disability during the six months prior to the effective date of coverage.

Sometimes loans are extended or refinanced. Most states allow the application of a pre-existing conditions provision to an extended or refinanced loan as long as both loans are insured under the same master group policy. However, if the amount of the new loan exceeds the amount of the old loan, then the insurer is allowed to apply the exclusion to the amount of the difference between the two loan balances.

Actively-at-Work Requirements

In many states, a credit disability insurer is allowed to impose on the borrower an actively-at-work requirement. As we defined in Chapter 4, an actively-at-work requirement specifies that an individual is not eligible for coverage unless he or she is at work and able to work on the effective date of coverage. In such states, the borrower is not eligible for coverage unless he or she is working 30 or more hours per week.

Examination of Claims

Although credit disability claims can raise considerations not found in other types of disability claims, the basic principles of evaluating disability claims still apply. This section contains information about disability claim processing that is unique to credit disability insurance.

Proof of Loss

At the onset of disability, the insured borrower must submit adequate proof of loss to the insurer. The initial proof of loss form used for credit disability claims typically contains four basic types of information:

- *the lender's statement*, which identifies the contract and certificate, the insured, the effective date of coverage, and the monthly benefit;
- *the insured's statement*, which states the cause of disability, the date of its onset, and a brief medical history;
- *the Attending Physician's Statement*, which confirms the insured's disability, diagnoses its causes, and gives dates of treatment and of hospitalization, as well as the prognosis of future disability; and
- *the employer's statement*, which discloses whether the disability is job-related and specifies the periods of time when the insured was absent from work because of the disability.

In most cases, proof of continuing disability must be submitted to the insurer periodically throughout the disability. Forms are sent by the insurer either directly to the insured or to the lender to be forwarded to the insured. A brief Attending Physician's Statement that indicates whether the insured is still disabled and receiving medical care is also usually required.

Sometimes an insurer may confirm that a debtor is totally and permanently disabled. In such cases, the insurer may agree to an advance payment to cover the remaining installments due on the indebtedness. Under such an arrangement, the lender and the insurer are saved the administrative expense of processing the claim and the benefit payment each month. In addition, the insurer saves the interest costs associated with the loan, since only the principal amount of the loan balance is repaid. The insured debtor is relieved of the need to continue to submit proof of loss forms. When the insurer makes such an advance payment to the lender, the insurer should protect itself from further obligations under the policy by obtaining a signed release from both the lender and the insured-debtor.

Claim Questions

Several claim questions can arise during the examination of a credit disability claim. There may be a question as to when the insurer's obligation for payment of disability benefits ceases. To illustrate, assume that Fran Willis has had a series of loans from one lending institution. Several times the lender has extended Fran's note in an attempt to help her during a financial crisis. Fran's most recent note was due to be repaid on August 1, but the lending institution extended the term to October 1. On August 15, Fran becomes disabled. As a general rule, the insurer's obligation for disability benefits ceases at the expiration date of the term of the original coverage unless additional credit disability coverage is issued. Thus, Fran was not covered at the time of disability. This principle applies when the disability coverage is for fixed amount loans, but not when the coverage is for outstanding loan balances on lines of credit.

The claim examiner may learn that the lender/policyholder has issued multiple certificates of insurance to the same debtor and that the total of the monthly indemnities exceeds the maximum authorized for the group. For example, assume that the Public Bank approved three loans to Mavis Biggens—a car loan for $9,000, a personal line of credit for $2,500, and a home equity loan for $10,000. Public Bank insured all loans with credit life and disability insurance from the Good Credit Insurance Company. Public Bank is authorized to issue coverage with a maximum monthly disability benefit of $350. Total monthly disability benefits payable in the event of Mavis' disability under all certificates of insurance equal $600. A claim examiner's position in a case such as the one just described, depends upon the wording of the group policy or group certificates. If the group policy contains protective language as to limits, the company might refund the premium for the excess amount and pay the maximum disability benefit authorized of $350. However, the company might be obligated to provide benefits on all the certificates, which in this situation equal $600.

Sometimes the initial proof of disability discloses that the insured's indebtedness has been discharged, and the company is then requested to make disability payments directly to the insured person. The claim examiner should review the group policy, the group certificate, and relevant state or case law. If all of these sources provide that the insurance terminates when the indebtedness is discharged, the company may deny liability on the ground that coverage has terminated.

MORTGAGE PROTECTION INSURANCE

Mortgage protection insurance pays the insured's remaining indebtedness on a mortgage in the event that the insured dies or becomes disabled and is unable to work. Residential mortgage life insurance is typically issued in the form of decreasing term life insurance either on the life of a single debtor or joint life insurance on the lives of two debtors with the benefit payable and the insurance ceasing upon the death of one of the two. The life insurance coverage is usually limited to the principal balance of the loan and does not cover interest or hazard insurance premiums.

Residential mortgage disability insurance usually provides a monthly benefit equal to the total monthly mortgage payment, including principal, interest, taxes, and hazard insurance premiums. A dollar maximum is set on this *benefit amount,* such as $500 or $750 a month. Until the mid-seventies, the maximum *benefit period* was graded according to the age at which total disability began; typically, a longer benefit period was allowed for disability due to injury than for disability due to sickness. Figure 16–1 shows a typical age-graded benefit schedule.

Maximum Benefit Period

If Total Disability Begins	For Disability Due to Injury	For Disability Due to Sickness
Prior to age 50	10 years	5 years
Between ages 50–55	4 years	2 years
Between ages 55–65	2 years	1 year

No disability benefit is payable beyond 66th birthday.

Figure 16-1.   Age-graded disability benefit table.

After incurring excessive loss ratios on mortgage disability plans sold in the 1950s and 1960s, many credit insurers began limiting disability benefits to a critical period, such as between 12 to 36 months after the onset of disability.

Underwriting of Mortgage Protection Insurance

Originally, mortgage life and disability insurance were sold in the same manner as credit insurance. Lenders offered the insurance to borrowers at the time of loan closing, and insurers performed little or no individual underwriting. The borrower was eligible to purchase the insurance if he or she did not exceed maximum age limits, typically age 65 for life insurance and age 55 or 60 for disability insurance. However, as the maximum amount of life and disability benefits available under these plans increased in accordance with the amounts of mortgage loans, individual underwriting became necessary. Today, the underwriter initially requires information about the proposed insured's age, occupation, height, and weight. In addition, the proposed insured must answer one or two general health questions.

If the proposed insured is advanced in age or indicates, in response to the health questions, that medical problems exist, an insurer usually requires information about the proposed insured's medical history. In such cases, the insurer often requires one or more of the following items: an Attending Physician's Statement, medical examination results, x-ray results, or blood test results. In addition, the underwriter will normally check the Medical Information Bureau (MIB) and the company's records to determine if the applicant has a history of medical impairments. After all medical information is compiled, the underwriter either accepts or rejects the application for insurance.

Examination of Claims

The examination of mortgage protection insurance claims is much like the examination of other types of life and disability insurance claims. The insurance is generally contestable for two years on the basis of statements made in the application. Investigations for misrepresentation follow the claim department's established procedures for investigation of any contestable claim and primarily involve the health history of the insured.

Mortgage protection life insurance typically includes a suicide provision which states that death benefits are not payable when death results from suicide during the contestable period. When a death, during the contestable period, is suspected to be a suicide, the investigation of the mode of death is quite extensive, requiring police reports, a coroner's report, and interviews with the deceased's family and friends.

One factor that can complicate the examination of claims for mortgage protection insurance benefits is errors made by the lender/policyholder. The lender/policyholder often takes applications, issues certificates, and calculates and collects premiums. Even if the insurer provides the lender/policyholder with formal written guidelines for the administration of the program, the diversity of employees handling the various administrative tasks can lead to a high number of errors. For example, the lender/policyholder may issue a certificate of insurance to someone whom the insurer has declined to cover, or the lender/policyholder may fail to attach a copy of the insurance application to the certificate of insurance. Depending upon the laws in the jurisdiction involved, the clerical error on the part of the lender/policyholder may be construed as an action of the insurer. The insurer may then be effectively estopped from invoking the contractual defenses needed to contest a claim.

Payment of Benefits

Mortgage protection insurance policies are characterized by comparatively large amounts of insurance and long terms of coverage. During the duration of such a policy, many things can occur to affect payment of the insurance benefit. For example, a mortgage may be transferred by a voluntary assignment as part of a divorce settlement. If the insurer is unaware of such a transfer, proceeds might be paid to an improper party. Therefore, any such changes must be carefully communicated between the lender/policyholder and the insurer.

Most mortgage protection policies give the insurer the right to require satisfactory evidence of insurability whenever the insured debtor's monthly mortgage payment is adjusted by reason of reamortization, deferment of principal payments, or a change in the maturity date of the mortgage. However, changes in monthly mortgage payments are more commonly caused by changes in the mortgage interest rate or by changes in taxes or insurance premiums. Policies and certificates generally provide that mortgage protection insurance will increase to cover such specified increases in the mortgage payment up to a maximum amount. For example, a policy may provide that mortgage protection insurance will increase in accordance with increases in the interest rate or property taxes up to a maximum of $50 per payment.

If a claim examiner receives a claim under a policy where the amount of insurance has increased as in the previous example, the examiner should determine the date of the change and verify the reason for the change. The date can be particularly important in administering a disability claim because if the disability occurred before the date of the increase in the mortgage payment, the company's liability is limited to the lesser amount.

When a death claim is paid under a mortgage protection insurance policy, the amount of the check sent to the lender is usually the outstanding balance of the debt as reported by the lender, plus any interest accrued from the date of death, plus any required charge for prepayment of the loan, minus any delinquent or deferred payments. If there is a discrepancy between the payment schedule in the certificate and the amount of outstanding indebtedness reported by the lender at the time of death, the claim examiner should learn the reason. Usually such a discrepancy is the result of the debtor's having missed payments or having paid only interest for several months.

Termination of Coverage

Mortgage protection insurance usually terminates on the earliest of *any* of the following events:

- termination of the group policy;
- repayment of the loan in full;
- transfer by the debtor of all interest in the loan security;
- expiration of the redemption period under a mortgage foreclosure or a sale of the debtor's interest in the loan security;
- assignment of the indebtedness by the lending institution;
- request by the debtor that the insurance be discontinued;
- failure of the debtor to pay a monthly premium contribution within 31 days of its due date, unless the lending institution advances the premium; and
- for disability insurance, attainment of the maximum age.

REGULATION OF GROUP CREDIT INSURANCE

As we mentioned at the beginning of the chapter, the lender is both the policyholder and the beneficiary of credit insurance. As policyholder, the lender is often in a position to receive fees or commissions on new credit insurance coverages and dividends or experience rating refunds on existing coverages. As beneficiary, the lender stands to profit from credit insurance coverage in excess of the amount of the loan. This unusual dual role has been blamed for occasional abuses that are contrary to the interests of debtors, such as

- *coercion to buy insurance*—some lenders/policyholders make the purchase of credit insurance a requirement for approval of a loan.

- *overinsurance or pyramiding*—some lenders/policyholders sell a new insurance policy on a refinanced loan without cancelling the old policy.
- *excessive premium charges*—some lenders/policyholders purchase insurance coverage from an insurer and then add an additional amount to the premium charged to the borrower.
- *failure to inform borrowers*—some lenders/policyholders neglect to inform borrowers that they have purchased insurance. Thus, no certificate or policy is issued to the borrower.

In response to these abuses, states have enacted credit insurance legislation based to a large extent on NAIC model bills. These state laws typically define eligible lending institutions and eligible debtors, set maximums on the amount and duration of covered loans, establish minimum group participation limits, and regulate premium rates and loss ratios. Overall, group credit insurance is regulated more stringently than are other types of group coverages.

Certain aspects of credit insurance are also regulated indirectly under the general banking and usury laws and under "truth-in-lending" consumer protection laws. These latter laws require that borrowers be given adequate information regarding the coverage, its costs, and their rights as debtors, which include the opportunity to decline the insurance if it is contributory. A borrower must not be pressured to accept the insurance on the mistaken belief that it is a requirement for obtaining a loan.

References

"Credit Insurance," *1985 ICA Group Insurance Workshop Notes*, 1–3.
"Credit Life," *1982 ICA Group Insurance Workshop Notes*, 90–92.
"Credit Life and Disability Insurance," *1980 ICA Group Insurance Workshop Notes*, 105–112.
Fagg, Gary. *Credit Life and Disability Insurance*. Springfield, OH: CLICO Management, Inc., 1986.
McDonald, James L. "Finance and Credit Life/Disability Claims," *1986 ICA Life Insurance Workshop Notes*, 19–25.

17

Annuity and Endowment Benefits

A life, medical, or disability insurance policy pays a benefit to an insured if some misfortune strikes, e.g., the insured dies, becomes sick, or becomes disabled. Annuities and endowments differ from life, medical, and disability insurance products in that the benefit payment under an annuity or endowment is not contingent upon the insured's loss.

In this chapter, we describe annuities and endowments. Our discussion focuses on individual insurance products designed for retirement needs. We also discuss the payout methods and the tax implications of the various payout methods.

ANNUITIES

An **annuity** is a contract entered into by an insurer and a purchaser. According to the terms of the contract, the purchaser promises to deposit a specified sum of money with the insurer. In return, the insurer guarantees income for a specified period, or for the lifetime of the person covered by the annuity, who is known as the **annuitant**. Most of the annuities sold by insurance companies are purchased by individuals to provide income for retirement. However, a person can also buy an annuity that will benefit another person or party—for example, a spouse, a child, or an organization.

Insurers design annuity contracts to satisfy the specific needs of the purchaser. The purchaser of an annuity contract can choose (1) when benefit payments will begin, (2) how premiums will be paid, (3) what the length of the benefit payment period will be, (4) how many lives will be insured under the annuity contract, and (5) whether benefit payments will be guaranteed or variable. Figure 17–1 illustrates various options available for annuities.

When Benefit Payments Begin

An annuity is classified as either an immediate or a deferred annuity depending upon when the benefit payments are scheduled to begin. Under the terms of an *immediate annuity*, benefit payments begin one benefit period after the annuity is purchased. For example, if an immediate annuity contract specifies that a benefit will be paid monthly, then the benefit payments will begin one month from the date of purchase. For immediate annuity contracts that specify an annual benefit payment, the first benefit payment will be paid one year from the purchase date.

For a *deferred annuity*, the annuity payment is scheduled to begin at some future date, called the maturity date. A person typically purchases a deferred annuity during his or her working years in anticipation of the need for retirement income. In such a case, the annuity's benefits are scheduled to begin on the anticipated retirement date of the prospective annuitant. If the prospective annuitant dies before the annuity payments begin, the amount paid for the annuity, plus interest, will be paid to a beneficiary designated by the purchaser of the annuity.

Method of Paying Premiums

The purchaser of an annuity may pay for it by submitting a single premium payment or by making installment payments over a period of time.

Single Premium Payments

An annuity purchased with a single premium payment may be a deferred or an immediate annuity. A single-premium deferred annuity will provide a larger annuity payment than will an otherwise identical single-premium immediate annuity because the deferred annuity will earn interest during the deferred period. The interest is then available to increase the annuity benefit payment amount. The single-premium annuity is particularly appropriate for situations in which an individual receives a lump sum of money—for example, from a life insurance policy, a retirement plan, or the sale of a business.

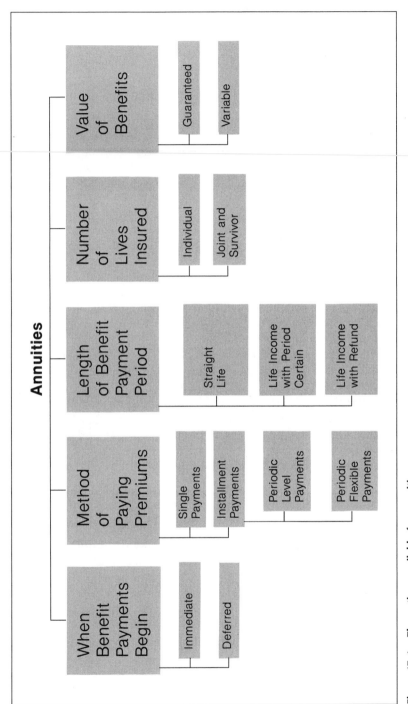

Figure 17-1. The options available for annuities.

Installment Payments

An individual may choose to pay for an annuity over a specified period of time by making periodic level premium payments or periodic flexible premium payments.

Periodic Level Premium Payments.   Under the periodic level premium payment method, the purchaser of the annuity pays equal premium amounts at regular intervals, such as annually, until either the date that the benefit payments are scheduled to begin or some other predetermined date. If the prospective annuitant dies before benefit payments begin, the premiums paid for the annuity, plus interest, will be refunded to the designated beneficiary.

Periodic Flexible Premium Payments.   According to the terms of the periodic flexible premium payment method, the purchaser of the annuity may vary the premium amount each year between a stated minimum and maximum amount. For example, such an annuity contract issued to Ellen Marsh may allow her to pay each year any premium amount that is between $250 and $1,000. This type of contract is particularly appropriate for self-employed individuals who do not know for certain the amount of their income each year.

A disadvantage of this type of contract is that the exact annuity benefit cannot be determined in advance of the contract's maturity date because the exact premium payment amounts are not known in advance. Annuity benefits are calculated on the contract's maturity date and are based upon the total of the premiums paid, the annuitant's sex, the age of the annuitant at the time annuity payments commence, and any refund features included in the contract. Some jurisdictions do not allow insurers to use sex as a factor in determining annuity payments.

Length of the Benefit Payment Period

Annuities can be classified according to the length of time over which benefit payments will be made. One type of annuity, an **annuity certain**, is guaranteed payable for a specified period of time, such as five years, regardless of whether the annuitant lives or dies. However, most types of annuities are termed **life annuities** because the length of the annuity payment is related to the length of the annuitant's life. There are three basic types of life annuities: the straight life annuity, the life income with period certain annuity, and the life income with refund annuity.

Straight Life Annuity

The **straight life annuity** provides annuity payments that are guaranteed to continue for as long as the annuitant lives. Annuity payments cease upon the annuitant's death even if the annuitant dies shortly after benefit payments begin. Because the straight life annuity does not pay a benefit to a beneficiary or to an estate after the annuitant's death, the annuitant receives the maximum amount of annuity benefit per dollar spent in premium outlay.

Life Income with Period Certain Annuity

The *life income with period certain annuity* provides that annuity payments will be made until the annuitant dies, or for at least a certain period even if the annuitant dies before the end of the period. The annuitant selects the guaranteed period, which is often five years or ten years. If the annuitant dies before the end of the guaranteed period, then the insurer will continue to make benefit payments to the annuitant's designated beneficiary until the end of the guaranteed period. For example, assume that Kirby Johnson purchased a life income annuity with a five-year period certain. Kirby names her sister Melissa as beneficiary. If Kirby dies two years after benefit payments begin, benefit payments will continue to be paid for another three years to Melissa. If Kirby survives the five-year guaranteed period, then the insurer will continue to pay annuity benefits to Kirby until Kirby's death. Upon Kirby's death, the insurer will have met its contractual obligations, and no benefits will be payable to Melissa.

Life Income with Refund Annuity

The *life income with refund annuity*, also called the refund annuity, provides benefits for the lifetime of the annuitant and guarantees that if the annuitant dies before the purchase price of the annuity has been paid out in benefits, then a refund will be made to a beneficiary chosen by the annuitant. The amount of the refund will be the difference between the amount that has been paid in annuity benefits and the purchase price of the annuity. If, for example, Winfield Scott purchases a life income with refund annuity for $40,000 but only receives $35,000 in annuity benefits before his death, then a $5,000 refund will be paid to Winfield's designated beneficiary.

Number of Lives to be Insured

An annuity contract may insure one or more lives. An annuity contract that covers two or more lives and which specifies that benefit payments will continue until both or all of the annuitants have died is called a *joint and survivor annuity*, or a *joint and last survivorship annuity*. Purchasers of such annuities are often married couples. When one spouse dies, the surviving spouse will continue to receive the annuity benefits for the rest of his or her life.

According to the terms of most joint and survivor annuities, the size of the annuity payment remains the same throughout the benefit payment period. However, some such annuities specify that the annuity payments will be reduced after the death of one of the annuitants. For example, assume that an annuity contract issued to a husband and wife pays a monthly benefit of $1,200. The annuity contract specifies that after the death of either the husband or the wife, the annuity benefit payable will be $600 per month, one-half of the $1,200 benefit amount.

Guaranteed or Variable Benefits

Traditionally, annuities have provided a guaranteed annuity benefit for a specified premium amount. However, the **variable annuity**, which was introduced in the mid–1950s, provides annuity payments that change according to the investment earnings of a special fund, called a separate account in the United States and a segregated account in Canada. A separate account, unlike an insurer's general account fund, has few investment restrictions and is invested primarily, or sometimes exclusively, in securities such as common stocks. Owners of variable annuities share in the investment gains and losses of the separate account. Thus, the purchaser of a variable annuity will profit from the separate account's investment gains but will suffer with the insurer if the separate account investments produce losses. Overall, the purchasers of variable annuities hope to lessen the impact of inflation on their retirement benefits.

TAX ISSUES

In the United States, an annuity may be either qualified or nonqualified for income tax purposes. The federal government does not tax the funds a person deposits into a **qualified annuity** until the funds are withdrawn. In other words, the amounts deposited into a qualified annuity, up to a stipulated maximum, are deductible from the depositor's gross income in the year the funds are deposited. Thus, the depositor pays no income taxes on these amounts until the funds are withdrawn from the annuity, resulting in deferred taxation for the depositor. Further, the interest earned on the funds in qualified annuities is not taxed until the funds are withdrawn. The advantage to this deferred taxation is that withdrawals made during a participant's retirement will theoretically be taxed at an income tax rate that is lower than the participant's income tax rate when the deposits were made. If a depositor places funds into a **nonqualified annuity**, then the depositor has already paid income taxes on the funds. Thus, at the time of withdrawal, the depositor will pay income taxes only on the interest earned on the funds.

In Canada, individuals who participate in a Registered Retirement Savings Plan (RRSP) can deduct their contribution, up to a stated maximum, from their gross income for income tax purposes. The amounts deposited into an RRSP and the interest earned on those amounts are not taxed until the funds are withdrawn from the account. Funds that have accumulated in an RRSP may be taken in a lump sum and used to purchase a life annuity. If an individual chooses to use the lump sum to purchase a life annuity, then the lump sum is excluded from the individual's gross income. However, the annuity payments are included in the individual's gross income in the year in which they are received. Nevertheless, by purchasing an annuity, the individual avoids paying a high rate of tax on an unusually large income received in one year.

In Canada, the manner of taxing income from nonregistered annuities depends, in part, upon (1) the date of acquisition of the annuity contract and (2) the date on which the annuity payments commenced. The income that accrues on currently-issued nonregistered annuities is taxed every three years rather than at the time the benefits become payable. However, the policyholder may elect annual accrual taxation if he or she wishes.

WITHDRAWALS FROM ANNUITIES

Funds in an annuity contract, whether taxed or untaxed, may be withdrawn by the annuitant at any time. However, in the United States withdrawals made before the annuitant reaches age 59½ are usually subject to a 10 percent federal tax penalty in addition to any standard income tax liability. The 10 percent tax penalty was instituted to discourage individuals from using annuity contracts as short-term investment contracts. Any benefits payable because of an annuitant's death or disability are not subject to the 10 percent tax penalty regardless of the insured's age.

In Canada, the withdrawal of funds from an annuity contract results in taxable income for the annuitant if the proceeds of the withdrawal exceed the adjusted cost base of the contract immediately prior to the disposition. The adjusted cost base is determined through a complex mathematical formula that is beyond the scope of this text.

In addition, some annuity contracts in both Canada and the United States charge the annuitant a surrender charge or a withdrawal fee if funds are withdrawn during the early years of the contract. The amount of the surrender charge usually decreases each year the contract is in effect until the charge is reduced to zero. Typically, a surrender charge is not applicable after a policy has been in force for ten years or more.

PAYMENT OF ANNUITY BENEFITS

The claim examiner's role in the payment process is to ensure that the terms of the annuity contract are fulfilled. Fulfillment of the contract's terms varies depending upon whether the annuitant is alive to receive the annuity benefits or whether payment is to be made to a beneficiary.

Payments to a Living Annuitant

In most insurance companies, the claim department sends an annuitant a notification letter approximately 60 to 90 days before the annuity contract's maturity date. If a payment schedule was elected at the time the annuity was purchased, the notification letter will describe the scheduled payment method. The notification letter will also outline any options that the annuitant may have with respect to changing the annuity's benefit payments. At the time the annuity matures, most insurers allow an annuitant to choose from four payment options. Generally, the annuitant may

- receive a lump sum payment of the annuity's value,
- leave the amount of the annuity's value with the insurer and receive only interest payments,
- receive the annuity's value in installment payments for a fixed period, or
- receive the annuity's value in a life annuity.

Calculation of the Benefit Payment

The annuity's value, or the amount of the total benefit due, under a fixed benefit annuity is a function of four factors:

- the total amount of the premiums paid, plus applicable interest,
- the annuitant's age when the annuity matures,
- the annuitant's sex (unless such a consideration is restricted by law), and
- the inclusion of any refund feature.

The value of a variable annuity is calculated using a system that expresses the premiums paid for the annuity as accumulation units. *Accumulation units* represent ownership shares in the total separate account. The number of accumulation units that a contract owner will receive from a given premium amount depends upon the value of the separate account at the time of each premium payment. For example, a premium payment of $300 might purchase 10 accumulation units in one year. However, if the value of the insurer's separate account decreases, that same $300 might purchase 14 accumulation units in the next year.

When the annuity benefit becomes payable, the accumulation units that have been purchased regularly during the established annuity premium payment period are applied to purchase **annuity units**. Thus, at retirement, the annuitant is entitled to receive the value of a fixed number of annuity units rather than a fixed number of benefit dollars. Periodically, the insurance company assigns the annuity units a given dollar value based on the investment returns of the separate account. For example, assume that in 1987, the value of an annuity unit was $10. Bram McKeithan, an annuitant with a matured annuity, is entitled to receive a monthly benefit of 15 annuity units. In 1987, Bram received a monthly annuity benefit of $150. However, in 1988, the insurer's investment earnings in the separate account increased so that the value of an annuity unit was increased to $12. Bram's monthly annuity benefit in 1988 was, therefore, $180.

Federal Income Tax Withholding

In the United States, annuity payments distributed either on a periodic basis or in a lump sum are subject to federal income tax withholding at the time of payment. However, by completing IRS Income Tax Form W-4P, the annuitant may elect not to have the insurer withhold any federal income tax. An annuitant who elects not to have any income tax withheld should be advised that he or she is still liable to pay any applicable federal income taxes. Some state regulations require insurance companies to withhold state income taxes from annuity payments and do not allow annuitants the option of electing not to have such taxes withheld.

Annuity Payments Made to a Beneficiary

Sometimes an annuitant dies either before an annuity matures or before all benefit payments have been made under a guaranteed installment or period option contract. In such cases, payment of the annuity contract's proceeds is made to the beneficiary designated by the annuitant.

Annuitant Dies Before Maturity Date

The beneficiary of an annuity contract may choose to receive the death benefit as a lump sum or may choose to accept one of the settlement options discussed previously. In the United States, beneficiaries other than the insured's spouse must receive all of the contract's proceeds within five years of the date of the annuitant's death. If the beneficiary of the annuity contract is the surviving spouse, the annuity contract may be continued in the name of the spouse as the annuitant. In such a case, the spouse may receive the exact benefits the annuitant would have received and for the same specified time period.

In the United States, the death benefit under an annuity contract does not qualify for total tax exclusion under the Internal Revenue Code because the annuity contract is not a life insurance policy. Therefore, if the amount of the death benefit, plus all dividends received by the annuitant, exceeds the sum of the premiums paid by the annuitant, the excess amount must be included in the beneficiary's gross income for tax purposes.

In Canada, the taxation of the death benefit depends upon the date of acquisition of the annuity contract. However, the basic rule is that if the death benefit exceeds the adjusted cost basis of the contract, then the resulting amount is subject to federal income tax.

Annuitant Dies During a Guaranteed Payment Period

If an annuitant dies during a guaranteed payment period, any remaining annuity payments will be made to the beneficiary designated by the annuitant in the contract. For a beneficiary other than a spouse, the remaining guaranteed payments must be distributed at least as rapidly as they would have been distributed by the method specified in the contract. The distribution must begin within one year after the annuitant's death.

In the United States, the beneficiary will not be taxed on income from the annuity unless the total amount the beneficiary receives, when added to any amounts received by the annuitant, exceeds the annuitant's investment in the contract. In other words, all amounts received by the beneficiary are exempt from tax until the investment in the contract has been recovered; thereafter, amounts received are taxable income to the beneficiary.

ENDOWMENTS

Endowment policies combine term life insurance with a savings element. If the insured dies during the endowment period, a death benefit is payable to a named beneficiary. If the insured lives to the maturity date of the endowment policy, the insured receives the endowment benefit.

Although endowment policies account for less than 0.5 percent of all insurance policies currently sold in the United States, and less than one percent of all policies sold in Canada, claim examiners still must be familiar with this product in order to process the millions of policies currently in force.

The Death Benefit

When a claim examiner receives a claim for a death benefit under an endowment policy, the claim is handled the same as any other claim under a term life insurance policy. As we discussed in Chapter 7, the claim examiner verifies the proof of loss and that the claim is in compliance with all of the provisions of the endowment policy. In most cases, after this review, the death benefit is paid with no need for any further investigation. The death benefit creates no taxable income for the beneficiary since the benefit qualifies as a life insurance benefit for income tax purposes.

The Endowment Benefit

A claim examiner processing the payment of an endowment benefit engages in many of the same activities as those required for processing an annuity benefit. The claim examiner notifies the owner of an endowment contract of the contract's maturity date. The different settlement options are presented, and the resulting tax consequences are described.

Settlement Options

The owner of an endowment policy generally may (1) receive the policy benefit in a lump sum, (2) leave the policy proceeds with the insurer to earn interest, (3) receive the policy proceeds in installment payments for a guaranteed period, or (4) receive the policy proceeds as a life income annuity.

Tax Considerations

The vast majority of endowment policyowners receive the endowment benefit in a lump sum. For United States income tax purposes, for the year in which the endowment benefit is received, a policyowner must include in his or her gross income any amount of the lump sum that exceeds the policyowner's investment in the contract. Investment in the contract is generally defined as the premiums paid by the policyowner less any dividends or withdrawals.

However, by electing one of the other settlement options, a policyowner may be able to spread the tax on the contract's investment gains over a period of years. If, prior to the policy's maturity date, the policyowner elects to leave the proceeds on deposit with the insurance company until a specified date, then the policyowner will be taxed only on the interest earned, until the remaining proceeds are withdrawn. Further, if within 60 days after an endowment becomes payable and before any payment is received, the policyowner elects to receive the endowment benefit either as a life income annuity or an installment annuity, then the policyowner will pay taxes only on the portion of the annuity payment that can be attributable to a gain over investment.

References

Pedoe, Arthur and Jack, Colin E. *Life Insurance, Annuities, and Pensions*, 3rd Edition. Toronto, CD: University of Toronto Press, 1978.

Pritchett, Travis S., Stinton, John E., Cox, Larry A., Schroath, Frederick W. *Individual Annuities as a Source of Retirement Income*. Atlanta, GA: LOMA, 1982.

The Tax Companion. Indianapolis, IN: Longman Financial Services Publishing, 1988.

Tax Facts on Life Insurance. Cincinnati, OH: NULaw Services, 1987.

Tax Manual: Annuities. Toronto, CD: Canadian Life and Health Insurance Association, Inc., 1989.

West, Carol T. "Annuities," *1988 ICA Life Insurance Workshop Notes*, 20–22.

18

Reinsurance

Just as an individual may turn to an insurance company in order to transfer a risk that is too great to bear alone, so also may an insurance company transfer to other insurers risks that are too great for the insurer to bear alone. **Reinsurance** is the process of transferring risk from one insurance company to another insurance company. The insurer seeking reinsurance is the **ceding company**, or the direct writing company. The insurer accepting the risk is the **reinsurer**. In some cases, a reinsurer may find it necessary to transfer part of a risk it has accepted to another reinsurer. Such a transaction is known as **retrocession**.

Reinsurance offers several advantages to the ceding company. First, reinsurance prevents depletion of the ceding company's capital or surplus in the event that the company experiences a number of unexpectedly large claims. Second, reinsurance reduces a ceding company's exposure to liability when introducing new types of policies or lines of insurance. Thus, a ceding company may more freely experiment with new lines of business or types of coverages when it can share the risk with a reinsurer. Third, reinsurance can increase a ceding company's capacity to accept new business and write policies of larger amounts than would otherwise be possible.

A reinsurer operates much like any other insurance company except

307

that a reinsurer's customers are the ceding companies, not the individual insureds. Individuals who are insured under a reinsured policy are rarely aware of the reinsurance arrangement since their contractual relationship remains solely with the ceding company. A reinsurer's claim department operates in a manner similar to that of all insurance companies; it is responsible for determining the reinsurer's liability for the claims submitted by ceding companies. In this chapter, we describe the claim considerations peculiar to reinsurance. However, before we can proceed with the claim considerations, we must first describe the various types of reinsurance arrangements.

REINSURANCE TREATIES

A **reinsurance treaty** is a contract between the reinsurer and the ceding company that sets forth the type of risks to be reinsured, the procedures by which the ceding company must submit business to the reinsurer, and the rights of the reinsurer in the underwriting and claim decision process. The treaty also specifies each party's obligations regarding premium taxes, policy reserves, policy dividends, cash surrender reimbursements, and supplementary benefits. There are two common types of reinsurance treaties: automatic and facultative.

Automatic Reinsurance Treaties

Under the terms of an **automatic reinsurance treaty**, the reinsurer agrees to provide reinsurance automatically for all amounts in excess of the ceding company's retention limit up to a specified maximum amount. The **retention limit** is the maximum amount of insurance that the insurer will carry at its own risk on any one individual. For example, a reinsurance treaty may specify that the ceding company will automatically cede to the reinsurer up to 300 percent of the ceding company's retention limit for a specified class of policies. Thus, if the ceding company's retention limit is $200,000 and the ceding company issues a $600,000 policy, then the reinsurer is bound to accept up to $400,000 of the risk amount.

Before the specific terms of the automatic treaty are set, the reinsurer reviews the provisions of the policies involved and the underwriting standards and claim practices of the ceding company. If an automatic method of reinsurance is then agreed to, the ceding company must comply with its regular underwriting practices. If the ceding company deviates from its regular underwriting practices, or if the ceding company changes the provisions of the policies being reinsured, the reinsurer may not be legally bound to accept the risk.

To eliminate selection against the reinsurer, the ceding company must cede to that reinsurer all accepted, eligible policies that are larger than the ceding company's retention limit. Further, most reinsurance treaties specify that the ceding company must carry at its own risk the full retention limit on each policy issued. For example, if a ceding company's retention limit for a particular $100,000 life insurance policy is $40,000, then the ceding company may cede $60,000 of that risk, but cannot reinsure any portion of the remaining $40,000. If an insurer were free to reinsure all of an insurance policy's risk, then the company might be tempted to ease its underwriting requirements.

An advantage of the automatic reinsurance treaty to the ceding company is that review and approval of each application by the reinsurer is not required. Therefore, the ceding company can issue policies for large amounts without delay. Automatic reinsurance treaties also usually provide coverage when an insured dies before the reinsurer has been notified that a risk has been ceded.

Facultative Reinsurance Treaties

A *facultative reinsurance treaty* allows a reinsurer to make an independent underwriting decision on each risk sent to it by a ceding company. The ceding company furnishes the reinsurer with a copy of the full underwriting file, which typically includes the application, copies of medical reports, and inspection reports. The reinsurer may request additional information from the ceding company if such information is necessary to underwrite the risk. After reviewing the information, the reinsurer either accepts a certain percentage of the risk and specifies the premium rate that the reinsurer will charge the ceding company or declines to insure any of the risk. If the reinsurer makes an offer, the ceding company is free to accept or reject that offer.

The primary advantage of the facultative reinsurance treaty is that the insurance application is subject to the scrutiny of at least two underwriters, one at the ceding company and others at the reinsurer. A major disadvantage to this method is increased processing costs since all applications and related documents must be copied and forwarded to the reinsurer for review. Another disadvantage is the increased time necessary to complete the underwriting process.

Combination Reinsurance Treaties

In some cases, a reinsurance treaty may specify a combination of the facultative and automatic methods. For example, assume that a ceding company has a retention limit of $2,500 of the monthly benefit for a certain class of disability policies. The reinsurance treaty specifies that $1,000 of the monthly indemnity benefit may be automatically reinsured. Any amounts in excess of a $3,500 monthly indemnity benefit ($2,500 retention limit + $1,000 automatic reinsurance) must be submitted facultatively to the reinsurer. If a particular policy provides a $5,000 monthly indemnity benefit, then the ceding company will retain $2,500 of the monthly risk, automatically cede $1,000 of the monthly risk, and submit $1,500 of the monthly risk to the reinsurer for a facultative analysis.

Changes to Retention Limits

In many instances, reinsurance is utilized by ceding companies that are experiencing rapid growth in new business. Reinsurance enables such companies to acquire new business faster than would otherwise be possible, given the company's capital and surplus condition. However, as the company grows, it may wish to rely less on reinsurance. In such situations, reinsurance treaties may provide that a ceding company can increase its retention limit on new business. There also may be a provision allowing the ceding company to reacquire a portion of the risk already ceded.

REINSURANCE PLANS

Just as insurance companies offer many different plans of insurance to applicants, so also do reinsurers offer different plans of reinsurance to ceding companies. The plan or plans of reinsurance are specified in the reinsurance treaty and can be divided into two major categories: proportional and nonproportional.

Proportional Plans of Reinsurance

With **proportional reinsurance**, the reinsurer shares a pro rata portion of the losses with the ceding company. The reinsurer's pro rata portion is stated in the reinsurance treaty. Proportional reinsurance is often used to reinsure individual life insurance policies. The three common types of proportional reinsurance plans are yearly renewable term, coinsurance, and modified coinsurance. Figure 18–1 is a comparative analysis of these three plans.

Yearly Renewable Term

Under the **yearly renewable term (YRT) reinsurance** plan, the ceding company buys reinsurance to cover the net amount at risk on a given policy. The **net amount at risk** is the face amount of the life insurance policy less the policy's reserve at the end of the policy year. Because the reserves for permanent life insurance policies increase each year, the net amounts

Plan	Responsibilities of Ceding Company	Advantages to Ceding Company
Yearly Renewable Term (YRT)	All Policy Reserves All Policy Dividends All Nonforfeiture Values	Simple to Administer Ceding Company Retains Investments Backing Policy Reserves
Coinsurance	A Pro-rata Share of Policy Reserves A Pro-rata Share of Policy Dividends A Pro-rata Share of Nonforfeiture Values	Reinsurer Maintains a Proportionate Share of the Reserves
Modified Coinsurance	All Policy Reserves A Pro Rata Share of Policy Dividends A Pro Rata Share of Nonforfeiture Values	Ceding Company's Assets are not Reduced

Figure 18-1. Comparative analysis of proportional reinsurance plans.

at risk decrease annually. Thus, the amount of reinsurance coverage needed for a particular permanent policy decreases each year. The reinsurance treaty typically includes a reinsurance schedule that shows the portion of the net amount at risk to be reinsured each year and the premium amount.

Under the YRT plan, the ceding company is responsible for policy reserves, policy dividends, and nonforfeiture values. Premiums paid by the ceding company to the reinsurer are based only on (1) the net amount at risk for the policy being reinsured and (2) the yearly renewable term rate for the attained age of the insured.

The primary advantages to a ceding company of the YRT reinsurance plan are that YRT is comparatively simple to administer and the ceding company retains more of the premium income under this reinsurance plan than under other reinsurance plans.

Coinsurance

Under a *coinsurance* plan, the liability of the reinsurer is a proportionate share of the face amount of insurance that has been ceded. For example, if a coinsurance plan specified that the reinsurer would be responsible for 60 percent of the liability for a $100,000 life insurance policy, then the reinsurer would pay $60,000 of the death benefit. In addition, the reinsurer is responsible for a pro rata share, in this situation 60 percent, of policy reserves, policy dividends, and nonforfeiture values. However, the reinsurer usually does not participate in policy loans.

For supplying the reinsurance and for the prorated responsibility of maintaining policy reserves, dividends, and nonforfeiture values, the reinsurer receives a pro rata share of the gross premium, minus an allowance for the ceding company's acquisition costs, premium taxes, and other expenses.

The primary advantage of coinsurance to the ceding company is that the reinsurer shares in maintaining policy reserves, paying policy dividends, and paying nonforfeiture values. Conversely, the primary disadvantage results from the requirement that the ceding company pay a portion of the premium to the reinsurer. Because of such payments, the assets of the ceding company do not grow as quickly as they would under the YRT method. Also, the recordkeeping necessary to determine prorated reserves, dividends, and premiums makes the coinsurance plan more complex to administer than the YRT plan.

Modified Coinsurance

The *modified coinsurance* plan of reinsurance is similar to the coinsurance plan in that (1) policy liability is on a pro rata basis, and (2) the reinsurer is responsible for a pro rata share of policy dividends and nonforfeiture values. The modified coinsurance plan differs, however, from the coinsurance plan in that the entire reserve for a policy is held by the ceding company. As we stated previously, the ceding company must increase the reserves for some types of life insurance each year. Under a modified coinsurance plan, the reinsurer pays to the ceding company an amount equal to the reinsurer's portion of the increase in the policy's reserve, less the interest the ceding company will earn on the amount of that increase. Thus, the assets of the ceding company are not diminished as a result of the reinsurance transaction.

Nonproportional Plans of Reinsurance

Nonproportional reinsurance plans are appropriate for situations in which the liability cannot be determined prior to the occurrence of the loss, such as in medical and disability insurance. Nonproportional reinsurance is also appropriate for insurers who wish to protect themselves against extraordinary loss experience. In other words, insurers who purchase nonproportional reinsurance are willing to retain the amount of a risk up to a certain point, beyond which they seek participation by a reinsurer. Many small insurers prefer proportional reinsurance plans for their medical and disability business because such reinsurance allows them to have partners to share the loss on every reinsured risk. There are three basic types of nonproportional reinsurance: stop-loss reinsurance, excess of loss per risk reinsurance, and catastrophe reinsurance.

Stop-Loss Reinsurance

Stop-loss reinsurance, also referred to as aggregate excess of loss reinsurance, is based on the total claim experience of a company for a specified line or lines of business during a period of time, usually twelve months. Under the *stop-loss reinsurance* plan, the reinsurer indemnifies the ceding company for a percentage (such as 90 percent) of total claim losses beyond a set point which may be either a predetermined dollar amount—e.g., the amount of all claims in excess of $10 million—or a percentage of the company's loss ratio—e.g., the amount of claims in excess of 125 percent of expected claims. Indemnification by the reinsurer is usually subject to a specified maximum limit.

Excess of Loss Per Risk Reinsurance

Excess of loss per risk reinsurance applies the principle of stop-loss reinsurance to individual policy claims. Under the excess of loss per risk plan, the reinsurer indemnifies the ceding company for a percentage of the amount of loss in excess of an agreed-upon point, usually up to a specified maximum amount.

Catastrophe Reinsurance

Catastrophe reinsurance protects a ceding company from a severe financial loss in the event that a single accident or a natural disaster involves several insureds. Under a catastrophe reinsurance treaty, the reinsurer agrees to pay the ceding company for losses in excess of a specified amount up to a maximum amount per catastrophe.

For example, assume that a car accident occurs in which four people insured under policies issued by the Best Friend Insurance Company die. The policies have face amounts of $125,000, $75,000, $50,000, and $25,000 for a total claim amount of $275,000. Best Friend has a catastrophic reinsurance treaty that specifies the following:

- a catastrophe is any event resulting in three or more covered deaths,
- the maximum liability of the reinsurer is $1 million per catastrophe and $75,000 per life, and
- Best Friend must incur total claim losses of $100,000 from a single catastrophe before the catastrophic reinsurance is payable.

In such a situation, Best Friend must pay $100,000 plus the $50,000 of the $125,000 policy that exceeds the reinsurer's maximum liability limit per life. Thus, the reinsurer will pay Best Friend a total of $125,000 [($275,000−$100,000)−$50,000)].

CLAIM CONSIDERATIONS

Reinsurers typically possess a highly skilled claim staff that is experienced in the medical, legal, and investigative aspects of claim administration. Nonetheless, just as the manager of a claim department cannot personally approve every claim processed by the department, neither can a reinsurer review every claim decision made by a ceding company on its reinsured business. Thus, the routine claim processing of reinsured policies is handled for the most part by the ceding company. However, reinsurance treaties frequently do allow the reinsurance company to participate with the primary carrier in claim decisions. In fact, a 1986 survey of 13 of the largest reinsurers ranked by total volume of reinsurance in force indicates that 46 percent of the reinsurers include clauses in their reinsurance treaties that require the ceding company to consult with the reinsurer prior to the claim decision. Whether a reinsurer chooses to utilize such a clause depends upon many factors including

- the reinsurer's level of confidence in the ceding company's claim handling ability,
- the amount of the reinsured risk,
- whether the policy is contestable, and
- the ceding company's desire for assistance.

When a claim is reinsured, both the reinsurer and the ceding company incur expenses. Regular and ongoing expenses, such as those for claim personnel and medical and legal staffs, are usually borne by the company that incurs them. However, one-time expenses for a particular claim—for example, inspection fees, costs of investigations and medical examinations, and court costs—may be split on a pro rata basis between the two companies.

Dispute Resolution

Sometimes the ceding company and the reinsurer disagree about a final claim decision. Some disagreements, such as those concerning compromise settlements, may be specifically covered by provisions of the reinsurance treaty. For example, the treaty may provide that the company with the larger potential loss is allowed to make the final decision on whether to offer a compromise settlement. However, all subjects that may result in future disagreements cannot be addressed within the reinsurance treaty.

In anticipation of such disagreements, the reinsurance treaty usually contains a provision that calls for the arbitration of disputes. Typically, a panel of three arbitrators will be appointed—one by the ceding company, one by the reinsurer, and a third is appointed by mutual agreement. In reaching a decision that will be binding on both the ceding company and the reinsurer, the arbitrators are instructed to consider the reinsurance treaty in its entirety, including any informal understandings that may exist between the ceding company and the reinsurer. The majority vote of the arbitrators is binding and there are no procedures for appeal.

Claim Notification

The ceding company is responsible for notifying the reinsurer about pending claims in a timely manner. Even in cases in which the reinsurer has no immediate liability, the ceding company still should report a claim to the reinsurer. For example, under an excess of loss plan of reinsurance, the ceding company has immediate liability up to a stated amount, at which point the reinsurer becomes liable. Although the reinsurer is not liable for the initial claim, that claim should still be reported so that the reinsurer can better estimate potential future liabilities. To encourage prompt notification of claims, a reinsurance treaty may contain a penalty clause that penalizes the ceding company for the late reporting of a claim.

Misstatement of Age or Sex

Occasionally, a discrepancy in an insured's age or sex is discovered at the time of claim. If the claim has been reinsured, there may be an adjustment of the benefits payable under the policy. In such a case, both the insurer and the reinsurer usually share on a pro rata basis in the amount of the adjustment.

Extra-Contractual Liability of Reinsurers

Sometimes after a claimant has been denied benefits under an insurance contract, the claimant will file a lawsuit in a court of law for breach of contract. If the court determines that the claimant was wrongfully denied benefits, then the court usually orders the insurer to pay the claimant the benefits specified in the insurance contract. In addition, the court may order the insurer to pay punitive damages, which, as we described in Chapter 9, is an amount in excess of the actual loss designed to punish the insurer for its behavior in wrongfully denying the claim.

At times, punitive damages are awarded under a policy that has been reinsured. A question then arises as to the reinsurer's liability, if any, to pay a portion of the extra-contractual obligation. There are conflicting points of view on the liability of the reinsurer. One view holds that a reinsurer shares a ceding company's total risk for a reinsured policy, including the risk of extra-contractual damages. Such a view is voiced most often in cases in which the reinsurer assisted the ceding company in the handling of the claim under which the punitive damages have been assessed.

However, the opposing point of view holds that extra-contractual damages are a risk separate and apart from the risk for which reinsurance was purchased and that a reinsurer makes no allowance in premium assessments for such damages. Further, opposing viewpoints hold that punitive awards are designed to deter some definite misconduct or perceived misconduct on the part of the ceding company. In cases in which a reinsurer does not assist a ceding company in the handling of a claim, then forcing the reinsurer to share in the extra-contractual award reduces the punitive effect on the ceding company.

To resolve the question of the reinsurer's extra-contractual liability, most reinsurance treaties now contain provisions designed to protect the reinsurer from participation in extra-contractual awards against the ceding company. A representative extra-contractual-damages provision reads in part:

> The Reinsurer shall not be liable nor shall any amounts be paid under this Agreement or otherwise for any extra-contractual damages . . .

However, interpretations of such provisions by the courts remain inconsistent. At the present, there is no industry standard that can enable insurers and reinsurers to act with certainty in this area.

References

Abba, Steven F. "Reinsurance Claim Considerations," *1983 ICA Life Insurance Workshop Notes*, 47–51.

Shields, Richard J. "Role of the Reinsurer in Claims Processing," *1986 ICA Life Insurance Workshop Notes*, 70–76.

Potter, James W. "To Re or Not to Re, that is the Question," *1988 ICA Health Insurance Workshop Notes*, 98–107.

Grossman, Eli A. *Life Reinsurance*, Atlanta, GA: LOMA, 1980.

A Contemporary Guide to Reinsurance. Atlanta, GA: Reinsurance Facilities Corporation, 1987.

Appendix

Appendix

Appendix

Guidelines for Investigating Accidental Death Claims

Checklist for Investigating Deaths When Disease is a Contributing Factor

(Basic questions: Policy in force? Contestable? Loss Covered?)

I. Insured's health history

What is the insured's medical background?
Is there a family history of disease?
Is old age a factor?
Are there any physical infirmities?
   Dizziness? Fainting spells? Seizures? Impaired vision or
      hearing?
Are there any disabilities?
Was the insured absent from work as a result of a medical
condition?

II. Insured's personal habits

Is there any evidence of drug or alcohol abuse?
What are the insured's dietary habits?
What are the insured's exercise habits?

III. Insured's medical treatment
What is the name of the family physician?
Any other attending physicians?
Was the insured admitted to any hospitals, asylums, sanatoriums,
   or rehabilitation programs?
Was the insured taking any medication or other treatments?

Checklist for Investigating Aviation Deaths

(Basic questions: Policy in force? Contestable? Loss Covered?)

I. Insured's health history

What is the insured's medical background?
Are there any physical infirmities?
    Dizziness? Fainting spells? Seizures? Impaired vision or
    hearing?

II. Insured's personal circumstances

Was the insured a licensed pilot?
    How long? How active?
Why was the insured aboard this aircraft?
Was the insured familiar with this type of aircraft?

III. Aircraft

What is the make and model of the aircraft?
Did the aircraft receive regular maintenance?
    How recently?
Is there any record of recent malfunctions?

IV. Circumstances surrounding crash

What was the cause of the crash?
Where was each body located?
What was the flight plan?
    Was the aircraft on course? On schedule?
What was the weather at the time of crash?

Checklist for Investigating Carbon Monoxide Deaths

(Basic questions: Policy in force? Contestable? Loss Covered?)

I. Car
What was the car's make, model, and serial number?
Was the car registered to the insured?
Where was the car usually kept?
Was the car in need of repairs?
Was the car's exhaust system in good repair?

II. Circumstances

Was the engine running?
Was the ignition on or off?
Was there any fuel remaining in the tank?
Were there indications that repairs were being made to the car?
Were the doors and windows open or closed?
Were the doors working properly?
Was the heater or air conditioner turned on?
Was the radio turned on?
Were the car lights turned on?
Was there a telephone in car?
Were there any indications of an attempted escape?

III. Garage (or room where death occurred)
Were the doors locked?
    If yes, from inside or outside?
Were the lights on?
What are the complete dimensions of the room?
Where are the doors and windows located?
Were the windows open or shut?
Was the air conditioning on or off?
Was there a telephone in the room?

IV. Weather on the day of death

What was the temperature?
What was the wind's direction and velocity?
What was the humidity?
Was there any precipitation?

Checklist for Investigating Drowning Deaths

(Basic questions: Policy in force? Contestable? Loss Covered?)

I. Insured

Was there a positive identification of the insured?
Was the insured able to swim?
    If yes, how well?
Why was the insured in the water?
Was the insured familiar with location's depth, currents, undertow?
What was the insured's distance from shore?
How was the insured clothed when recovered?
Were there any unusual marks of violence on the body?

II. Circumstances

What was the depth of the water?
What was the temperature of the water?
What was the temperature of the air?
What was the rate of the current?
What was the condition of the water?
    Calm? Rough?
Were there any hazards?
    Reefs? Debris?

III. Boat (if one was involved)

What was the boat's model, size, and registration number?
Was the boat equipped with life preservers?
Who was the person in charge of the boat?
Was the insured familiar with the boat?
Were there any mechanical malfunctions?
How should the boat have behaved in given weather conditions?
What was the boat's speed at time of drowning?
Were there any efforts to save the insured?
Were the decks slippery at time of drowning?
Were the guard rails up?

Checklist for Investigating Drug Cases

(Basic questions: Policy in force? Contestable? Loss Covered?)

I. Insured

What was the insured's general physical condition?
How long had the insured been using the drug in question?
    In what quantities?
Were any other drugs used by the insured?
Were there any unusual marks of violence on the body?
Were there any previous episodes of overdose?

II. Drug

What is the drug's name?
    Generic name? Brand name?
Is the drug legal or illegal?
Was the drug prescription or nonprescription?
    If prescribed . . .
        Name of prescribing physician?
        Why prescribed?
        When last refilled?
        What quantity?
    If nonprescription . . .
        How obtained?
        Quality of drug?
        Quantity of drug?

III. Circumstances

What was the position of the body?
How was the insured dressed?
Was there any evidence of attempts for help?
What were the results of the toxicology report?
Were there any indications that alcohol had also been ingested?
Any suggestion of a synergistic reaction?

Checklist for Investigating Deaths Resulting from Falls

(Basic questions: Policy in force? Contestable? Loss Covered?)

I. Insured

What was the insured's age?
What was the insured's physical condition?
Were there any chronic ailments or infirmities?
What footwear was the insured wearing at the time of fall?

II. Circumstances

What time of day did the fall occur?
What was the weather at the time of the fall?
Was the scene illuminated?
Why was insured at that location?
Was the insured familiar with the location?
Were there any hazards at the location?
    Slippery walks? Narrow steps? Obstructions?
Was the insured conscious after the fall?
    If so, what did insured say?

Checklist for Investigating Deaths Resulting from Falls or Jumps

(Basic questions: Policy in force? Contestable? Loss Covered?)

I. Insured

Why was the insured at the scene?
Had the insured ever been there before?
Was the insured familiar with heights?
What footwear was the insured wearing?
What activities were going on at the time?
Did the insured have torn fingernails or scraped hands?

II. Circumstances

What time of day did the fall occur?
What was the weather at the time of the fall?
Was the scene illuminated?
Did the insured scream or shout while falling?
What was the distance and angle of the insured's fall?
Was there any evidence that the insured tried to prevent the fall?
Did the insured fall from a window?
 If so, what was the size and height of window?
 Any obstructions by the window?
  Radiator? Screens?
Did the insured fall from a roof or parapet?
 If so, what was the height and thickness?
 Extension, if any, from wall?
Did the insured fall from a scaffold?
 If so, what are the dimensions? Safety belt in use?

Checklist for Investigating Fire Deaths

(Basic questions: Policy in force? Contestable? Loss Covered?)

I. Insured

Was there a positive identification of the insured?
What was the insured's general physical condition?
Why was the insured at the scene at that time?
Was the insured familiar with all exits?
Was there any evidence that the insured attempted to escape?
What was the cause of death?
>   Heat? Smoke inhalation?
How was the insured dressed?
>   Was the insured's clothing burned?

II. Circumstances

What was the cause of the fire?
>   Suspicious? Arson?
Was there any damage to the building and to contents?
How soon was the fire reported?
How soon did fire department arrive?
Was there a sprinkler system in the building?
>   If so, was it operating at time of fire?
Were there fire extinguishers?
What exits were available?
Were the exits locked?
Was there a telephone in the room?

Checklist for Investigating Gunshot Wound Deaths

(Basic questions: Policy in force? Contestable? Loss Covered?)

I. Insured

What was the insured's general physical condition?
Was the insured familiar with guns?
Was the insured familiar with the weapon used?
Was the insured right or left handed?
Was a paraffin test performed?
    Results?

II. Weapon

What was the type, make, caliber, and serial number of the gun?
Who was the owner of the gun?
    If not the insured, why did insured have it?
What was the gun's usual location?
Was the gun usually kept locked?
Was the gun usually kept loaded?
Was there a safety catch?
    Was it on or off?
What trigger pressure is required to fire the gun?
How many loaded and empty cartridges were there?
If rifle or shotgun, what is the length of the barrel?
Was the gun used frequently?
Was the gun used recently?

III. Circumstances

What was the location of the weapon?
What was the location of the body?
Was there any evidence of the gun being cleaned?
Was there any evidence of robbery/burglary?

Checklist for Investigating Traffic Accident Deaths

(Basic questions: Policy in force? Contestable? Loss Covered?)

I. Insured

What was the insured's age?
What was the insured's general health?
Were there any physical infirmities?
    Dizziness? Fainting spells? Seizures? Heart condition?

II. Vehicle (answer for each vehicle involved)

What is the vehicle's make, model, and serial number?
Name of driver and passengers?
Was the vehicle in need of repairs?
Were the brakes working?
Were the windows clean?
Who was the owner of the vehicle?

III. Location

Describe the street?
    Paved? How many lanes? Divided?
What was the condition of the street at time of the accident?
    Dry/slippery?
Where did the accident occur?
    On a curve? In an intersection? On a hill?
Were there any obtructions to visibility?

IV. Circumstances

What was the speed and direction of each vehicle?
At what point did the vehicles collide?
What was the position of the vehicles after collision?
What was the position of the body?
Were there any skid marks?
    If so, length and location?
Were there any ruptured tire or other defective parts?
Why was the insured at this location?
Was the insured familiar with this location?
Were the seat belts fastened?

V. Use of vehicle

Was the insured "at work" at the time of accident?
What was the essential purpose of the trip?
What was the insured's occupation and duties?
From where was the insured coming?
To where was the insured going?

Glossary

Glossary

absolute assignment. An irrevocable transfer of all of a policyowner's rights in a policy, usually made when the policyowner wishes to make a gift of a policy to another person or entity.

accidental death and dismemberment (AD&D) benefit. A policy benefit specifying that the full benefit amount will be paid if the insured loses any two limbs or the sight in both eyes as a result of an accident.

accidental death benefit (ADB) rider. A policy addition providing that, upon the accidental death of the insured, a benefit amount in addition to the death benefit amount of the policy will be paid to the beneficiary.

accidental means provision. An accidental death benefit provision stating that the benefits are payable if the insurer receives proof that the death of the insured was caused by accidental means.

accidental result provision. An accidental death benefit provision stating that the benefits are payable if the insurer receives proof that the death of the insured was the result of accidental bodily injury.

accumulation units. Ownership shares in a separate account.

actively-at-work provision. A group insurance policy condition that requires employees to be actively at work on the date their insurance would normally become effective in order to receive insurance coverage.

administrator. A person who is appointed by a probate court to manage a decedent's estate until all debts have been paid and the remaining assets in the estate have been distributed.

aggressorship. Occurs in a situation in which the insured makes an attack on another person in such a way as to invite deadly resistance from the other person.

all-cause deductibles. In health insurance, deductibles that must be satisfied only once per benefit period regardless of the cause of the claims.

annuitant. A person who receives annuity benefit payments.

annuity. A contract entered into by an insurer and a purchaser whereby the purchaser promises to deposit a specified sum of money with the insurer who, in turn, promises to provide a guarantee of income for a specified period or for the lifetime of the person covered by the annuity.

annuity certain. A type of annuity that is guaranteed payable for a specified period of time regardless of whether the annuitant lives or dies.

annuity units. Accumulation units that have been purchased regularly during an established annuity period.

antiselection. The tendency of persons who have a greater likelihood of loss also to have a greater tendency to buy and continue insurance coverage.

assignee. A person or party who receives through an assignment some or all of the rights of ownership in a life insurance policy.

assignment. The transfer of some or all of the rights of ownership in a life insurance policy to another person or entity.

assignment of benefits. An insured's grant of permission to an insurance company to pay insurance benefits directly to a provider of medical care, rather than to the insured.

assignor. A person or party who transfers some or all of the rights of ownership to another person or entity through an assignment of a life insurance policy.

Attending Physician's Statement (APS). A written statement from a physician that contains an insured's medical diagnosis, medical test results, record of medication, and dates of treatment.

attorney in fact. A layperson acting with a claimant's power of attorney regarding a claim.

automatic reinsurance treaty. An agreement by which a reinsurer agrees to provide reinsurance automatically for all amounts in excess of a ceding company's retention limit up to a specified maximum limit.

automatism. A condition in which a drug user takes repeated doses of a drug without realizing that the drug is being taken and without the intention of taking a lethal dosage.

balloon loan. A loan that requires monthly installment payments plus a lump-sum (balloon) payment at the loan's maturity date.

basic services. Under dental insurance, dental services, such as fillings, periodontics, and oral surgery, which are often covered at 80 percent of their reasonable and customary charges.

beneficiary. A person or entity who will receive the life insurance benefits payable upon the death of an insured. A person or entity who is named as the first receiver of life insurance benefits is known as the *primary beneficiary*. A person or entity designated to receive life insurance benefits if the primary beneficiary predeceases the insured is known as the *contingent beneficiary*.

binding receipt. An insurance premium receipt that usually provides temporary insurance coverage during the underwriting period.

birthday rule. A rule included in some coordination of benefits provisions, that specifies the manner in which benefits for dependent children are to be coordinated between two insurance plans.

buy-out. *See* **financial settlements.**

carry-over provision. A provision found in most medical expense policies stating that expenses incurred during the last three months of a benefit period, which are used to satisfy the current benefit period's deductible, may be used to satisfy any or all of the following benefit period's deductible.

case management. *Also known as* **large claim management, medical case management,** or **catastrophic claim management.** A cost-containment program designed to identify alternate, less costly methods of treatment for seriously ill patients without sacrificing the quality of care a patient receives.

cash deductible. *See* **deductible.**

cash surrender value. *See* **net cash value.**

catastrophe reinsurance. Reinsurance that protects a ceding company from a severe financial loss in the event that a single accident or a natural disaster involves several insureds.

catastrophic claim management. *See* **case management.**

causal relation requirements. Proof required by statute in Kansas, Missouri, Rhode Island, and Puerto Rico to show that the facts misrepresented in an application for insurance were related to the loss insured against.

ceding company. *Also known as* the **direct writing company.** An insurance company that seeks reinsurance.

certificate of indebtedness. A certificate issued to the beneficiary of a life insurance policy that specifies a guaranteed minimum interest rate and the frequency with which interest payments will be made under the interest settlement option.

change of condition provision. An insurance provision stipulating that, for a policy to become effective, all conditions described in the application must still be true at the time of delivery.

claim investigation. The process of obtaining necessary claim information in order to decide whether or not to pay a claim.

coinsurance plan. A type of reinsurance plan in which the ceding company pays the reinsurer a proportionate share of the premium paid, minus a proportionate share of the expenses associated with the policy. In return, the reinsurer agrees to share a proportionate share of the face amount of the insurance that has been ceded.

coinsurance provision. A stipulation found in most medical and dental insurance policies that requires an insured to pay a stated percentage of covered expenses.

collateral assignment. A transfer of some of the ownership rights in a life insurance policy. Collateral assignments are often made to secure a loan.

combination clause. A clause in a disability income contract that specifies a point at which the definition of total disability will no longer be based on an insured's inability to perform his or her "own occupation" but on the insured's inability to perform "any occupation."

common accident provision. A provision found in most major medical coverages stating that if an insured and one or more of his or her covered dependents are injured in the same accident, only one individual deductible amount will be taken from the total expenses incurred as a result of the accident. This provision is applicable only in contracts that do not include a waiver of deductible provision.

common disaster clause. *See* **short-term survivorship provision.**

community-property state. Any state in which, by law, a spouse is entitled to an equal share of income earned and, under most circumstances, to an equal share of property acquired by the other during the period of marriage.

commutation. *See* **financial settlements.**

comprehensive major medical plan. A major medical plan that covers virtually all types of medical expenses through a single major medical contract.

concurrent review. A component of a utilization review program that monitors an insured's care while the insured is hospitalized and encourages the dismissal of an insured from the hospital as soon as the insured's medical condition no longer warrants continued in-patient care.

conditional receipt. An insurance premium receipt that specifies standards or conditions the applicant must satisfy before the insurer will accept the applicant as an insurable risk. If the conditions are met, coverage becomes effective as of the date named on the receipt.

confirmation certificate. A certificate issued to the beneficiary of a life insurance policy that outlines the amount of life insurance proceeds in a retained asset account, the account number, and the current interest rate.

contestability. The process of disputing the validity of an insurance policy because of misrepresentation in the application.

contestable period. A time limit, usually two or three years, during which an insurer may contest or challenge the validity of a policy because of misrepresentation in the application.

conversion privilege. A term insurance policy provision that allows a policyowner to change the term insurance to a permanent insurance policy without providing evidence of insurability.

convertible term insurance policy. An insurance policy that contains a privilege allowing the policyowner to convert a term insurance policy to a permanent insurance policy without providing evidence of insurability.

corridor deductible. A fixed amount of money that an insured must pay for medical expenses after exhausting his or her basic medical expense benefits before major medical expense benefits are payable.

decreasing term life insurance. Insurance that provides a death benefit starting at a set face amount and then decreasing in some specified manner over the term of coverage.

deductible. *Also known as* **cash deductible** or **initial deductible.** The amount an insured must pay before an insurance company will make any benefit payments under a policy.

deferred annuity. An annuity under which benefit payments are scheduled to begin at some future date, called the maturity date.

dentist-consultant. A licensed dentist who understands the underwriting intent of dental plan language as well as the accepted standards of dental practice, and who advises insurers as to the appropriateness of dental treatment.

diagnostic related groups (DRGs).   A prospective payment method used in the Medicare Program, in which payment is not based on the number and kinds of medical services, but on the diagnosis of each patient.

direct writing company. *See* ***ceding company***.

disability buy-out insurance.   Insurance that provides cash funds to a business or professional partnership so that the business interests of a totally disabled partner or stockholder may be purchased if the disability is long-term or permanent.

discharge provision.   Legislation found in small estates statutes that releases from liability a person who makes the payment pursuant to the prescribed procedure to the same extent as if payment were being made to a court-appointed personal representative of a decedent.

dividends.   Periodic payments to shareholders from a corporation.

donor. *See* ***grantor***.

earnings.   Income such as salary, wages, profits, and other remuneration received for personal services rendered.

election period.   A 60-day period following notification of an insured's eligibility for COBRA continuation coverage, during which the individual can accept or decline the coverage.

elimination period. *Also known as* ***waiting period***. A specified number of days, typically 30 to 180 days, that must pass after the onset of total disability before any disability benefits are payable.

endorsement method.   A procedure for changing the beneficiary of a life insurance policy in which the change becomes effective when the policyowner submits the policy to the insurer and the insurer changes the name of the beneficiary on the policy.

endorsement. *See* ***rider***.

equivocal suicide.   An apparent suicide in which there is doubt about whether the deceased intended to die as a result of an apparently self-destructive act.

escheat laws. *See* ***unclaimed property***.

estate tax.   A tax on the transfer of property at death.

evidence of insurability.   Proof that an insured person continues to be an insurable risk.

excess of loss per risk.   In reinsurance, the application of the principle of stop-loss reinsurance to individual policy claims.

exculpatory statute.   Legislation in community-property states that allows an insurer to pay the proceeds of a life insurance policy in accordance with the terms of that policy without fear of double liability.

executor. A person, designated in a valid will, who is responsible for managing a decedent's estate until all debts have been paid and the remaining assets in the estate have been distributed.

facility of payment clause. A provision that allows an insurer to pay the whole amount or any part of a medical expense benefit to any institution or person to whom payment is owed for charges upon which the benefit is based or to a legal relative such as spouse, child, mother, or father.

facultative reinsurance treaty. An agreement allowing a reinsurer to make an independent underwriting decision on each risk sent to the reinsurer by a ceding company.

financial settlements. *Also known as* **commutations** or **buy-outs**. A lump sum payment by an insurer to a disabled insured that extinguishes the insurer's responsibility under the disability contract.

flexible-premium variable life. *See* **variable universal life insurance**.

foreseeability. The ability of an insured to have had a reasonable anticipation that harm or injury would be a likely result of a certain act or an omitted act.

fraudulent claim. A type of claim that occurs when a claimant intentionally uses false information in an attempt to collect policy proceeds.

good health provision. A provision contained in some group credit policies stating that a policy is void if the insured was not in good health when the application was signed or when the policy was delivered, whichever was specified in the contract.

grace period. A specified period of time after a premium is due, within which the premium may be paid without penalty and all coverage remains in force.

grantor. *Also known as* **trustor** or **donor**. A person who sets up a trust.

group life insurance. Insurance that provides life insurance coverage for a group of people under one contract, called a master contract.

guaranteed insurability (GI) rider. A policy addition that gives the policyowner the right to purchase additional insurance of the same type as the original policy on specified dates for specified amounts without supplying additional evidence of insurability.

guardian. A person who is appointed by a court to be legally responsible for another person who, because of age or incapacity, is legally incompetent. The guardian can sign a valid release for a policy's benefits.

Health Maintenance Organization (HMO). An organization that provides health care on a prepaid basis to subscribing members. Subscribers are treated by HMO physicians and are not charged for the cost of the service, but may be responsible for a small co-payment.

hearsay evidence. Evidence based on what someone has been told but has not actually witnessed.

hold harmless release. A discharge stating that a payee will reimburse an insurance company in the event that a subsequent claimant successfully challenges the disbursement of the policy's proceeds.

hospice care. Medical treatment designed to ease the physical and psychological pain associated with a terminal illness rather than to cure the illness; this treatment includes counseling the patient and family members.

immediate annuity. An annuity under which benefit payments begin one benefit period after the annuity is purchased.

incentive coinsurance provisions. Provisions included in some dental policies that promote regular dental care by specifying that insurers will pay a higher percentage of dental expenses if the insured receives regular dental examinations.

incident of ownership. Any policy right including the right to (1) change the beneficiary, (2) cancel or surrender the policy, (3) assign the policy, (4) obtain a policy loan, or (5) use the policy as collateral for a loan.

income replacement benefit. *See recovery benefit.*

incontestability provision. A clause in life and health insurance policies stating that after a policy has been in effect for a specified period of time (1) from the policy issue date, and (2) during the lifetime of the insured, the validity of the policy will be incontestable.

increasing term life insurance. Insurance that provides a death benefit starting at a set face amount and then increasing in some specified manner over the term of coverage.

individual fraud. A type of medical insurance fraud committed by individuals on their medical expense claims in order to obtain benefits in excess of their medical expenses.

individual life insurance. Life insurance that typically covers only one person (exception: family policies) and that is issued in relatively unrestricted maximum face amounts.

initial deductible. *See deductible.*

installment certificate. A certificate issued to the beneficiary of a life insurance policy that specifies the amount of each benefit payment and/or the period during which benefit payments will be made under a settlement option. An installment certificate also specifies whether a beneficiary is allowed to withdraw all or part of the funds during the payment period.

installment loans. Fixed-amount, fixed-term loans that are repayable in equal monthly payments.

insurability provision. An insurance provision stipulating that, for a policy to become effective, the insured must still be insurable at the time of policy delivery according to the underwriting rules and practices of the company.

integrated deductible. A type of deductible included in some major medical expense plans that can be satisfied by amounts paid by the insured under basic medical expense plans.

inter vivos trust. *See* **living trust.**

interim insurance agreements. *See* **temporary insurance agreements.**

internal replacement. The surrender of one life insurance policy in order to buy another insurance policy that is issued by the same insurer.

interpleader. An action at law whereby an insurer holding property belonging to someone else submits to a court the question of who is rightfully entitled to the property.

irrevocable beneficiary. A beneficiary whose interest in a life insurance policy cannot be changed or revoked unless the irrevocable beneficiary dies or gives written consent to a change of beneficiary.

joint and survivor annuity. *Also known as* ***joint and last survivorship annuity.*** An annuity contract covering two or more lives specifying that benefit payments will continue until both or all of the annuitants have died.

joint credit life insurance. Credit life insurance that pays the full benefit amount to a lender upon the death of any of the loan cosigners.

large claim management. *See* **case management.**

late remittance offer. A communication to the owner of a lapsed life insurance policy specifying that the insurer will accept an overdue premium after the expiration of the grace period and will reinstate the policy without requiring the completion of a reinstatement application or the submission of evidence of insurability.

level term life insurance. Insurance that provides a death benefit that remains the same over the period specified.

lien. A charge on real or personal property that is established to satisfy a debt or obligation.

life income with period certain annuity. An annuity with a provision stating that benefit payments will be made until the annuitant dies, or for at least a certain period even if the annuitant dies before the end of the period.

life income with refund annuity. *Also known as* **refund annuity.** An annuity that provides benefits for the lifetime of the annuitant and guarantees that if the annuitant dies before the purchase price of the annuity has been paid out in benefits, then a refund will be paid to a beneficiary.

living trust. *Also known as* **inter vivos trust.** A type of trust created through a formal agreement to take effect during the life of the grantor.

long-form reinstatement application. A reinstatement application similar to a policy application in that both address the long-term health history of the insured.

major services. Under dental insurance, dental services, such as inlays, crowns, prosthodontics, and orthodontics, which are often covered at 50 percent of their reasonable and customary charges.

master contract. A legal contract between an insurer and a group policyholder; the master contract provides insurance coverage for many individual lives.

material fact. A fact that is relevant to an insurance company's underwriting decision to insure a policy.

matrimonial regime. In Quebec, a legal arrangement selected by spouses or imposed by law that regulates the ownership and disposal of the property of the spouses during the course of their marriage.

maximum benefit period. The maximum period during which disability income benefits will be paid.

maximum benefits for related confinements provision. A provision included in basic hospital and surgical policies that limits the maximum benefits for all hospital confinements and for all surgery performed during one period of sickness or for any single injury.

medical case management. *See* **case management.**

medical necessity provision. A condition included in most major medical expense plans, stating that medical services that are educational or experimental in nature are not eligible for coverage.

Medicare carve-out. Medical expense coverage offered by employers to retired employees that reduces medical expense benefits to the extent that those benefits are provided by Medicare.

Medicare supplement approach. Medical expense coverage offered by employers to retired employees that provides benefits for certain expenses not covered under Medicare.

minimum deposit arrangement. An arrangement whereby a policyowner can apply the first-year cash value of a policy to the initial premium amount.

misstatement of age or sex provision. A policy provision that allows insurers to make adjustments in a policy's benefit if the insurer or the policyowner discovers that the age or sex of the insured is incorrect as stated in the policy.

modified coinsurance plan. A plan of reinsurance similar to a coinsurance plan in that a policy's liability is on a pro rata basis, and the reinsurer is responsible for a pro rata share of policy dividends and nonforfeiture values. However, under a modified coinsurance plan, the entire reserve for a policy is held by the ceding company.

mortgage protection insurance. Long-term credit insurance designed to insure home mortgages.

net amount at risk. The face amount of a life insurance policy less the policy's reserve at the end of a policy year.

net cash value. *Also known as* **cash surrender value** *or* **surrender value**. The amount of money that a policyowner may receive if he or she cancels his or her whole life insurance coverage and surrenders the policy to the company.

nonduplication of benefits. A method of coordinating medical expense benefit payments between two insurance carriers that allows the secondary carrier to pay the difference, if any, between the amount paid by the primary plan and the amount that would have been payable by the secondary plan had that plan been the primary plan.

nonforfeiture options. Policy options that allow a policyowner who is surrendering a policy with a cash value to determine what is to be done with the net cash value of the policy.

nonqualified annuity. A type of annuity in the United States funded with money that has already been taxed by the federal government in the year in which the funds are deposited.

nonresident alien. A person who is not a citizen of the United States but who is living in the United States for a short period in order to accomplish a definite purpose.

nonretroactive disability benefits. A type of disability benefit that is payable for the period of disability following an elimination period.

open-ended loan. A loan in which the amount of money lent is unspecified and the amount of debt can vary throughout the period of the loan, decreasing, increasing, or remaining the same.

outliers. Medicare patients whose illnesses are unique and whose conditions may not be classifiable under one of the diagnostic related groups.

overinsurance. A situation that occurs when a person insured under two or more insurance policies can collect total benefits in excess of actual losses incurred.

partial disability. A medical condition that prevents an insured from working full-time or completing one or more important job duties.

participation limit. *See* **relation of earnings to insurance clause**.

peer review committee. A panel of licensed dentists that resolves disputes between an insurer and a dentist.

per-cause deductibles. In health insurance, a term used to classify deductibles that must be satisfied for each injury or illness incurred by an insured during a benefit period.

permanent and total disability. A condition that prevents an insured from returning to any gainful employment.

policy anniversary. The anniversary of the date on which a policy was issued.

policy lapse. The termination of an insurance policy because of non-payment of premiums.

policy loan. A loan that is made to a policyowner by an insurance company and which is secured by the cash value of the policyowner's whole life insurance policy. The policy loan cannot exceed the policy's cash value.

preadmission review. A component of a utilization review program that requires an insured person, or that person's physician, to obtain prior authorization from an insurer before any non-emergency hospitalization.

preauthorization of benefits. *See* **predetermination of benefits provision.**

precertification of benefits. *See* **predetermination of benefits provision.**

predetermination of benefits provision. *Also known as* **preauthorization of benefits, precertification of benefits,** *or* **pretreatment review.** A provision often included in dental policies; the provision specifies that when dental treatments are expected to exceed a stated level, such as $100, $150, or $200, the dentist should submit to the insurer the proposed treatment plan for the patient so that the insurer can determine the amount payable by the dental plan.

pre-existing condition. (1) In individual health insurance, an injury that occurred or sickness that first manifested itself before the policy was issued and that was not disclosed on the application. (2) In group health insurance, a condition for which an individual received medical care during the three months immediately prior to the effective date of the coverage in a group policy.

preferred beneficiary. In Canada, prior to July 1, 1962, a beneficiary of a life insurance policy who was a member of the life insured's family and who was given special rights.

presumptive disability. A condition that, if present, automatically causes an insured to be considered totally disabled. Examples of presumptive disabilities include irrecoverable loss of sight in both eyes, the severance of both entire hands or both entire feet, or the severance of one entire foot and one entire hand.

pretreatment review. *See* **predetermination of benefits provision.**

prima facie *evidence.* A set of facts that, in the absence of evidence to dispute them, will entitle the bearer to whatever he or she seeks.

primary provider of benefits. In a coordination of benefits situation, the medical expense plan that pays the full benefits provided by its plan before any benefits are paid by another medical expense plan.

principal. In a loan transaction, the amount of money originally borrowed.

probationary period. See **waiting period.**

proportional reinsurance. A form of reinsurance in which a reinsurer shares a pro rata portion of the losses with a ceding company.

provider fraud. A type of medical insurance fraud that is initiated by a medical care provider on patients' claims in order to increase the provider's own income.

proximate cause of death. An event that is directly responsible for a death or an event that initiates an unbroken chain of events that lead to death.

public curator. In Quebec, a public officer authorized by the government to administer the property of persons who have disappeared.

punitive damages. An amount that a court may order an insurer to pay in excess of the insurance benefits specified in an insurance contract. Punitive damages are designed to punish an insurer for its behavior in wrongfully denying a claim.

qualified annuity. A type of annuity in the United States funded with money that is deductible, up to a stated maximum, from the depositor's gross income in the year in which the funds are deposited.

reasonable and customary charge. A fee most frequently charged by surgeons of similar specialization and experience in a given geographical area for a specified surgical procedure.

recording method. A procedure for changing the beneficiary of a life insurance policy in which the change becomes effective when the company receives written notification of the policyowner's desire to change the beneficiary designation from one person to another.

recovery benefit. *Also known as* **income replacement benefit.** A disability benefit payable after an insured satisfies a qualification or an elimination period, returns to work, and then suffers a loss of earnings directly resulting from a preceding total or partial disability.

reinstatement provisions. Provisions included in life and health insurance policies that permit a policyowner to restore a lapsed policy to in-force status by meeting certain requirements.

reinsurance. The process of transferring risk from one insurance company to another insurance company.

reinsurance treaty. A contract between a reinsurer and a ceding company which sets forth the type of risks to be reinsured, the procedures by which the ceding company must submit business to the reinsurer, and the rights of the reinsurer in the underwriting and claim decision process.

reinsurer. An insurance company that accepts a transfer of risk from another insurance company.

relation of earnings to insurance clause. *Also known as* a **participation limit.** A clause included in some guaranteed renewable or noncancellable individual disability policies that limits the amount of benefits in which an insurer will participate when the total amount of disability benefits from all insurers exceeds an insured's usual earnings.

renewable term life insurance policy. An insurance policy that gives the policyowner the option to renew the insurance coverage at the end of the specified term without submitting evidence that the insured person continues to be an insurable risk.

rescission. A legal remedy, usually based upon material misrepresentation in an insurance application; in rescission, an insurer seeks to void a policy.

resident alien. A person who is not a citizen of the United States but who is living indefinitely in the United States.

residual benefit for partial disability. A disability income benefit payment that is made to a partially disabled insured and that varies according to the percentage of the insured's income that is lost during a period of partial disability.

result clause. A type of war hazard exclusion that excludes payment of benefits for losses resulting from war or acts of war.

retained asset account (RAA). An interest-bearing money market checking account that is established by an insurer for the beneficiary of a life insurance policy, and into which the insurer deposits the policy's death benefit.

retention limit. The maximum amount of insurance that an insurer will carry at its own risk on any one individual.

retroactive disability benefits. A type of disability benefit that is payable retroactively from the date of disability, once an elimination period has been satisfied.

retrocession. The process in which one reinsurer cedes its excess risk to a second reinsurer.

retrospective payment method. A medical expense payment method that provides benefits after costs are incurred by the insured; this method encourages hospitals and physicians to provide the maximum level of care to a patient, but does not provide incentives for insureds or medical care providers to cut or control medical expenses.

retrospective review. A component of a utilization review program that provides an insurer with periodic reports on physicians' practice patterns and hospitals' average lengths-of-stay.

revocable beneficiary. A beneficiary whose interest in a life insurance policy can be revoked at any time by the policyowner.

rider. *Also known as* **endorsement**. A policy addition that becomes a part of the insurance contract and is as legally effective as any other part of the policy; a rider can provide a supplementary benefit or, increase the death benefit, or limit a policy's coverage.

right of survivorship. A stipulation sometimes included in assignments of life insurance policies which provides that if an assignee dies, the assignee's survivors are entitled to his or her portion of the assignment.

segregated account. *See* **separate account.**

sentinel effect. The tendency of hospitals involved in hospital audit programs to carefully prepare hospital bills because they expect their bills to be reviewed in detail by insurers.

separate account. *Also known as* a **segregated account** in Canada. An investment account maintained separately from an insurance company's general account in order to manage funds for nonguaranteed (variable) insurance products. A separate account has few investment restrictions and is invested primarily in securities such as common stocks.

settlement. *See* **financial settlement.**

shareholder. Owner of a corporation.

short-form reinstatement application. A reinstatement application that guards against reinstatements by insureds whose condition has changed drastically since the premium due date; a short-form reinstatement application must be completed within a comparatively short period, such as 30 to 90 days after the end of the grace period.

short-term survivorship provision. *Also known as* a **common disaster clause.** A life insurance policy provision which states that payment of policy proceeds to a beneficiary is dependent upon the beneficiary's being alive for a specified period, such as 15 days or 30 days, following the death of the insured.

single-payment loan. A short-term loan that is repaid in a single sum at the loan's maturity date.

six and six exclusion. A pre-existing conditions exclusion commonly used in credit disability policies, which states that an insured's disability is not covered if the insured was treated for the condition within six months prior to the effective date of coverage, and becomes disabled from that same condition within six months after the effective date of coverage.

small estates statutes. Legislation that enables an insurer to pay relatively small amounts of policy proceeds to an estate without involved court proceedings. Summary statutes and affidavit statutes are two common types of small estates statutes.

spouse and children's insurance rider. An addition to any type of permanent life insurance policy to provide coverage for a spouse and/or children.

status clause. A type of war hazard exclusion that excludes payment of benefits for losses resulting while an insured is in military service.

stop-loss reinsurance plan. A reinsurance plan in which a reinsurer indemnifies a ceding company for a percentage of total claim losses beyond a set point; the percentage may be either a predetermined dollar amount or a percentage of the ceding company's loss ratio.

straight life annuity. An annuity in which the benefit payments are guaranteed to continue for as long as the annuitant lives.

superimposed major medical plan. A major medical plan that is coordinated with various basic medical expense coverages and that provides benefits for expenses that exceed these coverages.

surgical schedule. In a health insurance policy, a list of common surgical procedures and the maximum benefit amount that an insurer will pay for each procedure.

surrender value. *See* ***net cash value.***

synergistic reaction. A combined action of two or more drugs ingested at the same time that results in a total effect that is greater than if the two drugs had been taken independently.

TEFRA corridor. The required difference between a universal life insurance policy's face amount and the policy's cash value.

temporary insurance agreements. *Also known as* ***temporary insurance receipts*** and ***interim insurance agreements.*** Legal agreements between an insurer and a proposed insured that provide a guaranteed amount of temporary life insurance coverage for a specific period of time, usually the underwriting period.

tenants in common. People who share title and use of an estate, but who have no right of survivorship.

term life insurance. Insurance issued to provide coverage for a specified period of time or term. Term life insurance pays a benefit only if the insured dies within a specified period of coverage.

testamentary trust. A trust that is created by a provision in the will of a grantor/insured and that does not become effective until the death of the grantor/insured.

Third Party Administrator (TPA). An organization that administers insurance benefits but accepts no responsibility for providing funds to pay claims.

third-party applicant. One who applies for insurance on the life of another person.

trust. A legal arrangement whereby one person or corporation holds and administers property for the benefit of one or more other persons.

trustee. A person or corporation responsible for administering property for the benefit of one or more other persons.

trustor. *See* ***grantor***.

unclaimed property statutes. *Also known as* ***escheat laws***. Statutes that regulate funds held by insurance companies or other organizations for which no owner can be found. Insurers typically hold unclaimed property for seven years. If the rightful owner is not found during this time, the property is turned over to the state.

underwriting. The process insurers use to assess and classify the potential degree of risk that a proposed insured represents.

universal life II. *See* ***variable universal life insurance***.

utilization review program. A cost-containment program that evaluates the appropriateness, necessity, and quality of health care provided at various stages in its delivery.

variable annuity. An annuity that provides annuity payments that vary according to the investment earnings of a special fund, called a separate account.

variable life insurance policy. A life insurance policy that remains in force during the insured's entire life, provided that premium payments are made as specified. Benefits and cash value depend on the investment performance of a separate account (U.S.) or a segregated account (Canada).

variable universal life insurance policy. *Also known as* ***universal life II*** and ***flexible-premium variable life***. A life insurance policy that combines the premium and death benefit flexibility of universal life with the investment flexibility and risk of variable life insurance.

voluntary trust. A trust that is created informally by the terms of a beneficiary provision in an insurance contract.

waiting period. *See* ***elimination period***.

waiting period. *Also known as* ***probationary period***. A period of time, usually one to six months, that must pass after a new employee is hired before that new employee is eligible for group insurance coverage.

waiver of deductible provision. A provision found in some major medical coverages that waives a claimant's initial deductible if the claimant's medical expenses are a result of an accidental injury.

waiver-of-premium benefit. A rider or policy provision under which the insurer promises to forego collection of a policy's premium if an insured becomes totally disabled, and if the total disability continues for a specified length of time. The waiver-of-premium benefit remains in effect for as long as the insured's total disability continues.

whole life insurance. Insurance issued to provide coverage for an insured's entire lifetime, as long as the premiums specified in the contract are paid.

yearly renewable term (YRT) reinsurance. A type of reinsurance plan in which a ceding company buys reinsurance to cover the net amount at risk on a given policy.

Index

Index